Better Homes and Gardens®

Holiday Decorations
You Can Make

Contents

BETTER HOMES AND GARDENS BOOKS

Editorial Director: Don Cooley
Managing Editor: Malcolm E. Robinson • Art Director: John Berg
Asst. Managing Editor: Lawrence D. Clayton • Asst. Art Director: Randall Yontz
Designers: Faith Berven, Harijs Priekulis

Introduction

Making the most of each holiday during the year is what *Holiday Decorations You Can Make* is all about. This year, add to the fun by creating decorations for your home that reflect the spirit of the day you are celebrating.

On the pages that follow, you will find a multitude of exciting decorating projects that represent the talents of many fine designers. The four-color photos will spur you to action, and the detailed instructions will ensure the successful completion of your decorations.

Just think of how much fun it will be for the whole family to make Christmas decorations for every room in the home—also for the front door, entryway, and your yard. There is even one chapter geared to the tastes and talents of 6- to 12-year-olds. It is jam-packed with easy-to-do holiday projects that youngsters will love making.

Other holidays throughout the year are featured, too. Included are decorations for New Year's Eve, St. Valentine's Day, St. Patrick's Day, Easter, Halloween, Thanksgiving, Jewish holidays, and patriotic holidays.

This book has something that will appeal to everyone in your family—all ages, all interests, and all degrees of expertise. Simply decide what you want to make, assemble all the materials, and get started on your project.

The doorway on the opposite page fairly shouts "Merry Christmas." Pine boughs, toy instruments, and fake fruit are attached to a block of plastic foam and combined with ribbons to ornament the door. Use tubs of poinsettias as an integral part of the overall theme. Ivy growing on the trellis is a year-round decoration that also adds a festive Yuletide touch to the doorway.

Chapter 1

Christmas Trees

Inside each person lives the small child who gazed in awe at the huge, twinkling Christmas tree and dreamed of sugarplums and Santa Claus during that long, long wait till Christmas. To that small child, viewing the Christmas tree was a glimpse into a land of enchantment. To an adult, it is a return to the dreams of childhood.

You can carry this dreamworld into decorating your home with Christmas trees. Purchase a live or man-made tree reminiscent of your childhood Christmas tree and decorate it with breathtakingly beautiful ornaments. Or, select a more contemporary, novel approach—make your own holiday tree. You may wish to extend the 'natural' decorating trend to fashioning a tree from bamboo, milkweed pods, or fruits. Or, you may decide to create a small tree from fabric, paper, or plastic. If space permits, you may even want to display a traditional tree in the living room or family room and decorate the rest of your home with unusual handmade miniature trees. And, don't forget tree skirts—the final touch to a perfect tree.

Above all, never settle for the same Christmas tree decorations year after year. Add variety to your holiday scheme by treating your elegant room-size tree to a new look. And, make one or more miniature trees to extend the holiday mood to other rooms in your home.

The traditional Christmas tree shown at left is at home in the wood-paneled room where a crackling fire in the fireplace adds further enchantment to the season. Red, white, and blue wrappings on the packages add emphasis to the tree ornaments.

Choosing and caring for your tree

Selecting the perfect Christmas tree is one of the highlights of the holiday preparations for many families.

The most exciting adventure is to take your family to an area where you can choose and cut your own tree; if this is not possible, make a family outing to several lots to select the special tree that you can all enjoy.

If you're looking for a tree that will last for more than a week or two, you have an alternative. You can purchase a balled-and-burlapped tree, which first can be the focal point of your holiday decorations and then can be planted in the yard when the Christmas season ends.

Regardless of which type you decide on, your choice will be simplified if you know about the characteristics of various species.

Species of evergreens

There is no particular species of evergreen that can be considered the best all-around Christmas tree because each variety has its own characteristics and people have their own preferences. The following brief descriptions of the five species that are most widely grown and sold—although not all necessarily are available in your area—should help in making your selection.

The balsam fir has short, flat, dark green needles, which usually are rounded at the tips. The needles are arranged in a feather-like pattern on grayish, finely hairy twigs. These twigs grow at right angles to each branch, resembling crosses (perhaps this is one of the reasons for their popularity at Christmas), and the rounded bud tips are coated with a waxy pitch. The bark of the balsam is gray or brown, thin, and smooth.

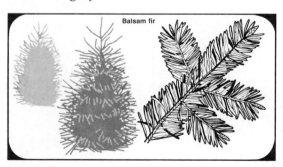

Balsam fir

The Douglas fir, another short-needled fir, has needles that are attached around the twig. The needles are short-stalked, soft, and pliable, and are dark yellow green or blue green. While most fir trees have rounded buds, the Douglas fir has reddish brown buds that narrow at the tip into a sharp point.

The eastern red cedar usually is easy to identify because of its extremely short, dark blue green, scale-like leaves. The leading shoots bear needlelike leaves almost half an

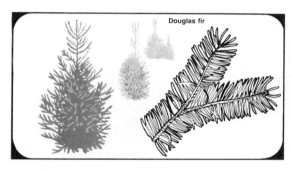

Douglas fir

inch long, and the leafy twigs are rounded or four-angled and slender.

The Scotch pine, a fast-growing tree, has longer needles than the balsam and Douglas firs. The needles grow in clusters of two and are dark blue green in color, usually twisted, and from 1½ to 2½ inches long. However, within the past several years, varieties have been produced with shorter needles. With proper pruning and trimming, you can make the Scotch pine very bushy, a desirable characteristic for a Christmas tree. It is a popular tree, partly because it holds its needles longer than most other trees. The Scotch pine has cones between two and five inches long. The bark is scaly and bright orange red, darker on older trees.

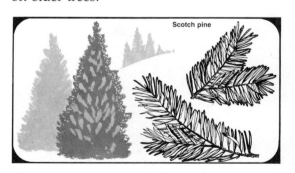

Scotch pine

The white pines, both eastern and western varieties, are very much alike, with silvery blue green needles that are soft to the touch. However, the slender eastern pine needles are quite long—2½ to 5 inches—and are grouped together in clusters of five, whereas the needles of the western white pine are noticeably shorter and stouter.

How to select a cut tree

Once you've decided which variety of evergreen you prefer, follow these guidelines when you make your selection:
• To save time—yours and the salesperson's—determine the size and shape of tree you want before going tree shopping.
• The needles on the tree should be resilient, not brittle. Run your fingers down a branch to ensure that the needles adhere to each twig.
• Shake or bounce the tree on the ground lightly to see that the needles are firmly attached to the branches. If only a few of the needles drop off, the tree is still fresh and should retain its freshness throughout the holiday season.
• Limbs should be strong enough to hold ornaments and strings of electric lights.
• Tree should have a strong fragrance and good, green color for the species.
• Check the tree for freshness, cleanness, health, and trimming, and be sure it displays the best qualities of the species.
• Keep in mind the height of the room where the tree will stand. Avoid buying a tree that is too tall for your room, since you will have to pay more for it than is necessary, and you'll have the extra work of sawing off a foot or two at the bottom of the tree to make it fit your room height.

The formula for tree symmetry is this: the width of the lowest branches should measure about half of the tree's height. If your tree's shape leaves something to be desired, you can remedy this easily by trimming or removing unwanted branches and drilling small holes in the tree trunk. Then, insert small branches or trimmings to eliminate bare spots. Also, arrange the ornaments and lights so they camouflage the less-than-perfect tree. If your tree will be in a corner or against a wall or window, economize by buying a tree that's shapely only on one side. A one-sided tree can be an advantage in a small room, too—it takes up less floor space and makes the room appear larger.

Balled-and-burlapped trees

Why not let your Christmas tree do double duty? If you are in the market for an evergreen to work into your landscape, order a balled-and-burlapped one from your nurseryman. Decorate it and display it indoors for Christmas, then plant it outdoors after the holidays are over.

When the tree arrives, let the ball soak up some water in a tub, then remove the burlap and allow the surplus water to drain away. Next, wrap the ball in a sheet of plastic and tie the plastic securely with twine. Spray the foliage with antidessicant (available at most garden centers). This solution, which is also good for cut Christmas trees, dries out in a thin, transparent film that allows the passage of oxygen and carbon dioxide during the life processes, yet, at the same time, prevents a loss of moisture and drying out of the needles.

Place the tree in your house a couple of days before the holidays, but don't keep it indoors longer than a week or it may not survive when you plant it outdoors.

If you live in an area with a cold climate, plant the evergreen in a hole that was dug before the ground was frozen, and that was mulched to prevent freezing.

Care of the cut holiday tree

Try not to set up your tree too soon before Christmas. When you bring the tree home, cut the butt of the tree at a diagonal about one inch above the original cut—this opens the pores and aids in the absorption of water. Be sure to keep the tree in a cool, shaded spot outdoors or in an unheated room of your home until you set it up. Also, remember to keep the tree in a container of water.

Before you set the tree in the container, saw the butt again, squaring off the diagonal. This facilitates placing the tree in the stand as well as aiding absorption.

When you set up the tree, place it firmly in a tree stand and keep the water level continuously above the cut. You may need to add from a pint to a quart of water each day. Sprinkling water on the branches and needles before you decorate your Christmas tree also will help it to retain its freshness.

When you take the tree down after the holidays, wrap an old sheet around it while you remove it to avoid leaving a trail of needles through your house.

How to select a man-made tree

Although there's still nothing that can compare with an evergreen that is fresh, fragrant, and well shaped, artificial Christmas trees are gaining wider acceptance each year.

One reason for the booming sales of man-made trees is the difficulty of buying healthy, shapely trees in many sections of the country. Another is a concern for the environment; some people prefer to leave evergreens growing in their natural habitat where their beauty can be enjoyed for years to come. Other factors are the safety and convenience of an artifical tree. Apartment and condominium dwellers often are urged to have artificial trees because they are nonflammable; also, there isn't the chore of disposing of evergreens and of cleaning up needles in the halls.

When you are shopping for an artificial Christmas tree, be sure to look for a label or tag identifying the tree as flame retardant, which means that it is self-extinguishing. The tree will melt or char if it is exposed to an open flame, but it will not burn. If you haven't shopped for a man-made tree recently, you may be surprised by the forest of selection. There's Scotch pine, Douglas fir, Scandinavian spruce, balsam, and a host of others. There are two general types of artificial trees—soft needle and hard needle. The soft-needle type has four-inch needles with a soft, featherlike quality. The hard-needle tree, on the other hand, has slightly smaller needles and a crisper appearance.

Man-made Christmas trees are often a combination of shades of green. Some have light green tips to simulate new growth and others intermingle green and slate blue needles the same as their live counterparts.

You have a choice of outswept, upswept, or downswept branches. The decision is purely personal, although the outswept style is the most popular because of its fuller, fatter shape. Tree heights vary from 2 to 12½ feet. When you are selecting a tree, consider the overall shape rather than height alone.

Use only miniature lights on man-made trees; larger bulbs generate too much heat. Most miniature or midget lights burn cool, so they won't melt needles on artificial trees or burn children or pets. Avoid the ceramic-coated or translucent bulbs. Instead, consider the new 'optic sprays.' Their tiny hairlike strands contain no electricity; instead, they pick up light from below.

Christmas tree safety

Don't let that beloved symbol of the Christmas season be a fire hazard. Always remember that dry, resinous evergreens are highly flammable and can be consumed by fire almost explosively. Also keep in mind the following important tips:

● Use freshly cut trees with moisture-filled needles. These are safer than trees that have been cut weeks before.
● Avoid placing your tree near anything that gives off heat—fireplace, radiator, electric heater, or television.
● Never use open flames, such as lighted candles, on or near the tree.
● Don't buy any tree lights that lack the U.L. (Underwriters' Laboratory) label.
● Never leave your Christmas tree lights on when there is no one in the house.
● Check the electric light cords close to your tree for frayed or worn spots, which easily could lead to a fire.
● Do not overload the electric circuits.
● Avoid playing with electrically operated toys directly under the Christmas tree.
● If you plan to decorate your tree with spray-on flocking and angel hair, spray the tree with snow first, then add the angel hair. Remember that angel hair, by itself, will not burn nor will the spray-on flocking. But snow sprayed onto angel hair adds up to a combustible material.
● Hang only unbreakable baubles on the lower branches, which are easily reached by a child's inquisitive fingers or a curious cat. Save the fragile ornaments for the higher and inaccessible branches.
● If someone accidently drops and shatters a glass ornament while trimming the tree, it's best to use a dampened paper towel to help pick up the tiny ornament fragments from the floor. Don't attempt to pick them up with your fingers.

If you follow all these guidelines, you can be reasonably certain of having an attractive tree that will remain fresh indoors for more than a week and a holiday season that will be free from Christmas tree mishaps.

The **Christmas tree at right** is scaled to the size of the room and is decorated to coordinate with the room's decor. Instructions for making the ornaments are given on page 58.

How to decorate Christmas trees.

The custom of decorating Christmas trees is a part of the holiday season that everyone anticipates with joy. Although the traditions that surround evergreens reach back to ancient days, the present style of the holiday tree became established in the last century.

In many ways, decorating ideas remain unchanged from the time that the first trimmed trees appeared in Germany. An early description mentions paper roses, apples, wafers, and sweets as ornaments—all still are part of our traditional tree decorations. A feeling of nostalgia permeates the air when you see a tree trimmed with candy canes, gingerbread men, and garlands of stringed popcorn and cranberries—highlighted with lights.

Some people traditionally make the tree trimming ritual strictly a family affair Usually, this takes place on Christmas Eve or perhaps a few days earlier. Others enjoy inviting friends to share in this festive annual event. It's a big part of their holiday entertaining, and they serve a buffet meal accompanied by a punch bowl filled with eggnog or a sparkling punch.

You can lavish ornaments on a tree so that the tree radiates with jewel-like splendor, or you can use very few ornaments other than strings of lights and enjoy the natural beauty of the evergreen. In between these two extremes there is a wide range of decorating schemes possible.

Electrifying ideas for Christmas

Come Christmastime, and everyone's an electrician of sorts. Maybe you've decided that this year you're going all out with holiday lighting in your home, perhaps even brighten up the neighborhood with an outdoor tree. If so, save yourself the frustration of faulty wiring—blown fuses, bulbs that won't burn, and switches that fail—with proper equipment and preparation. Here are

◄ **Trim your tree** like the one at left, with pine cones, clusters of berries, and pods—all in brown, woodsy tones—to play up a back-to-nature theme and to emphasize the wood tones.

some background facts that will help you choose and use Christmas tree lights wisely, as well as beautifully.

Estimate how many lights you will need on the Christmas tree by measuring the height of the tree (in feet) times the width of the tree at its widest part. Then, multiply by three. For example, on a six-foot tree that is four feet wide, you'll need 72 lights to illuminate it effectively.

If you are purchasing new strings of lights, get those that have individually lighted bulbs so that other bulbs in the set will still light when a burned-out bulb remains in the socket. And, be sure that the lights you buy have the U.L. approval so you'll be covered by your insurance policy in the event that you have a fire. Also, when you purchase outdoor lights, be sure to read the U.L. label and information on the box, which will indicate whether or not the lights are intended for use outdoors.

String the lights on the tree first and get them securely in place before adding any other ornaments or trim. Be sure to distribute the lights as evenly as possible, and at the same time, try to arrange the electric cord so that it is unobtrusive.

Exterior lighting tips

In planning the lighting for an outdoor tree, keep in mind that you probably will have to use one or more extension cords, so make sure the wire is large enough to carry the electrical load that is required of it.

Number 18 wire is big enough for most lines, but use number 16 for lines over 15 feet long or those that have a number of lights in the circuit. Waterproof the extension cord connections used outside with a small plastic bag. Cut out the bottom of the bag and slip it over the connection. Tie both ends tightly around the cord with a piece of twine.

Before stringing the lights on the tree, connect all of the strings and plug them in to see if you have any burned-out bulbs or shorts in the circuit. Also, arrange the older bulbs in such a way that if any of them burn out when they are in position you'll be able to replace them easily.

Under-the-tree trims

When trimming your tree, don't forget to add a rug under the tree or a tree skirt. Choose colors and motifs that harmonize with your Christmas decorations.

Under-the-tree rug

Use cutouts from leftover Christmas cards to trim the circular felt rug at the right. The rug measures 36 inches in diameter.

The traditional Christmas symbols—old Santa himself, a prancing reindeer, a tree surrounded by packages, a cluster of candles, a beribboned wreath, a trio of bells, an assortment of gaily colored ornaments, and a flaming red poinsettia or any other Christmasy bloom—are perfect for this project.

Arrange the designs on the felt so they present a pleasing appearance, then pin the cutouts in place. Completely cover each picture cutout with a piece of nylon net. (For eight designs, buy ½ yard of 72-inch-wide flesh-colored netting.)

Stitch around each card to hold it in position. (Select thin cards to make sewing with a needle and thread easier.) Use beads and sequins for eyes, eyebrows, mouth, and any other facial features. Stitch sequins and beads through the card and felt, choosing harmonious colors to work with. When making the poinsettia design, use seed beads in different shades of red. String the beads in rows, then go back over every two or three beads and stitch them securely.

When the greeting card cutout is completely covered, cut away the net and pull out the thread you used to hold it in place. On a card where a face is in evidence—such as Santa's—do not remove the net. This will give the face more depth.

If you prefer to adapt this same pattern to a tree skirt instead, draw a straight line with chalk between two designs all the way to the center, then cut on the line with a scissors. With a pair of pinking shears, cut a tiny circle to fit around tree trunk.

For the border trim, choose a metallic or sequin-studded braid and stitch or glue around outer edge. If you prefer to back the rug or skirt, cut another piece of fabric smaller. Blindstitch or glue pieces together.

Tree skirt

Fold a piece of velveteen in half lengthwise; cut in two sections. Lay sections right side up atop each other. Make paper pattern from diagram shown on this page; pin to velveteen, then cut through two thicknesses. Sew straight edges together; press seams flat. You'll have two side seams; place them together. Cut down center of back scallop.

Cut lining; follow the same procedure as you did above. Sew the lining to the velveteen, right sides together. Turn the skirt right side out; sew the opening closed. Cut four trees (see sketch) from green felt. Cut out the colored sections; follow the diagram for placing. Glue into place on skirt.

Cut out girl and boy figures—two each—from felt. Glue the faces down first, then all other sections. Glue the face features last. When the glue dries, machine-stitch.

Glue orange pompons to the peaks of the girls' hats and to the treetops. Make the tassels from hot pink yarn to sew between the scallops on the outer edge.

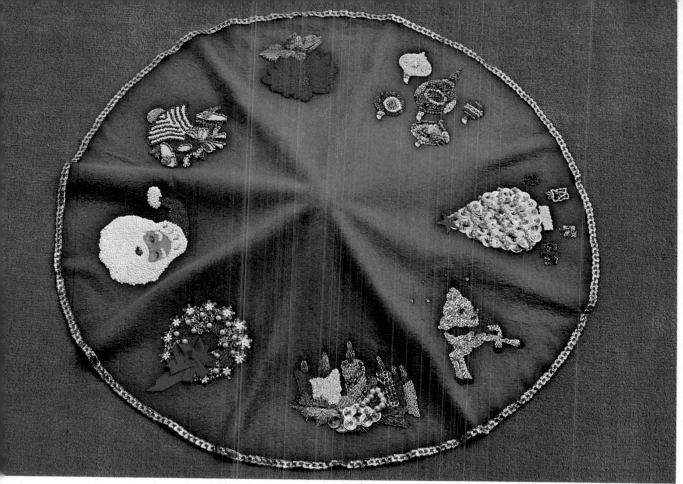

Under-the-tree rug

Tree skirt

Christmas trees to make

Turning your hand to making Christmas trees does wonders for your holiday decorating scheme. You can place small trees on tables, mantels, wall shelves, chests, and buffets. Also, this is one project in which the entire family can participate. Be sure to start early in the season and let each family member contribute ideas, time, and talent. Once you get started, you'll want to place a small tree in every room of your home.

When Christmas is over, pack the trees away carefully in storage boxes and use them again the next year.

Fabric, ribbon, and braid

Create a variety of novel holiday trees with bits and scraps of fabric and small amounts of ribbon, braid, and decorative trims. The designs that follow are just a sampling of the many small trees you can make.

Eyelet ruffling of cotton or nylon has a particularly feminine appearance that makes this petite Christmas tree especially appealing in a young girl's bedroom or as an unexpected surprise in a guest bedroom. All you have to do is cover a 20-inch-high plastic foam cone with ruffling and velvet bows (both available at notions counters).

First, pin the eyelet ruffling to the foam base in layers that overlap slightly. Next, embellish the eyelet with dainty velvet bows pinned atop the ruffles. For the bows, use narrow velvet ribbon and add tiny gold balls for a teardrop effect. Finally, attach a sturdy base to the plastic foam cone to support the tree. Feel free to alter colors according to your decorating scheme.

A Maypole tree made of shiny satin ribbon and glass balls proves that this pretty ornament can make its debut in December just as well as in the merry month of May.

For the tree base, use a glass candy dish with a perforated rim. If you don't have one tucked away in your cupboard, purchase an inexpensive one from a variety store.

To construct the tree, fill the dish with a firm base of plastic foam, and insert an 18-inch-long dowel in the center. Spray both dish and dowel with gold paint, and glue 16 pieces of ribbon to the top of the dowel.

Cut the ribbon strips long enough so you can loop them through the lace-lined rim of the candy dish and still have one inch left over. Before you attach the last two ribbon streamers, fill the candy dish with shiny glass ornaments underneath the ribbons. For a final touch, top your Maypole tree with a shiny ornament.

If your tastes lean toward more subdued materials, you may choose to follow these same instructions but use velvet ribbon instead of the shiny satin ribbon for streamers.

Fabrics and coat hangers are the secret ingredients for this severely tailored holiday tree that will fit into any contemporary room setting with dignity.

First, remove the hooks from ten wood hangers and cover them with black and white plaid fabric. Next, add a row of black ball fringe along the outside curve of each end.

To hold the hangers in place, cover two pieces of 2x42-inch cardboard with matching fabric. Glue the fabric firmly to the cardboard. Every seven inches, glue two hangers on one piece of the tree trunk. Weight the tree down with books until the glue is dry. Wrap a narrow piece of the same fabric around and around, using lots of glue so the joining will be firm, or use fabric tape to keep the hangers in place. Glue the other 2-inch piece over the center to cover the joinings.

Assemble the cardboard triangles and trim them with scraps of fabric, as shown.

Calico, polka dots, and gingham checks that decorate this small tree are completely in tune with the country style that is so popular in home decorating and fashions today.

To make this frilly tabletopper, cut an assortment of brightly colored fabric remnants into strips that vary in width from one to four inches. Be sure to cut these strips with your pinking shears to eliminate tedious hemming, then gather them evenly and hand-stitch each strip individually.

Starting at the top of a 16-inch-tall foam cone tree base and using straight pins, attach one row of ruffling at a time. Pin the top nine rows of ruffles into the cone. Add the remaining rows to the bottom edge of the ruffled layer (not to the cone itself) before handstitching. Use a four-inch base for the

Eyelet ruffling tree

Maypole tree

Fabric and coat hanger tree

Calico, polka dots, and gingham tree

Patchwork tree

Sewing notions tree

Velvet bows and pine cones

Tiered table tree

tree, cover it with fabric, and attach it securely to the tree cone.

This patchwork Christmas tree will appeal to little folks, and making it will appeal to everyone who likes to cut and paste. It is a good evening project for the family.

To build one like this, make a wire tree frame and cover it with sturdy cardboard. Glue the prefinished patches onto this base.

Make each patch colorful and unique—with designs glued in each patch. Use pictures on old Christmas cards for patterns for designs. Cut the designs out of felt and glue them to the patches before gluing the felt patches to the tree. Also, stitch around the edge of each patch before gluing it to the tree. For the tree base, cover a wood circle with felt and edge it with ball fringe.

Velvet bows and tiny pine cones are the principal ingredients in this festive small tree. Start with a plastic foam cone and spray it with brown paint. Next, drill holes in the ends of small pine cones and insert wires that have been dipped in glue. Stick the wires into the foam base so that the pine cones are distributed evenly all around, and spray them gently with gold metallic paint.

Make the bows of ½-inch-wide green velvet ribbon. Pierce each small bow with a nail, and stick the nail into the foam base and glue a jewel to the head of the nail. Glue more jewels to small glass ball ornaments with wire stems, and attach them to the tree. Mount on a base in scale with the tree.

A tree made of sewing notions provides a creative challenge for the home sewing enthusiast. The first step is to make an exhaustive search for every piece of leftover braid, ribbon, rickrack, yarn, and fringe from your sewing basket that will lend itself to holiday tree decorations. Combine colors and textures that are harmonious.

Next, cover a plastic foam cone with green felt, securing the felt with either pins or glue. Then, gather the trims into flowerlike rosettes, arrange them in a pleasing design, and pin them to the cone so they overlap.

To complete this colorful and ingenious tree for your home, use a compote for a tree base. The one shown here is made of brass, but you may want to use a ceramic or glass compote instead.

This opulent tiered table tree is fashioned of loops of heavy crepe paper in brilliant shades of lime and traditional holiday green.

The first step in making this elegant tree is to spray a 3-inch, a 2½-inch, and a 2-inch plastic foam ball and a 32-inch-long wood dowel (pointed at the top) with green paint. Then, thread the balls onto the dowel, which you must anchor securely in the base. The base used here is a paper-covered food container that has been sprayed gold. Place a large lump of florist's clay inside the covered container, and anchor the dowel in it. The clay also will add weight and prevent the tall tree from toppling over.

Now, stack four 9x10-inch pieces of heavy crepe paper (cut on the crossgrain). Use a double amount of layers if a lighter weight crepe paper is used. Sew or staple the layers together 1½ inches from the longest edge. (See sketch at left.) Cut into one-inch strips up to the stitches or staples. Loop each strip back to the stitching, as shown in the illustration; staple to itself. Pin it around a 3-inch foam ball. Repeat this procedure, but cut from paper 9x7½ inches for the 2½-inch ball; and 8x6 inches for the 2-inch ball. Cut the strips proportionately narrower for the smaller sized balls.

Curl a strip for the top and glue it around the dowel just below the finial. Stick artificial

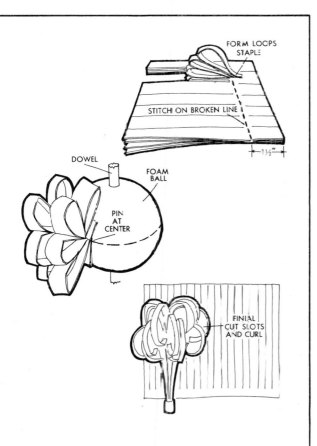

FORM LOOPS
STAPLE

STITCH ON BROKEN LINE

1½"

DOWEL

FOAM BALL

PIN AT CENTER

FINIAL
CUT SLOTS AND CURL

red berries and white fruit into the foam balls between the loops. Add a shiny finial to top it off, and arrange greens, ornaments, and small packages around the bottom.

Natural materials for trees

The use of natural materials for making small Christmas trees has great appeal for almost everyone. Whenever you're walking through your garden or the woods, or along the beach, keep your eyes open for pods, berries, twigs, leaves, nutshells, and seashells—all are likely candidates for creating small trees for the holiday season. Even if you live in a big city high-rise where you can't collect your own materials, you can always shop for natural materials at your florist shop, variety store, or supermarket. And speaking of supermarkets, don't forget that you can use fruit—apples, oranges, limes, and lemons—for decorating small trees with equal aplomb.

All it takes to convert materials that are a product of nature's handiwork into trees of beauty is a little imagination and a desire to put your nimble fingers to work.

The 6-foot-tall bamboo beauty shown on the opposite page is made of ordinary bamboo fishing poles that you can find at most hardware or sporting goods stores.

Cut the bamboo poles into graduated lengths; on the one pictured here, the lowest branch measures 48 inches long, and the top one measures 6 inches long. After you have cut and sanded all of the lengths of bamboo, drill a ¾-inch hole in the center of each pole. For the tree trunk, cut a piece of ½-inch galvanized pipe to the desired height. Thread this into a four-way coupling base.

Assemble the branches on the trunk of the tree, then spray the entire tree with several coats of paint. Add trim touches of satin-finish balls, a number of tailored silk tassels, and honeycomb garlands, laced with twinkling tree lights. Tuck artificial bamboo leaves into the drilled holes of the branches. You can easily alter the dimensions of this type of tree to fit the room in which you wish to display it proudly.

Lemons and spicy-scented pomander balls provide the inspiration for this delightful table topper. When you incorporate this holiday tree into your decorating scheme, a fragrant, spicy aroma will permeate the air.

First, cut a 6-inch circle of plywood for the base of the tree. Next, bore a hole in the center and insert a 20-inch-long dowel. Now, make a cone of chicken wire and attach it over the dowel tree trunk.

Push tree ornament hangers into the back of the lemons. Then, hang them on the chicken wire in tiers, starting at the bottom of the tree. To make the pomander balls, select firm apples, oranges, or lemons; then stud the fruit with enough whole cloves to cover the entire fruit. Set the balls in a mixture of ½ cup of ground cinnamon, nutmeg, allspice, ginger, and a cup of powdered orrisroot for several days.

Tie each pomander ball with a printed, polka dotted, striped, or plaid ribbon, and attach the balls to the cone with ornament hooks. To make the top-of-the-tree ornament, place cinnamon sticks over pipe cleaners and arrange them in a jaunty fashion. Also, intersperse cinnamon sticks in between the lemons and pomander balls to add a three-dimensional effect.

Milkweed pods are used to make this handsome tree. Collect the pods early, then store them in a dry place until you are ready to use them.

To reproduce this design, start by cleaning the 'fur' out of the inside of the pods. Be sure that the pods are in halves and free from dust and dirt before you paint them.

Next, arrange the pods on a thick layer of paper, insides up, and spray the insides with gold paint (see illustration). When they are thoroughly dry, turn the pods over and spray the outsides with green paint. At the same time, spray the plastic foam cone tree base green to help camouflage any spaces between the pods that will remain exposed.

Then, start at the bottom of the cone and pin on the pods, placing the pins toward the top of the pod (see illustration). Layer the pods to the top of the cone and finish the tree with a golden treetop ornament for a touch of glamour. Use a shallow container as the base for the tree and display the tree in a commanding position.

Novel trees you can make

Anyone with an average amount of dexterity and patience can make a Christmas tree that he or she will be proud to display during the holiday season.

This is your big chance to be as inventive as you wish; you can create your tree out of materials that range all the way from the

Bamboo tree

Lemons and pomander balls

Milkweed pod tree

The illustration below, left, shows how to spray-paint the milkweed pods; the one below, right, shows how to layer them on the base.

Tree of wooden boxes

Mexican tree

Pennsylvania Dutch tree

Egg carton spectaculars

most ordinary to the most unlikely. The designs on the pages that follow will inspire you to immediate action.

This tree of wooden boxes, which you can make easily with the aid of a hand or power saw, will add beauty to any wall. Cut the Christmas tree shape (including tree stand) from a sheet of ¼-inch plywood and spray it green. When it is dry, arrange small blocks of wood in various sizes and shapes on it.

Cut colorful gift wrapping paper to fit each block. Brush the top of each block with white glue and press the block onto the paper smoothly. Glue sides of block and fold paper over as if you were wrapping a gift.

When the glue dries, brush a tiny line of glue over the sides and the top where the gold cord will go. Do not put glue on the back of the box. Press the cord in place; snip at the bottom edge; secure the edges with glue. Glue the packages on the tree.

Using nails ¼ inch longer than the packages are thick, nail each box to the tree where the cords cross. Tie bows of matching cord and glue them over the nails. Cover the tree stand with felt or burlap, and glue on felt or burlap trim. Finish the tree with a coat of clear plastic spray.

This Mexican tree, a south-of-the-border variety that has that one-of-a-kind distinction, doesn't require any special skills to make. It's made from ordinary cardboard and rug yarn in bright, happy colors. And, all you have to know is how to cut and paste.

First, draw a tree shape on newspaper, measuring 19x24 inches, with the trunk extending one inch below the bottom edge of the tree. Fold the paper in half, then draw a scalloped edge. Draw another tree shape 2½ inches smaller in the center of the first tree. Cut out this design and use it for a pattern when you cut the tree from corrugated cardboard.

Cut a corrugated cardboard strip 2x23 inches; mark at the center, then mark in half again. Score at the three halfway points with a razor blade, then bend the strip away from the cut into a square for the tree base. Secure with masking tape.

Cut another strip of cardboard 3x2 inches. Make a cut halfway through the center of the strip. Slip the trunk of the tree through the cut in the strip, centering it to make a stand as you would for a paper doll. Set the tree on the stand inside the square base, letting the tree rest diagonally on the stand.

To make the top of the base, cut two half squares (triangles) the same size as the base; fit them up to and against the tree trunk. Cut another piece the same size as the bottom of the base. Tape these pieces in place. Tape the bottom edges of the tree to the top side of the base. This will hold the tree firmly in position.

Draw the details for the trim on the tree, making each side a different design. Fill in the solid areas by gluing on rug yarn; glue heavy yarn to the cut cardboard edges and base. Dribble glue in a line the width of one strand of yarn. Use your fingertips to push each new row up to the next one. Cut the yarn when you change colors.

Pennsylvania Dutch motifs adorn this quaint wall tree. Use it in your own home, or pleat it accordion-style and send it as a thoughtful and personal gift to a faraway friend on your Christmas gift list.

Cut the tree from two sheets of 30x40-inch medium-weight mat board. Place the boards on a smooth cutting surface with the two 40-inch sides touching. Draw the triangular tree shape, dividing it into seven 9-inch-high sections and leaving one inch of space between each section. Cover each section with self-adhering green paper, and bring the paper around to the back of the section.

Cut the decorations from gift wrapping or other colored paper. Or, you can copy large designs from a youngster's coloring book. Use rubber cement to glue the sections together and to glue the rows of decorative motifs in position.

Lay all of the completed sections on the floor (right side down) and space them one inch apart. Glue lengths of one-inch-wide green grosgrain ribbon (10 yards in all) on the back to hold all the sections together.

Egg carton spectaculars might well be the title for these small trees.

For the one at the left, cut the tree and its base in one piece from a 24-inch sheet of plastic foam. Then, spray the entire piece with iridescent gold glitter. Cut the stars out of egg carton cups and spray them gold, too. Insert a small Christmas ball in the center of each one before you glue them to the flat tree. Finally, add beads on pins, bead sprays, and glass ornaments. Mount the tree on the wall with a picture hanger.

Another artistic egg carton effort is the one on the right. Cut any size of base from a sheet of plastic foam. Cover the base with a coat of gold spray paint.

Cut out sections of egg cartons to form the petals of the roses. Spray each rose gold. Use green velour paper to form the bows and to make the stripes that separate the rows of roses. Pin sprays of gold beads through the ribbon bands to help keep them in position and to add an extra decorative touch.

A tree of Santa faces smartly decorates a party room or a child's room. To duplicate this tree that encompasses both traditional and sleekly contemporary design, first make a tree frame out of lath or shutter slats (about 1 inch wide). Attach the 'branches' (5½, 7, 8½, 10, 11½, and 13 inches long) to a 39-inch-high 'trunk.' Leave 4½ inches from the top branch to the tip of the tree and space the branches 3½ inches apart. Lacquer the tree red. Glue white wooden beads or buttons on the front at the intersections of the branches and the trunk.

Use a pepper can for the tree base. Pour plaster of paris into the can and prop up the tree until the plaster is completely set. Cover the can with white felt and add stripes of red felt or vinyl tape.

Next, purchase 12 small tops at a toy department and paint jovial Santa faces on them. Put screw eyes in the tops of the tops and on the ends of the branches. Attach the tops to the tree with a small wire loop (jump ring) through each screw eye. For the finial, cut a 3-inch-diameter circle of white cardboard, and glue the top of a large lacquered spool to it. Glue a white bead to the center of the spool; affix the treetop ornament to the top of the stately red and white tree.

Pinwheels and candy canes are natural go-togethers for youngsters of all ages. Here, they go together to form a lighthearted tree.

Start with 10 plastic foam candy canes. Remove the spirally wrapped ribbon and arrange the canes (upside down) in the shape of a tree. You'll want to cut off some of the extra straight parts of the top canes to use for the lower part of the tree trunk. Pin the canes together with corsage pins, then tie them with ordinary white sewing thread. Pin ten large plastic pinwheels and four smaller pinwheels into the foam candy cane tree with push pins.

This clay pots-and-saucers tree, a clever concoction shaped to resemble a small Christmas tree, is constructed by slipping clay flowerpots and saucers over a 25-inch-long dowel. Drill one-inch holes in the center of the bottom of clay pots and saucers. Then, invert the bottom pot and stack the others as shown in the sketch below, spacing three-inch collars cut from paper towel cores and covered with adhesive-backed vinyl between the pots and saucers. Glue at the top and bottom to hold each section firmly.

Fill the tiers with candy canes, bonbons, and hard candies. Top with message made from cardboard letters, painted or covered with paper. Glue each letter to a dowel stick and insert in the upper pot.

A wicker wall tree is ideal against a paneled background. First, spray-paint a half wicker tree bright red. Measure the solid bands on the wicker frame and cut strips of green burlap 2½ to 3 times this length. For the lower band, this burlap strip should be 4 inches wide; for the three center bands, 3 inches wide; and for the top band, 2 inches.

Fray the edge of the burlap in about one inch from the outside on all strips. Gather each strip by running spool wire through the centers. Then, wire all but the top strip of burlap to the solid bands of wicker.

Add ornaments to the center of each burlap band. Use chenille-stemmed balls and satin apples to which you've added 4-inch pieces of chenille stem dipped in glue and pushed into small holes drilled in the apples. Wire the apples and balls in place by going through burlap to wicker frame with stems, then bending them to hold them securely.

Tree of Santa faces

Pinwheels 'n candy canes

Clay pots and saucers

Wicker wall tree

For the top of the tree, bunch together a group of burlap ravelings, twice the height of the top section. Wire the bunched ravelings at the top center. To fasten to the top of the tree, stretch the ravelings down over the frame on the top section, wrapping them with another piece of raveling to hold them in place. Then, wire the top gathered strip of burlap over the raw edges. Wire on a short length of gold beads and glue a narrow red felt strip between the beads. Add a satin apple to the top and a huge felt bow wired to the tree trunk.

Contemporary Christmas trees

Even though the Christmas holidays are steeped in tradition, why not inject a contemporary spirit into your holiday decorations?

On these pages are several contemporary tree designs. Each of them will complement today's modern furnishings.

The lacy-looking, ceiling-high tree is made of 14-gauge expanded metal branches reinforced by a ⅜-inch cold rolled steel rod placed on the underside of each branch. A one-inch pipe is welded to the branches for support. Each level of pipe is graded in size from wide at the bottom to narrow at the top in order to form a tree shape. Cut the one-inch pipe into 10-inch sections for each group of four branches. Use a center pole of ¾-inch pipe, with three legs welded to it, to stabilize the tree and serve as a tree stand.

After you have made the frame, spray it several times with flat white paint. Then, wire the tree so you can arrange candle lights on the tip and center of each branch. Mask off the candles and flock the tree with a home flocking kit, using a vacuum cleaner to blow the flocking through the branches. This will give a lacy effect to the branches. Flock with several light applications, allowing each coat to dry completely.

Now, the tree is ready to slip on the one-inch pipe over the ¾-inch center pole that supports it. Trim the tree with artificial

◀ **The elegance of the lacy-looking tree** at the left conceals the fact that it's made of metal. It is shown here in a ceiling-high version.

This abstract tree and matching candleholders ▶ make an attractive grouping for a table, buffet, or chest. Instructions are on page 28.

27

Hawaiian plumeria blossoms strung as leis, garlands of white crown flower blossoms, satin balls in three sizes, and Japanese tassels.

The three-tiered stylized tree and matching candleholders pictured on page 27 make an attractive grouping. You can make this unusual trio from cardboard and wood dowels supported by a wood base. The cardboard pieces are covered with scraps of velvet and other fabric and are attached in geometric design, with masking tape on the inside. Attach the fabric to the cardboard surface with glue. Conceal the joints with gold braid.

The abstract tree has a 5x5-inch base with ¾-inch dowel center. Three triangle units in graduated sizes fit over the dowel.

The largest candleholder has a 5x5-inch wood base (one inch thick). Wood dowel fits into hole cut in the center. Height is 10 inches. You can purchase holders for the candles in hardware stores. The triangles are 6x6 inches. Second holder has same size base and is eight inches tall. Triangles are 4½x4½x4½ inches.

The golden tree, which resembles a palm tree called neanthebella, has leaves made from gold foil. Cut through several thicknesses of foil at one time to speed up the leaf-making process. Cover the wire with gold floral tape to back the leaves, then bend each leaf into shape before attaching it to the branch. Use a ½-inch wood dowel for a center support. Decorate the tree with green silk balls, and arrange gift packages wrapped in colors coordinated with the tree colors.

Oilcloth trees offer a high-style wet look that is completely in tune with rooms that feature contemporary furnishings. They will make an attractive grouping on a coffee table, a buffet, or a low mantel.

Use plastic foam cones in graduated sizes for bases. Pull oilcloth taut over each cone, then staple securely in place. Trim the trees with paper medallions, tree toppers, and tiny packages that you can fasten on with glue and pins. Choose oilcloth in colors, designs, and patterns that are lively and harmonize with your other holiday decorations.

To make the cowhide bead tree, use a 6-foot-high wood garden trellis, and turn it upside down. Cut off the center stake to make the bottom level, and trim off the protruding side edges. Use any 12x18x24-inch box for the chest. Cover both the trellis and chest with cowhide or velour paper. Arrange cup hooks at the outside edges of the trellis, and drape strands of mahogany beads up to 12 inches

from the top. Drive four 2-inch nails into the top of the trellis, draping strands of beads across for center loops.

Use a Christmas handkerchief mounted on cardboard as a treetop ornament. Trim it with burlap braid which also outlines the center edge of the trellis.

Trim the covered chest base with leather strips and upholstery tacks. Wrap the gift boxes with plastic-coated shelf paper in a harmonizing color, and tie with yarn and gold rickrack. Arrange them in the chest.

The pyramid tree (pictured on page 30), adorned with feather-trimmed angels, will add a glamorous note to a tabletop or desk. To assemble the parts for this pyramid tree, cut four elongated triangles (20 inches tall x 7 inches across the bottom) and a 7x7-inch base from construction board.

Cover the triangles with pink velvet, and glue all four sides together to form the tree. Glue a double row of gold cording along all borders. Attach a gold foil tassel to the top. At each corner of each triangle, hang one pink teardrop crystal bead.

Use a coffee can for the base and cover it with pink velvet. Drill a hole in the can lid and screw a wooden dowel into it. Fill the can with plaster of paris (to act as a weight), and seal the can. Glue a double row of gold cording around the top and bottom edges of the base. Cover the wood dowel tree trunk with gold cording.

Cut angels from construction board and attach hands made from gold wire cording. Cover angels with pink velvet. Glue on small pieces of mirror. Glue cording completely around angel forms as a border. Glue on small stick balls for heads. Attach halos made from gold wire cording to backs of heads. Attach pink feather to each side of angels.

Insert gold wire trumpet into stick ball (about where mouth would be) and let rest between hands. Glue and pin angels onto tree.

The angel tree, pictured on page 30, is basically three cones joined together by dowels. For the base, drill ⅜-inch holes in the center of a newel post, a 6-inch wooden salad bowl, and a 6-inch square wood block. Join these with a dowel, and glue in place.

Drill another hole in center of a 12-inch plywood circle and on top of newel post. Place a 36-inch-long dowel through holes.

For the tree, cut quarter circles with 25-, 19-, and 7-inch radii from medium-weight cardboard. Assemble by fitting the largest

Golden tree

Oilcloth trees

Cowhide bead tree

cone around the plywood circle (see illustration on page 30). Glue the overlap together. Hold the cone together with pins until the glue dries. When it is dry, trim off points of cone to fit the dowel through; measure and mark 12½ inches up from the bottom. Slide onto dowel. Repeat for the second and third cones. Cover with burlap or a coat of paint. Trim with lengths of gold metallic rope.

To make each angel, cut out back from cardboard (see sketch). Fold up flaps; glue in place. Cut and glue craft sticks or tongue depressors, as shown, for the body sides. To form the front panel of gown, glue craft sticks to body sides. Cut arms and hands from popsicle sticks, then paint sleeves and gown white. Cut wings and cover with gold foil paper. Position on back of angel.

Glue 4-inch chenille stems between wings. Glue arms to bottom of wings. For head, string two ⅜-inch wood beads and a 1-inch wood bead on the stem. Glue lace to the top bead. Crown with a gold star. See directions on page 30 for star. Add scalloped dress trims cut from gold foil paper. Glue a ½x2-inch gold strip for collar. Add wire loop to neck

Pyramid tree

Crocheted tree

Angel tree

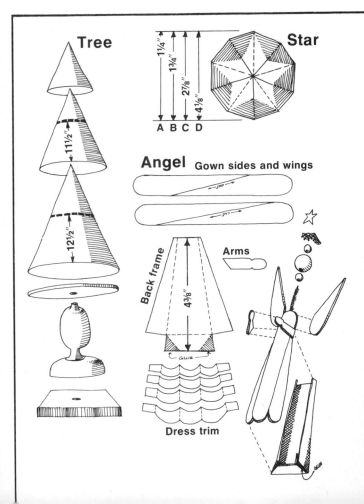

Tree

Star

1 1/4"
1 3/4"
2 7/8"
4 1/8"

A B C D

11 1/2"

12 1/2"

Angel Gown sides and wings

Back frame

4 3/8"

GLUE

Arms

Dress trim

(under collar) for hanging. Place seven angels on the bottom row; four on the top row.

Use gold tagboard, base metal, or heavy gold foil paper for the stars. Make 11 of A (1¼ inches) for angel crown; 16 of B (1¾ inches) to use around base; 47 of C (2⅞ inches) — use 28 for bottom tier, 15 for middle tier, and 4 for top tier; and 2 of D (4⅛ inches) for treetop. Cut dotted lines in shaded areas. Score all solid lines on one side and score all broken lines on the reverse side. Fold under the shaded areas.

The blue crocheted tree starts with a cone-shaped foundation. To make this foundation, use a 15-inch-square piece of flexible cardboard and draw a curved line diagonally across to form a quarter circle for foundation of tree. Cut along the curved line. Form cone, with the base measuring 4½ inches in diameter and tapering to a point at the tip. Secure firmly in place with tape or staple in place. Cover the cone with crepe paper.

Next, make the crocheted cover, starting at the tip, with 2 strands of crochet cotton in Parakeet blue held together, ch 4. Join with sl st to form ring. 1st rnd: ch 5 to measure 1 inch; *yarn over hook, draw up a loop in ring to same height as ch-5, (yarn over and draw through 2 loops) twice—1 inch dc made. Repeat from * 7 times more. Join with sl st to top of ch-5—8 dc. 2nd rnd: ch 8 to measure 1½ inches; yarn over hook, draw up a loop in same place as joining to same height as ch-8, (yarn over and draw through 2 loops) twice—1½ inch dc made; * ch 1, make a 1½-inch dc in next dc.

Repeat from * around, ending with ch 1. Join to top of ch-8 dc and 8 ch-1 sps. Hereafter, make dc's same height as starting ch-8 of rnd and join to top of starting chain of rnd. 3rd rnd: ch 8 to measure as before, *2 dc in next dc, ch 1. Repeat from * around. Join—16 dc and 8 ch-1 sps. 4th rnd: ch 8, dc in each dc and in each ch-1 sp around. Join—24 dc. Try crochet over cone as work progresses to check fit. 5th rnd: ch 8, *dc in next dc, 2 dc in next dc—inc made. Repeat from * around. Join—36 dc. 6th rnd: ch 8, dc in each dc around. Join—36 dc.

7th rnd: ch 8, increasing 9 dc evenly spaced, dc in each dc around. Join—45 dc. 8th and 9th rnds: repeat 6th and 7th rnds—54 dc on 7th rnd. 10th rnd: ch 8, increasing 6 dc evenly spaced, dc in each dc around. Join—60 dc. 11th rnd: Repeat 6th rnd. Leaving a 10-inch end of thread, break off and fasten. Slip

crochet over cone, allowing last rnd to extend beyond base of cone. Thread end of thread into a needle and draw tops of sts of last rnd closely together under base of cone; fasten.

Large flowers (make 31): starting at center with 2 strands of thread held together, ch 4. Join with sl st to form ring. Ch 9 to measure 1¾ inches. Make 25 1¾-inch dc in ring. Join. Leaving a 10-inch end, break off and fasten. Thread end of thread into a needle and make running sts through tops of sts. Stuff flower with some yarn; draw sts together and fasten. Leave remaining thread for sewing flower to crocheted cover on cone.

Small flowers (make 6): starting at center with 2 strands of thread held together, ch 4. Join with sl st to form ring. Ch 8 to measure 1½ inches. Make 18 1½-inch dc in ring. Join. Finish same way as for large flower above.

Twin leaves (make 64): with 2 strands of thread held together, *ch 12; make a 1-inch dc in 6th ch from hook and in each of next 4 ch, ch 3, skip next ch, sc in next ch to complete first leaf. Repeat from * once; drop loop from hook, insert hook through hole of a bangle and draw dropped loop through, ch 1, sl st in sc of first leaf. Leaving an 8-inch thread for sewing, break off.

Ball (make 8): starting at center with 2 strands of thread held together, ch 4. Join with sl st to form ring. 1st rnd: 6 sc in ring. 2nd rnd: 2 sc in each sc—12 sc. Next 4 rnds: sc in each sc around. Leaving an 8-inch end, break off; fasten. Finish same as large flower.

Sew one large flower to top of cone. Then, arrange remaining flowers and balls over the cone; sew in place. Stitch centers of twin leaves between flowers and balls.

Crochet abbreviations	
ch	chain
sc	single crochet
dc	double crochet
sl st	slip stitch
sp (s)	space (s)
rnd	round
inc	increase
st (s)	stitch (es)
comp	completely
sk	skip
co	continue

* Repeat whatever follows * as many times as specified ( ) Do what is in parenthesis number of times indicated.

Chapter 2

Trims for Trees

Make every December 25 the most memorable Christmas ever by concocting your own tree decorations. And, to make it even more rewarding, let the whole family join forces and contribute time, talent, and energy to this project. This pooling of talent will generate ideas that are definitely not run-of-the-mill.

Take a look at the ornaments in this chapter, and choose those that will give your tree a flattering, new look.

The yarn ornaments in the photo at the left were made with the help of a sewing machine. Why not duplicate some of them? To make the pink and orange teardrop at the far left, wind yarn around a 1½x12-inch strip of construction paper. Sew down center, trim yarn and paper, then tear paper away and shake yarn hard to twist. Tie ends together to form a teardrop; add a pompon at the top.

To make the wreath at the upper far right, wind a 2x10-inch strip of paper with three layers of green yarn. Sew down the center twice; tear away paper between loops. Wind yarn around a 9-inch length of No. 20 wire and bend into a circle. Twist wire ends and tie yarn ends; trim with a yarn bow.

For the others, wind yarn around paper, insert wire along one edge, then stitch wire in place. Remove paper and bend wire into desired shapes. Trim with balls or pompons.

Here's your opportunity to experiment with unusual color combinations of yarn. And, you can cut down on the hours needed to make the assortment of yarn ornaments shown in the picture at the left if you use your sewing machine.

Trims from yarn

Yarn may seem like an unlikely candidate for Christmas tree decorations, but it has many advantages: you can choose from an almost unlimited array of colors; it's easy to work with; and since it's unbreakable, even if you have small children with inquisitive fingers, there is no safety problem.

Crocheted ornaments

You can crochet the entire group of ornaments shown on pages 35, 36, and 37 with a few skeins of yarn and a crochet hook. Then, add some tiny round mirrors, beads, brilliants, or heavy metallic foil to decorate them.

For the variegated star, you will need about 10 yards of variegated yarn, two yards of green knitting worsted, a size H crochet hook, and two tablespoons of wallpaper paste.

Star (make two): with variegated yarn, ch 4. Join with sl st to form ring. 1st rnd: ch 1, in ring make (sc, ch 7) 5 times. Join to first sc— 5 loops made. 2nd rnd: ch 1, (in next loop make 4 sc, ch 3; and 4 sc) 5 times. Join; break off; fasten. With wrong sides tog, using green and catching only inside loops of each edge, sew stars tog, making 2 overcast sts in each st around. With green make a 9-inch chain for hanger. Sew ends tog to form a loop, and sew to one point on star.

Mix wallpaper paste with 8 to 10 tablespoons of water. Leave the hanger free, and saturate the star with paste. Squeeze out, then pull back in shape; hang up to dry.

The beaded ball requires ½ ounce each of a light and a dark color of fingering yarn, a No. 1 steel crochet hook, and 150 beads.

Starting at center with dark color, ch 6. Join with sl st to form ring. 1st rnd: ch 4, dc in ring (ch 1, dc in ring) 14 times; ch 1. Join with sl st to 3rd ch of first ch-4—15 dc and 15 ch-1 sps made. Break off; turn. 2nd rnd: attach light color to any dc, ch-4,* in next ch-1 sp make dc, ch 1 and dc, ch 1, dc in next dc, ch 1. Repeat from * around ending with ch 1, join to 3rd ch of ch-4. Break off; turn.

3rd and 4th rnds: alternating colors, repeat 2nd rnd twice. 5th rnd: string 150 beads onto dark color. With wrong side of last rnd facing, attach dark to any dc, ch 1, sc in same dc where yarn was attached, *ch 2, insert hook

in next dc and draw loop through, slip up a bead, yarn over hook and draw through 2 loops on hook—bead sc made; (ch 2, sc in next dc) 3 times. Repeat from * around. Break off and fasten. Holding one strand of each color together, make a 10-inch chain. Join with sl st to first ch to form hanger. Break off and fasten. Sew a hanger to the center.

For the pompon ball, you will need 1 ounce of pink knitting worsted, a 3-inch white foam ball, 1 bead and 1 sequin for each pompon, and long straight pins.

For each pompon, wind yarn around three fingers 15 times. Break off. Tie strands tog at center; cut loops at each end and trim. Slip a bead onto pin. Then slip sequin onto same pin. Stick beaded pin through center of pompon; then into white foam ball. Make necessary number to cover ball.

The three-color star requires only a few yards each of pink, purple, and orange knitting worsted, a size G crochet hook, 3 large teardrop rhinestones, and 4 tablespoons of wallpaper paste.

Make 3 motifs—one each of pink, purple, and orange. Motif: ch 4, join with sl st to form ring. 1st rnd; ch 1, 8 sc in ring. Join. 2nd rnd: ch 6, dc in same place as joining sl st, * ch 1, in next sc make dc, ch 3 and dc. Repeat from * 6 times more; ch 1, join to 3rd ch of ch-6. 3rd rnd: *ch 1, in next ch-3 sp make sc, ch 1, dc, ch 5, sl st in 5th ch from hook, dc, ch 1 and sc—point made; ch 1, sl st in next ch-1 sp. Repeat from * around. Join, break off, and fasten.

Use wrong side of crochet as right side of star. With right sides tog, overcast the edges of 4 points of purple and pink motifs tog. Then, overcast 4 points of orange motif to the 4 free points of pink motif. Overcast remaining 4 purple and 4 orange points tog. With purple, make a 9-inch chain for hanging. Sew ends together to form a loop and sew to top. Mix wallpaper paste with 12 to 15 tablespoons of water. Leaving hanger free, saturate star with paste, squeeze out, pull back in 3-division shape, and hang up to dry. When thoroughly dry, glue a glittering teardrop to the center of each motif.

The multicolor crocheted link chain requires 2 ounces of rainbow knitting worsted and a size H crochet hook.

First link: ch 20. Join with sl st to first ch to form a ring. Ch 3, dc in each ch around. Join to top of ch-3. Break off. Second link: ch 20, pass the end of ch-20 through last link made. Join with sl st to first ch of ch-20 to form ring. Complete same as first link. Join links together.

For the three-dimensional square, you'll need 2 ounces each of rose and green knitting worsted, a size H crochet hook, and heavy foil or metallic gift wrap paper.

Motif (make 3): wire rose, ch 6. Join with sl st to form ring. 1st rnd: ch 4, 3 tr in ring, * ch 4, 4 tr in same ring. Repeat from * twice; ch 4. Join to top of ch-4—4 bls and 4 sps made. 2nd rnd: ch 1, sc in same place as joining sl st, * sc in each tr to within ch-4 sp, 6 sc in sp. Repeat from * around. Join to first sc. Break off and fasten. 3rd rnd: attach green to same sc where last joining was made, ch 4, tr in next 5 sc, * 2 tr in next sc, ch 4, 2 tr in next sc, tr in next 8 sc. Repeat from * around ending with 2 tr in last 2 sc. Join. 4th rnd: repeat 2nd rnd. Break off and fasten.

Cut a piece of foil or gift wrap same size as motif; pin to wrong side of motif. With foil sides tog, sew 2 edges of 1st and 2nd motifs tog. Then, sew 2 edges of 3rd motif to remaining 2 edges of 2nd motif. Sew remaining 2 edges of 3rd motif to remaining edges of 1st motif. With green, make a 7-inch chain for hanger. Sew ends tog to form a loop and screw to top.

The sunburst takes 1 ounce of light orange and a few yards of dark orange knitting worsted, a size H crochet hook, and 2 mirrors, 2 inches in diameter.

Motif (make 2): with light orange, ch 4. Join with sl st to form ring. 1st rnd: 7 sc in ring. 2nd rnd: 2 sc in each sc—14 sc made. 3rd rnd: (sc in next sc, 2 sc in next sc) 7 times —21 sc. 4th rnd: working in back loops only, * in next sc make sc and hdc; in next sc make dc and tr; in next sc make dc and hdc. Repeat from * around—7 points. Break off and fasten. Center: attach dark orange to remaining front loop of any sc on 3rd rnd, ch 4, * skip front loop of next sc, dc in front loop of next sc, ch 1. Repeat from * around. Join to 3rd ch of ch-4. Break off; leave 8-inch length of yarn. Place a mirror in center of motif.

Thread a needle with 8-inch length and run through tops of dc's. Draw up tightly to hold mirror in place and fasten. With wrong sides of motifs tog, attach light orange to a sc between points * working in the center

Crocheted tree ornaments

loop of each st on each edge, make sc in next 2 sts, in tr make sc, ch 3 and sc, sc in next 2 sts, sl st in next sc. Repeat from * around, ending with sl st in place where yarn was attached. For hanger, make 8-inch chain and sl st in same place as last sl st. Break off; fasten.

Crochet abbreviations	
ch	chain
sc	single crochet
hdc	half double crochet
dc	double crochet
tr	treble crochet
st	stitch
sl st	slip stitch
rnd	round
tog	together
bl	block
sp	space
( )	do what is in parenthesis the number of times indicated
*	repeat whatever follows the * as many times as specified

35

These crocheted tree decorations will add to the excitement of Christmas morning because they have pockets to hold small treasures. Fill them with tiny toys for the little ones, an unexpected piece of jewelry for Mom, or a key chain or money clip for Dad. Make these from small amounts of knitting worsted, using a size 1 crochet hook.

Square pocket ornament with fringe: with variegated yarn, ch 30, sl st to first ch (top of bag), ch 1. Rnd 1: 1 sc in each ch around, sl st to first sc (30 sc), ch 1. Rnds 2 through 9: *1 sc in each sc around, sl to first sc (30 sc), ch 1. Repeat from * for each rnd. On rnd 9 omit ch 1. Fasten off. Rnds 10 through 13: attach plain color yarn and repeat rnd 2. On rnd 13 omit ch 1. Fasten off. Rnds 14 through 17: attach variegated yarn and repeat rnd 10. On rnd 17, omit ch 1. Fasten off.

To finish: attach plain yarn to top of bag in first ch st sp. 1 sc in each sp around, sl st to first sc. Ch 25 and attach to opposite side of bag for handle. Fasten off.

Fringe: cut 15 5-inch strands of plain yarn. Fold one strand in half and draw through both edges at bottom. Pull cut ends through loop to knot. Repeat with the other 14 strands to close bag and make fringe. Sew the bell to top center front of the bag.

Star pocket ornament: (Make two): with 1st color, starting at center, ch 4, sl st to first ch to form ring. Rnd 1: 10 sc in center of ring, sl st to first sc. Rnd 2: ch 4, 1 sc in 2nd ch from hook, 1 sc in each of next 2 ch sts, *sk next sc on rnd 1 and sl st in next sc, ch 4, 1 sc in 2nd ch from hook, 1 sc in next 2 ch sts. Repeat from * 3 times, sl st to first sl st; fasten off.

(Makes 5 points.) Rnd 3: attach 2nd color to top st of any point, 1 sc in same sp, * sk next 2 sc, work cluster of 5 dc in sl st sp, 1 sc in top of next point. Repeat from * 4 times. Sl to first sc. Fasten off.

Rnd 4: picking up back loops of rnd 3, attach 3rd color in any sp, 1 sc in same sp, 1 sc in each sp around (30 sc), sl st to first sc. Fasten off. Rnd 5: attach 4th color to any sc midway between 2 points, sl st in same sp, * 1 sc in next sc, 1 hdc in next sc, 2 dc in next sc, ch 2, sl st in 2nd ch from hook (picot), 2 dc in same sc sp with last dc, 1 hdc in next sc, 1

sc in next sl st, sl st in next sc. Repeat from * around 4 times, sl st to first sl st. Fasten off.

Assembling: place 2 star shapes wrong sides together. Leave open at top between 2 points. With 4th color yarn, whipstitch together through top back loops around star. Attach 4th color yarn to one of points at side of opening, ch 25 and attach to other side of opening for handle. Fasten off. Make a 2-inch pompon; attach to bottom center point.

Square diamond (not visible): make 2 sqs. Starting at center, with first color ch 4, sl st to first ch to form ring. Rnd 1: ch 3 (counts as 1 dc), 3 dc in center of ring, ch 1, * 4 dc in center of ring, ch 1. Repeat from * 2 times. Sl st to top of ch 3 to join (16 dc in all). Fasten off. Rnd 2: attach second color in any ch-1 corner, 1 sc, ch 2, 1 sc in same sp, * 1 sc in top of next 4 dc, 1 sc in next ch-1 sp, ch 2, 1 sc in same sp. Repeat from * around, sl st to first sc. Fasten off. Rnd 3: attach 3rd color in corner sp, ch 3 (counts as 1 dc). 1 dc in same sp, ch 2, 2 dc in same sp, * 1 dc in each of next 5 sc, 2 dc in next corner sp, ch 2, 2 dc in same sp. Repeat from * around, sl to top of first dc. Fasten off. Rnd 4: attach 2nd color in corner sp, 1 sc in same sp, ch 2, 1 sc in same sp, *1 sc in next 9 dc sps, 1 sc in next corner sp, ch 2, 1 sc in same sp. Repeat from * around sl st to first sc. Fasten off.

Assembling: place squares wrong sides together and mark opening 2 inches down from top point on either side. Whipstitch sides together, leaving open between marks. Attach yarn to one top corner, ch 15, fasten to top corner of opposite square to form a hanger. Make a 36-strand, 3-inch-long yarn tassel. Attach the tassel to the bottom of the diamond.

Cornucopia (not shown): crochet a square, following the instructions above, except make the square 1 inch larger all around. Bring the two opposite corners together and whipstitch a seam to form a cornucopia. Attach a yarn tassel to the bottom point. Fasten a 1-inch brass ring to the top point.

These brightly colored crocheted tree decorations ▶ are holiday versions of miniature tote bags. The night before Christmas, fill them with gift packages for every member of the family.

Needlepoint hang-ups stitched on canvas

Needlepoint news

Whether you're a novice with a needle or a past master of needlepoint, you'll enjoy trimming your Christmas tree with these creative masterpieces. For the thrifty-minded, this is a wonderful opportunity to make good use of scraps of needlepoint canvas and wool. For the recycling enthusiast, it will be rewarding to utilize plastic berry boxes as a base for needlepoint stitching.

For the needlepoint ornaments stitched on needlepoint canvas, use single thread canvas (10 meshes per inch). Work the designs in bright colors of yarn, following the charts. Bind the edges of the canvas with masking tape to prevent raveling. Follow the graphs shown here to make the designs. (One square on the graph equals one mesh on the canvas.) Fill in the canvas with half-cross stitches

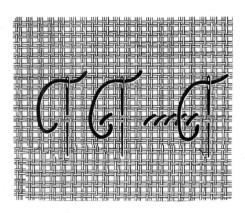

(see sketch, opposite page, left), always bringing the needle out at the bottom of the stitch, working over one mesh of the canvas. Always stitch in the same direction—from the lower left to the upper right.

When you have completed the stitching, remove the masking tape and steam press

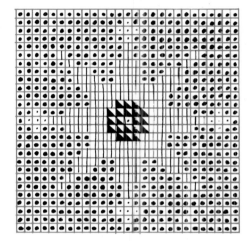

each piece on the wrong side. For the oblong ornaments, use half-inch-thick plastic foam cut to whatever size you wish. For the thicker versions, use a double thickness of foam. Trim the canvas, leaving ½ inch around the edges. Pin the canvas to the foam base; glue down the edges of the canvas to the edges of the foam base. Use rubber bands to hold

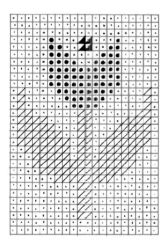

down the canvas while the glue dries. When the glue is dry, cover the edges with thick yarn and glue it down.

For the pyramid decoration, cut four triangles from cardboard—2⅝ inches at the base by 3 inches on the side. Cut one 2⅝ inches square. Tape these together to form the

Plastic berry boxes with coverups

pyramid. Cut felt pieces to fit the bottom and two sides. Stitch the side and bottom edge of the needlepoint triangles to the felt with a catch stitch. Insert the pyramid; stitch the other needlepoint sides.

Plastic berry boxes are a good substitute for needlepoint canvas, as you can see from the ornaments shown above. And, the boxes are a no-cost retrievable item. Experiment with unusual color combinations of yarn gift tie, or use double strands of knitting worsted for equal effectiveness. To make these ornaments, you will need only a basic knowledge of the simplest needlepoint stitches.

Instead of using regular needlepoint canvas, use pieces cut from ordinary plastic berry boxes for the bases, cutting two of each shape desired. Alternate the horizontal and the vertical stitches, one abutting the other, on the same grid. Overcast the stitches around the outside of each shape.

Finish the yarn ends at the beginning and the end by weaving under the stitches. At the top of each decoration, make a loop for hanging. Trim with a fluffy yarn tassel.

Fun with felt

Look at the diversity of color scheming you can bring into play with these felt trims. Use them on your Christmas tree, at the table to hold place cards, or any spot where you want a touch of brightness.

Felt bouquets

The only materials you need for these baskets of flowers are small amounts of felt, disposable broiler or cookie sheet foil, and glue.

To make the basket, cut a 5-inch circle from broiler or cookie sheet foil and another from felt. Coat each with adhesive and join.

On metal side, draw a 1-inch circle in center. Cut 16 evenly spaced slits to center circle; snip off every other section. This leaves eight sections to form basket. Overlap sections slightly all around, placing glue on inside of basket at each overlap.

For handles, cut foil in 3/16-inch-wide strips —enough for a length of 24 inches—and join into one long strip; cover with same color felt. Spiral handle strips around a No. 3 knitting needle. Glue to basket.

To make flowers, draw petals and leaves freehand, then trace designs onto felt-covered foil. Cut out shapes with scissors.

Felt bouquets

Slip No. 30 wire stems through petals; anchor a pleasing arrangement inside baskets with wire and glue. Keep flower arrangements low inside baskets so handles will slip over the branches easily.

To construct chains, spiral the foil strips around a pencil or dowel, then put together as you would old-fashioned paper chains. Affix flowers on some of the links. Make the flowers the same as for the baskets. Join two together and attach to chain links.

Felt dolls

These delightful little folks can hang on your tree to amuse your family, or you can use them as stocking stuffers or party favors.

1. For the boy, cut ½-inch foam in shape of body, ¼ inch smaller than pattern for clothes. Cut a back and front for each pattern piece.

Hands and sleeves are cut double (cut 4). Glue felt head on foam base. Glue yellow yarn in place. Glue shirt, pants, and shoes. Add detail to collar; glue to shirt. Put detail on shoes (use liquid embroidery and tiny gold beads). Glue hat to head; glue white grosgrain ribbon around hat, and top the hat with two pompons.

2, 3, 4, and 5. Enlarge doll patterns (see sketch); make two copies—one for cutting out pieces, and one for reference.

Turn second copy to back side; draw in each detail carefully with transfer pencil. Place, transfer side down, on a piece of beige or pink felt, making it larger than the doll itself. Press with an iron to make transfer. (This makes placement of pieces easy.)

Cut all pieces from scraps of felt and tiny cotton prints. Lay fusible bonding material over doll, cutting out face area and hair line. Pin cutout pieces in place, using transfer lines as a guide. Press fabric pieces in place, according to package instructions for bonding material.

Embroider features that are too tiny to cut from fabric. Cut a second felt piece for back side. Stitch front and back together, stuffing with cotton as you go.

6. For the girl (lower right in photo), cut out the pieces according to the sketch; glue felt head to foam base, as for the boy above. Put detail on the shoes. Glue on red dress. Add lace and bows to the apron; glue fronts together. Glue to dress. Glue the hands and sleeves together; add to apron. Add lace trim, hat, and ribbon trim.

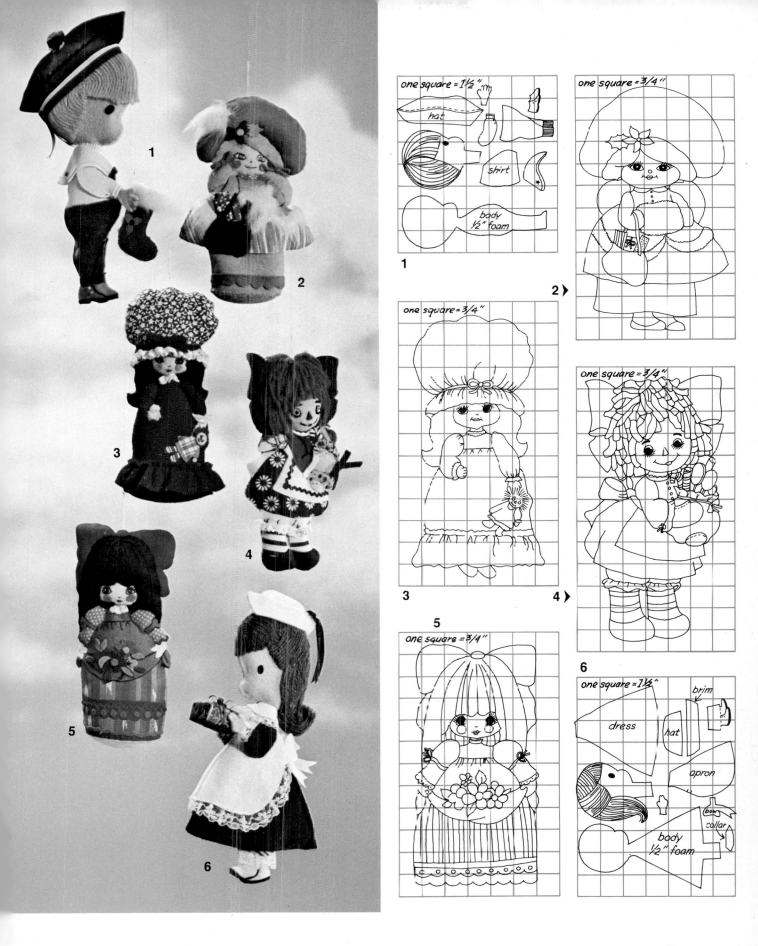

one square = 1½"
hat
shirt
body ½" foam
1

one square = ¾"
2 ▶

one square = ¾"
3

one square = ¾"
4 ▶

one square = ¾"
5

6

one square = 1½"
brim
dress
hat
apron
body ½" foam
bow
collar

Thread-covered balls

Hollowed-out ball

Ribbon and lace ornaments

Bell and ball ornaments

Plastic foam coverups

It's like waving a magic wand and converting Cinderella's pumpkin into a handsome coach when you start with ordinary plastic foam bases and deck them out in finery.

Thread-covered balls

Use satin or plastic foam balls (the kind you can stick pins into and hold crochet cotton or silk sewing thread in place as you wind it around balls) in assorted sizes to make these decorations (opposite page, top left).

Directions are for a five-inch-diameter ball. Adjust directions accordingly for smaller balls. Mark the North Pole (top), South Pole (bottom), and opposite points at east and west with straight pins. These points should be equally spaced on a circumference. Mark middle front and middle back, too.

Start winding No. 8 crochet cotton or silk sewing thread. Hold end of background color (gold) at top; wind around ball. Lay thread an inch to the left of the front pin, and along the right side of the top pin.

The second round goes ⅛ inch to the left of the first thread at the back (along the left side of the bottom pin) ⅛ inch to the right of the first thread at the front, and along the right side of the top pin.

Continue moving ⅛ inch to the left in back, and ⅛ inch to the right in front. Cross threads at top and bottom until ball is covered, except for 2-inch space front and back. Cut off. Thread end of thread into a large needle; sew through crossover point and/or the ball itself to fasten.

Make another layer (same color), using east and west pins as the crossover points.

Start with another color (white) at the top; wind ⁵⁄₁₆ inch to right of back pin, to left of bottom pin, ⁵⁄₁₆ inch to left of front pin, and to right of top pin. Wind second strand exactly next to first one, crossing top and bottom. Leave a small space after the first two. Wind third and fourth strands next to each other. You should have four pairs of threads before the front and back pins, and four pairs after to form a ⅝-inch panel front and back of eight pairs of threads.

Repeat the above procedure with the same color, using the east and west pins as poles.

This forms a 4-pointed star, with a grid where all the threads cross.

Mark the NE, NW, SW, and SE points on the circumference. Any pin may be removed once point it marks is established on ball.

With a contrasting color (red), repeat the last two panels; use newly marked points as crossover points. This forms an 8-pointed star with points of alternating colors.

Using this same technique, wind 6 threads of a dark color (navy or black) on *each* side of *each* panel; form an outlined 8-pointed star, with another 8-pointed star inside it, and an octagon in the center.

Using the second 'star' color (red), wind a ⁵⁄₁₆-inch strip on each side of each panel of the first 'star' color. (NS-EW). Each white-striped part will now have a dark outline with a red stripe on each side of it.

Do the same with the 'opposite' color (white) along the remaining points; (NE-SW, NW-SE). The eight points will be of equal size but opposite colors.

Wind four strands of black or navy around the circumference (the points of the star) without crossing. Wind four strands of white on each side of dark strips.

Wind a ¼-inch-wide pale pink strip on each side of the NE-SW, NW-SE points.

Attach a double cord and large tassels to the bottom, and a cord for hanging at the top.

Bells, balls, and stars

It's easy to make a collection of exquisite bell, ball, and star ornaments such as those at the upper right, lower left, and lower right of the opposite page when you start with plastic foam bases. Look through your craft cupboard for lace, ribbon, braid, buttons, and other assorted tack-ons for trimming them.

Either pin or glue the trim to the plastic foam bases. If you use white glue, allow it to thicken to a syrupy consistency before applying it to the foam. For trims that do not adhere well, pin them directly onto the shapes until dry, then remove the pins.

After the basic forms have been covered, add finishing touches of lace, ribbons, embroidery, handpressed posies, or old postcard cutouts. Attach tassels with straight pins.

Wax isn't only for museums

For unsurpassed elegance, trim your tree with wax-coated ornaments. They will bring you pleasure for many years to come. For the base, use white plastic foam balls with slightly irregular surfaces that require some sanding. Or, if you prefer, use the kind resembling stiff crystalline, and cover the surface of the ball with tissue paper first.

When making these eye-pleasing ornaments, be sure your finished design has continuity. Achieve this by using all the same pictures or by selecting pictures that have a similar background, artistic style, and scale. Keep a file of favorites.

When you've selected compatible pictures, tear off edges in a downward motion so the white of the paper will not be visible. The thinner the card, the better it will adhere to the ball. Turn card over and peel off back carefully (see picture 1). Next, turn card over to picture side and make one-inch tears toward center from edge to help card bend around ball. Try not to tear into vital areas of picture. Sand ball and place cards around ball to check for fit and appearance. Corners of card should touch at top.

For paste, mix three tablespoons cellulose powder with enough water to make it thick and creamy. Paste will last for months if you keep it stored in a sealed jar.

To make the hanger for ball, cut a generous length of cord or monofilament fishing line. Double and tie ends of cord around head of a pin. Use a darning needle to push pin into foam ball until head of pin is below surface of plastic ball. Fill this indentation and any other dents in the ball with freshly mixed spackle. Allow to dry thoroughly, then sand surface smooth.

Hold cards on ball and mark center, top, bottom, and sides to avoid overlapping and unevenness. Put cellulose paste on back of first card. Center the card, following marks. Smooth card out from center to torn sections, overlapping to avoid any wrinkling. Smooth card down quickly and carefully (picture 2). Then, put a matching card in middle of opposite side. If the corners overlap, tear off part of cards so they just meet. Let ball dry.

To give continuity of color, mix a color with acrylic paints that harmonizes with the background of the cards. Using a watercolor brush, apply paint to all areas not covered with cards and let it dry.

To prepare paraffin, place aluminum foil in bottom of electric skillet for easy cleaning. Add ½ inch of water; set heat at 250°. Place one-inch squares of paraffin in tuna cans. Turn to 200° when wax melts.

Next, brush on thin coats of wax over entire area of ornaments. Use several coats, but not enough to obscure the images on the cards (picture 3). (If the wax is opaque, the temperature may be too low.) For easy wax application, stand the ball in a tumbler or bowl. Wax the upper half, let it dry, turn the ball, and wax the lower half.

Scrape off any excess wax with an old paring knife (picture 4). If you hit a projection caused by a wrinkle in the card, press this area down lightly, apply wax over it, and scrape it again. When the entire ball is smooth and even, rub finished ornament with an old terry-cloth towel to add sheen.

◀ **A warm, subtle glow emanates** from these wax-coated wonders. Best of all, they're made of simple, inexpensive, commonly available materials.

1 **2** **3** **4**

Cardboard capers

When you're assembling materials to use for making Christmas tree decorations, don't forget to salvage pieces of cardboard, heavyweight paper, tagboard, or mat board. All three of the treetop ornaments shown on these pages start with one of these materials.

Five-pointed star

To make this yarn-covered star, draw a pattern on heavy cardboard, following sketch given here. Draw a circle with a radius of 5½ inches. Point A on sketch equals half the radius. Using radius on compass of distance from A to B, swing an arc from A to find point C. For point D, use radius of distance from B to C, swinging arc from B. Use length from B to D to find points E, F, G around circle. Draw lines between points, forming a star.

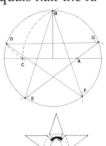

Cut out the star, then cut one-inch slots in it, as shown in the second sketch. Bend heavy wire around the star, allowing the end to follow edge of slot; tape in place. (Star is covered with yarn, so the wire will be hidden.) Bend end of wire to serve as ornament hanger.

Put glue on all of the sections together; weave yarn over and under in slots. Wind points in same manner from the center to the tips. At the tips, run the yarn ends under the wrapped area. Make center pompons of pink and red yarn.

Woven star

To make this wondrous beauty, cut a 6-sided shape from mat board (see sketch in the next column). Sharpen one end of five wood chopsticks; trim to desired length. Leave sixth one long enough to anchor to the tree. Glue sticks to every other point of hexagon, turn, and secure remaining sticks on opposite side. Spray with flat black paint. Trim with self-adhering paper or vinyl. Glue wooden beads in place. Put glue on alternating sticks as stays for the first row of crochet thread.

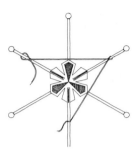

Tie thread and wrap around sticks to create a triangle. Open spacing around stick results from winding thread two or three times around stick before carrying it to the next one. When triangle is complete, tie thread and turn piece over; repeat weaving on remaining sticks. Brush knots with glue; clip threads.

Eight-pointed star

To make the yarn-trimmed ornament shown here in blue and gold, fold a 6-inch-square piece of heavyweight paper, cardboard, or tagboard into 16 squares (each measuring 1½x1½ inches). Turn paper over, fold on diagonals, corner to corner, then points to center of square (solid lines on sketch). Cut lines A to B on sketch. Hold square with horizontal folds up; pop all dots from underneath. Paper will fall into a ball with all dots on outside points. All horizontal and vertical folds will become mountains; the diagonals valleys.

On one folded square, glue or tape all sections marked '1' over all sections marked '2', matching folds. Repeat all steps on second square of paper. Place open points into position. This makes a sturdy, double-wall structure. Since it will be hidden by arms, use any type of paper you wish.

To make points: measure base on one triangle on polyhedron; use this measurement as radius of circle. Each point takes a quarter circle. On quarter circle, measure and fold into four equal parts. Fold under ½-inch tabs, as shown in the sketch. Overlap section 4 on section 1; glue. Bend up tabs; glue to points.

Before attaching last arm, make a hole through remaining point of polyhedron and through ball; cut opposite point with a pointed tool such as a knitting needle. Thread a piece of heavy wire through, bending end over polyhedron point; secure wire with masking tape. Spiral wire for attaching finial to tree. Glue remaining arm to point. Trim with colored yarn that you make into pompons for each point.

46

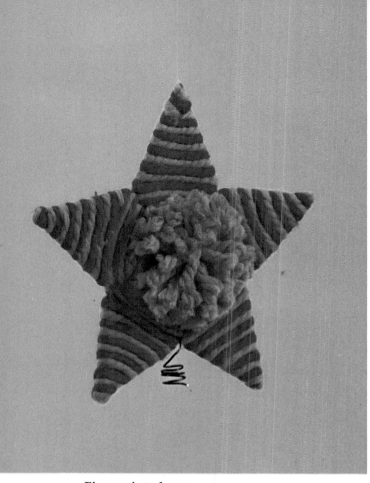

Five-pointed star

Woven star

Eight-pointed star

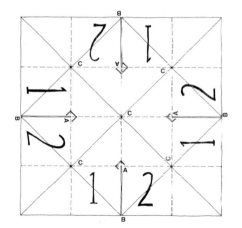

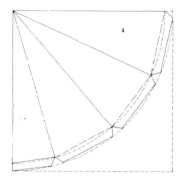

Finds from nature

Don't forget Mother Nature as a source for materials when you are collecting items to use in tree trim craft projects. The instructions that follow make use of eggs, seeds, pods, and wood. You'll enjoy testing your creative skills by using these simple objects.

Start with eggs

Decorated eggs are colorful and are fun to make. Start with blown eggshells (see instructions below) or use plastic foam eggs, then add your own decorations.

These wax-coated seed balls are a joy to make and beautiful to behold. Even the younger members of the family can participate because they are so simple to make. For the bases, choose either plastic foam shapes or hens' eggs. If you use the latter, make a hole in both ends (one larger than the other) and blow into the smaller hole at one end, forcing out the contents of the egg through the larger hole at the other end.

Select seeds small enough to conform to the oval egg shape—such as seeds from squash, melons, barley, or rice. If you wish to darken the natural color of the seeds, toast them in a 200° to 250° oven.

To string the egg for hanging as a tree ornament, cut 18-inch lengths of heavy thread or fishline. Thread a small bead or pearl onto the line and tie in the center. Thread the two ends of the line into the smaller hole of the egg and out of the larger hole. Add a drop of glue on the hole; draw the bead to it and glue the bead to the larger hole.

Brush glue on a small section of the egg, then arrange the seeds on the egg in even rows. Overlap the seeds slightly for a textured look, and allow them to dry. In a can set in a saucepan of water, melt pieces of old white candles or paraffin used for canning. When it is melted, remove it from the heat and wait

from 5 to 10 minutes. Dip a teaspoon in to see if the wax will coat the spoon. If it is too hot, let it cool longer. If it is too cold, reheat it and test the wax again. When it is ready, hold the egg by the string, dip it in the wax, and roll it around. One coat should be sufficient to cover the egg.

Eggheads, which can double as tree ornaments or table decorations, can be as ornate and colorful as you wish. Why not have a family contest to see who uses the most ingenuity when designing the eggs?

Some of the eggheads shown below are colored with acrylic paints; others are tinted with egg dye. You might even want to leave some of the eggs their natural color, then dress them in holiday finery.

Glue on bottle caps or segments that have been cut from egg cartons for the hats. Paint the faces, and glue strips of paper ribbon to simulate hair.

On the plaster-trimmed eggs, place spackle in a squeeze bottle and apply squiggles from the bottle. When the spackle is dry, paint the eggs with tempera or acrylic paints. Finally, preserve eggs with a coat of shellac.

Use these to trim your tree or as place cards for a whimsical table setting. Also, make some extras to hang in a cluster in various lengths over the breakfast table.

These eggs, decorated with seeds and coated with wax, are so easy to make that even the youngest members of the family can participate. Use squash or melon seeds, rice, or barley.

49

Egghead collection

The collection of tastefully decorated eggs on the opposite page (top photo) could well be the focal point of the festive holiday season. These blown-out eggs and overscale plastic eggs, suspended from pungent fir branches, are covered with acrylic paints and adorned with jewels, cord, and braid.

The flowerpot egg shown at the left in the photo is made of a hen's egg, with the contents blown out according to the directions on page 49. Cut a hole at each end of the shell with a craft knife or a razor blade. Glue the stem from a broken wine glass or goblet into one end. Paint the egg with tempera paints, and add the decorative trim with a felt tip pen. Insert a spray of dried flowers or greenery in the top of the decoration.

Hanging eggs make exciting tree decorations. Use eggshells or plastic foam egg shapes and trim them with paint and jewels. First, draw the design on with pencil. Then, paint the egg with tempera paints. Decorate the eggs with jewels you collect from discarded or broken jewelry, or buttons, Glue the jewels on; also glue on bands of metallic braid or ribbon for a finishing touch.

The standing egg, decorated in natural earth tones, is made simply from a plastic egg that once served as a prosaic hosiery package. First, bore a hole through the bottom of the egg and insert a stem from a broken wine glass. Secure it with white glue. Draw the design on with a pencil. Paint the design with tempera, and finish your creation with a coat of clear varnish or acrylic spray to add a long-lasting lustrous finish.

The egg cage at the far right, designed to resemble a graceful gazebo, will make a stunning tabletop ornament.

Assemble the cage from a precut wooden base, ⅛-inch wooden dowels, cardboard, a copper disk (used for copper enameling and available at hobby or craft shops), and a wooden turned knob or drawer pull.

Cut the four sides and square top from cardboard, following illustration in the next column. Glue the parts together. Cut a piece of cardboard to fit the top of the wooden base. Glue the beads to the centers of the four posts. Glue posts into inside corners of top and onto corners of cardboard base. Paint the cage with stark white latex wall paint. Blow the contents from an egg. Transfer a wallpaper design from the wall covering to the egg by drawing it on lightly with pencil. Paint the design with tempera paints. With a

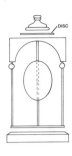

pair of small scissors, enlarge the holes at each end of the egg so they will accommodate a ⅛-inch dowel rod cut to the height of the cage. Paint the dowel white, the same as the cage, then push it through the egg and glue it in place. Glue the dowel and egg to the inside of the cage. Be sure that the dowel is centered.

Place the cardboard structure on the wooden base and glue it in place. Glue the copper disk on top of the structure, and glue on the wooden knob for a finial.

These happy characters, with engaging grins on their faces, guarantee to evoke a jovial holiday spirit from all who view them.

To create these smile-inviting ornaments, use eggs as foundations. For each one, cut four pieces of fast-setting plaster of paris surgical bandage (available from surgical supply stores) five inches wide and long enough to go around the egg. Trim the bandage edges and dip one strip at a time into warm water. Apply the wet bandage to the egg, smoothing with your fingers. If bandage starts to dry while you are working with it, dip fingers in water. Apply the next strip to overlap the first; continue adding the other strips until the whole egg is covered.

Cut five inches of sturdy, lightweight wire and push into the top for a hanger. When the plaster has dried, paint the egg with gesso. Draw face on with a pencil, then paint all with acrylic paint. Outline face with gold paint. Attach a bell to the end of the wire hanger and paint wire and bell gold.

Pods with glamour

Milkweed pods collected along the roadside adorn the tree shown here. To make these unique decorations, split pods in half and decorate them any way you want. Spray-paint the outside of the pods in colors to enhance your room. When paint dries, brush insides of some with glue and dust them with glitter. Glue a spangle centered with a rhinestone in opening of pod.

On others, brush glue only along front edges and dust with glitter. Glue ball fringe, pompons, or spangles to the pods, or suspend beads and balls in the openings. Make a hole at the top of the pods and string metallic string or braid through to form a hanger.

Hanging and standing egg decorations

Happy faces

Pods with glamour

Jolly jigsaw cutouts

There was a time when small dolls and toys were painstakingly whittled by hand by Father or Grandfather. He would start with a single block of wood and whittle slowly and carefully until each feature could pass his critical inspection. These handcrafted wooden toys are now treasured by collectors.

Now that the jigsaw has eliminated so much of the manual labor involved in woodworking projects, you can do surprising

things with wood in very little time. This is one of the easiest tools to use skillfully, and one of the safest. With all these virtues, it's no wonder that the jigsaw's the natural choice for making wooden toys for children.

All it takes to make the ornaments shown on these two pages is a few basic woodworking tools, some scraps of plywood, paint, dowels, beads, staples, and a modest amount of woodworking know-how.

The storybook characters shown on the opposite page will delight small children. And their cost will delight you—you can make the grouping from a single sheet of ⅛-inch-thick plywood measuring 12x18 inches. First, trace the patterns (see sketch) onto the wood with a pencil, then cut out the pieces with a jigsaw along the tracing lines. Give each piece a coat of white oil-base paint to act as a sealer. Sand the pieces lightly after the paint is completely dry.

Paint the articles of clothing and the facial features with enamel for a hard, glossy finish, or use acrylic paints. Paint the lighter parts of the decorations first, then proceed to the darker colors.

Notice the heads with dotted lines in the sketch. Use wooden beads for these heads. Hold them in place with one-inch pieces of pipe cleaner glued to the back of the body through the hole in the bead head.

These cutout characters have movable arms and legs. Make them of ⅛-inch-thick plywood, and cut the pieces out with a jigsaw. Use ⅛-inch diameter dowel sticks for the arms and legs (A). Use small beads (B) for the hands. Sand the ends of the dowels slightly so they will fit into the beads. Drill ⅛-inch holes in the wooden shoes (C), and glue the legs into the holes.

Using a small bit, drill holes in the body where indicated on the sketches and in the ends of the arms and legs. Insert small electrical staples in the tops of the heads for hanging. Thread the staple with cord. Paint the dolls with two coats of gesso, then with acrylic paints. When the paint is completely dry, give all of the dolls a final coat of gloss polymer medium. Join the dolls together with large jump rings (D). Add wigs made of yarn to the bareheaded dolls.

Shapely tree ornaments

Making molded Christmas tree ornaments offers unlimited opportunities for those of you who enjoy creating truly original decorations. Historically, natural clay has been transformed into artifacts through the addition of heat. Now, you can start dabbling in this ancient art simply by using baker's clay, resin in liquid or pellet form, glass that is melted or broken into tiny crumbs, plastic clay, or plastic crystals.

You may become so enthralled with this craft that you decide to enroll in a ceramics class at your nearest art center after you have completed your molded tree decorations.

Baker's clay know-how

Grownups as well as youngsters get a bang out of working with versatile baker's clay. The timeless technique of shaping baker's clay ornaments allows you to roll out, cut, or mold the clay and then bake it like homemade cookies. Baker's clay requires only three ordinary household ingredients—flour, salt, and water from the tap.

To make the dough, combine four cups of flour and one cup of salt; add 1½ cups of water all at once. Stir the mixture until all of the dry ingredients are moistened. (Each recipe makes enough clay for one dozen ornaments of average size.)

Knead the dough on a lightly floured tabletop for at least five minutes. The dough will hold together and have a velvety texture. Roll out the parts for the desired shape; place on a cookie sheet and bake in a moderate oven (350°) for 30 to 45 minutes or until the dough appears slightly browned around the edges, as for sugar cookies. (The baking time will vary with the thickness of the dough and the length of time that the dough has been exposed to the air before baking.) You can double-test for doneness by pressing down on them with a cloth-covered finger. If there's no indentation on the clay, they are done.

Remove the cookie sheet from the oven and let the clay cool for about 10 minutes. Then, lift the ornaments from the cookie sheet to a wire rack with a metal spatula. Spray them with a clear varnish or plastic. (Either is available at hobby or craft shops.) This spray will seal out all moisture, thereby preserving the trims for years. Otherwise, the high salt content absorbs moisture from the atmosphere. If this happens, your lovely ornaments will not retain their shape. In other words, that's the way the cookie crumbles.

After spraying the baker's clay figures with clear varnish or plastic, paint the ornaments with oil, watercolor, poster paint, food coloring, or acrylics. You may wish to leave some of them their natural color or divide portions and paint on trims for added brilliance.

If you wish, coat the entire ornament with a decoupage solution after the paint dries. It takes about 15 minutes in a warm room for this to dry. (Be sure to check decoupage instructions regarding the proper ventilation, if you are applying it indoors.)

Use baker's clay dough within five hours after mixing it. As you work with the clay, store the unused portion in a plastic bag to keep it moist. *Caution:* neither the raw dough nor the baked forms should be eaten. Keep it out of reach of tiny tots who can't resist sampling everything they see.

These lacy snowflake ornaments (right, bottom) add a touch of delicacy to any Christmas tree. Make the ornament centers from a small ball of dough, about the size of a doughnut center. Press the ball down on an ungreased baking sheet until the dough is about two inches in diameter and one inch thick. For the star center shapes, use a cookie cutter for a pattern.

Attach the circles by taking a small ball of dough, rolling it between your fingers, and 'gluing' it to the center ball with water applied with a small paintbrush. Press holes in the dough balls with the handle of a paintbrush or other instrument.

For the squiggly effect, knead a ⅜-inch-thick roll of clay about 12 inches long, just as you would with regular modeling clay. Shape it around the dough center in a scallop effect. Push the scallops against the center with the brush handle; use water for an adhering agent where the pieces of dough meet.

For the textured designs, impress a patterned button into the designs, then remove the button. Bake the ornaments in the oven according to the instructions given above.

Baker's clay and plastic clay ornaments

Lacy snowflake ornaments

Color your snowflake ornaments by brushing on acrylic paints in lively fluorescent hues. After the paint is thoroughly dry, brush or spray on a coat of clear gloss varnish to add a lustrous finish.

These bright trinkets (above) are made of baker's clay and plastic clay. You can use your oven to bake them.

For the fat cat, roll out plastic clay and shape it. Then, make coils of the clay and position them on the cat shape to make the collar, the front legs, and the tail. Shape small balls for the cat's eyes, nose, and centers of his ears.

For the angel candleholder, mold the clay over two fingers, forming a simple, round-topped cone. Roll out clay coils for the angel's hair (a coiffure, no less) and the arms. Use small beads of clay to make her eyes. Cut out the wings and attach them to the body of the angel. Then, push a small, spiral candle into the top of her head.

To cure these plastic clay figures, place them on a foil-covered cookie sheet in a cold oven. Turn the heat to 200° for 15 minutes, then turn off the heat and remove them from the oven. If the pieces are more than ½ inch thick, they may require a slightly longer curing time. Dress them up by decorating

From melted glass to stitchmarker rings

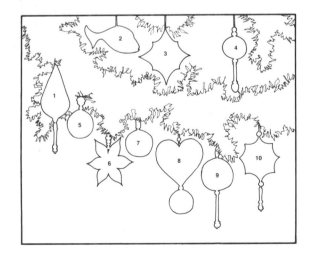

them with acrylic paints. Use motifs that are reminiscent of the holiday season.

The rest of the ornaments at the top of page 55 are made of baker's clay. Roll out the dough, then shape the various designs with cookie cutters or a knife. If the dough is to be left unpainted, sprinkle on some extra salt before you bake it to give a sparkling effect. If the design is to be used as a tree-top ornament, insert a fastener for attaching the ornament to the tree.

Bake the ornaments in a preheated 325° to 350° oven for half an hour. After cooling the baker's clay designs, color them with poster or acrylic paints. To preserve the designs, dip them in clear plastic film.

Resin, glass, and plastic

You can make glittering translucent ornaments of ethereal beauty from resin in liquid or pellet form, melted glass scraps and crumbs, and plastic crystals. Process these decorations in a miniature ceramic kiln or in the oven of your kitchen range.

The breathtaking array of translucent ornaments shown on the opposite page are made up of a variety of materials that run the gamut from melted glass to knitting stitchmarker rings. (The drawing below the photo provides the key to locating the instructions for each individual ornament.)

These gem-like ornaments are a good introductory project for working with clay, glass, and resin. They are fired on an inexpensive miniature ceramic kiln that operates from an ordinary electrical outlet. Once you have mastered the basics with these materials, you can expand into more ambitious projects.

A. First, shape the clay coil frame. Next, clean the frame with a moist sponge when the clay is leather hard.

B. Next, arrange the clay forms on a plaster bat. Place paper towels on top of them, and weight down the forms lightly until they are dry. Fire the clay to maturity.

C. Trace the shapes of the apertures on a sheet of acetate, cut the piece slightly larger than the opening, then tape it to the backside of the form, carefully sealing all of the edges.

D. Fill the openings with catalyzed resin, tinted or clear, and arrange the imbedded pieces in an interesting design.

E. When the resin is hard, peel away the acetate and clean any residue of resin from the back of the hard clay with a cloth that has been dampened in acetate.

F. Press small coils of florist clay or plasteline around the fired clay outlines or drapery rings to serve as a dam so the resin won't spill over (see diagram A).

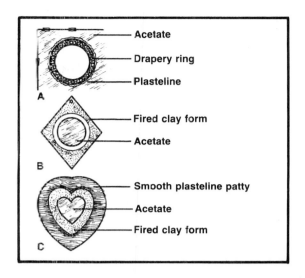

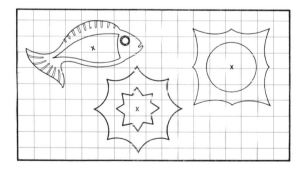

G. Seal the large openings in the cutout forms with matching shapes of acetate, taped to the underside of the decoration (see diagram B above). If the forms happen to be warped or uneven, press them lightly into smooth plasteline until they are level (see diagram C above).

H. Where the parts in the various ornaments are joined with clay coil frames, as in the snowflake (6) or the teardrop (1), glue them with liquid clay (slip). Cut the other frames freehand, following the paper patterns (see sample below, in the opposite column), from ¼-inch-thick clay sheets with windows (X) cut out of centers.

Following are the instructions for making the individual ornaments. (The numbers given below correspond with those in the drawing on the opposite page.)

1. *The white teardrop* is fashioned from clear and colored resin, plastic cafe curtain rings cut in half, a melted bottle neck, and melted glass scraps.

2. *The fish* is constructed of clear resin, melted glass crumbs, and green and white knitting stitchmarker rings.

3. *The star* features colored resin, white insulated staples arranged in a circular pattern, slices of patterned glass rods, and melted marbles.

4. *This dazzling round ornament* is made of a glass drapery ring filled with clear resin and the mainspring from an old, discarded clock. The shimmering dangles are made of glass tubing and wire.

5. *Here's another round ornament.* This glass drapery ring is filled with pastel blue resin and slices of pearly shells.

6. *The snowflake* shown on page 56 has a clay coil frame, glued together with liquid clay (slip), and filled with clear and colored resin.

7. *This circular ornament* (shown on page 56) is filled with amber resin and decorated with small screw eyes, melted glass, and half-round pearls.

8. *The heart* shown on page 56 is made of colored resin, plastic curtain rings, large beads, hors d'oeuvre picks, and the cutout middle of the heart. All of the above ornaments are framed with clay coils.

9. *Here's another circular ornament* (shown on page 56). This one is framed with drapery rings, filled with clear resin, and decorated with half-round glass beads. Make the dangles from glass tubing and wire.

10. *The octagonal-shaped ornament* is made of colored resin and has a glass dangle.

The trims with the appearance of stained glass shown at the top of the opposite page have polystyrene cooking crystals, metal cafe curtain rings, and white glue as their principal ingredients.

Arrange the cafe curtain rings on wax paper and glue them together with white glue in the design you want. When the glue dries, place the form on aluminum foil on a baking sheet. Next, hook a thin wire through the top of the ornament for the hanging piece and fill the sections with polystyrene cooking crystals, bits of marbles, old glass beads, and scraps of glass. Position these glass pieces in the center of the ring sections, along with edges, or in whatever design you like best.

To achieve a cracked or bubbly appearance, cook the ornaments in the oven of your kitchen range at 350° for 20 minutes. Allow a longer time if you wish the windows to have a transparent look.

Do not place these ornaments in direct sunlight or near any heat source, as the polystyrene pellets will liquefy if reheated.

The rattan ornaments in geometric designs shown on the opposite page, left, bear a striking resemblance to cathedral stained glass windows. The rattan shapes provide the framework for the resin that holds bits of colored glass in place. First, brush-paint the frames with metallic gold paint. (Don't use spray paint because the clear boat resin that holds the colored glass in place will float off of sprayed gilt.)

Before you paint these rattan forms, attach hanging swivels to the tops. Let them hang until the paint dries, then lay the frames on cellophane paper. (Foil can also be used, but the cellophane generally lies smoother and peels off more easily than foil.)

Arrange small pieces of colored glass in the frame. You can use slag, stained glass, broken bottles—some melted first in the ceramic kiln at 1450° until softened. Use brighter colors than you desire for the finished ornaments. (Colors fade when the resin is poured over the glass.) Finish by pouring liquid boat resin into the framework, filling to the top level of the rattan. (Liquid resin works better than resin pellets.) Let the resin harden overnight, then peel off cellophane.

You can use these ornaments as tree decorations. However, they are equally suitable as mobile decorations.

Plastic crystals were used to make the handsome Christmas tree ornaments on the tree shown on page 11. Purchase these in colors to match your room from your hobby shop.

Draw designs (the ones shown on this tree are in the shapes of birds and stars) on cardboard and cut them out. To make the molds for these ornaments, use extra-heavy-duty foil. Cut the foil ¼ inch larger than the cardboard patterns, and turn up the edges to form a pan. Pour the crystals in to fill the pan. Bake in a 400° oven from 5 to 8 minutes. Allow more time for a larger pattern. Bake until the design is solid.

Take the crystal design out of the pan and place it on a wooden board. To keep it from curling, weight it down with books or other heavy objects. When ornaments are cool, use a hot wire to punch a hole in the desired place for a hanging wire.

The picture cutouts that are shown at the far right of the opposite page are imbedded in resin crystals.

To make these striking decorations, spray metal cheese carton lids with furniture wax; wipe off the excess. Next, place a heavy layer of resin crystals in the bottom to half-fill the mold. Cover this layer with colored tissue paper, pictures, doilies, or other designs. Now, place a second layer of resin crystals over the pattern and fill the mold. Place the mold on a baking sheet and bake in a 350° oven for 45 minutes, or until the crystals are clear. Cool ornaments in the molds until they pop out easily.

As a final touch, file the edges if they are not smooth. Glue braid around the edges of the ornaments and drill a hole in the top to use for a hanging wire or string.

58

Polystyrene framed with curtain rings

Rattan ornaments

Picture cutouts in resin

Paper ornaments

If you can manipulate your fingers to cut, fold, and glue paper, you can convert ordinary tissue paper into enchanting designs, such as those pictured above.

Start with a 20x20-inch tissue paper square, fold it into a triangle, and, starting at the wide end, fold the paper over and over until you have a strip about ½ inch wide. Press the strips with your fingers and apply gloss polymer medium as you fold. (This serves as an adhesive as well as a gloss finish.) To form the bodies of these designs, roll the strips into circles or ovals.

The angel is made by rolling the tissue paper strips into an oval about 6 inches high. Use part of another strip for the dress out-line. Roll three pink strips into a circle for the head and glue to the body. Make wings and halo by gluing four sheets of tissue paper together. Cut out wings and halo and coat with gloss medium. Glue to body and head.

The bird is made by rolling two circles (one for the head, another for the body) and joining them with a neck strip that's wound around both the neck and the body. Cut 4x2-inch pieces and fold for the head feathers; use 8x2-inch pieces for tail feathers. Fold to ¼-inch-wide strips, roll ends, and glue.

The sunburst is made by rolling one strip of yellow and two strips of orange tissue into a circle. Glue two strips of red orange together by overlapping the ends. Then, wrap this long strip once around the circle. Next, form sunburst points with the remaining portion of the strip, gluing the base of the points onto the center circle of the design.

60

The **snow lady** requires three tissue strips for the head, and four for the body. Roll them into circles and glue the circles together. For the broom handle, roll a lollipop stick in a piece of brown tissue paper, applying gloss medium as you roll. Make the arms of two 3¼-inch tissue strips, glue around the broom handle, then glue onto the body.

The **oval ornament** is constructed of one white, one green, and one red strip rolled into an oval about 4½ inches high. Make the outside row of two more red strips rolled into circles at each end, then glued to oval.

The **bluebird** is basically two circles glued together. The head is made of two tissue strips; the body is three strips. Glue the head to the body. Make the tail with a 14-inch strip looped to form feathers and glue it to the body. Cut a 3x5-inch piece of yellow tissue paper for the feet. Fold into a ⅜-inch-wide

strip, then bend the strip into a V-shape. Cut V-shaped feet in both ends of the strip and glue feet to the body. Follow these same instructions for making the beak.

The **butterfly** has an oval body about four inches long. Loop and shape the top and bottom wings, using one strip for each wing. Make the antenna from a pipe cleaner bent into a U-shape with ends curled around a pencil, and glue it in place.

Santa is made in the same manner as the snow lady. Make the arms of 3-inch pieces of red strip. Cut the beard, gloves, and hat from four layers of tissue glued together. Add a white tissue circle for the hat's pompon.

The **flower** starts with a center circle. Next, add petal loops, leaving a space between first and last petal for stem. Fold a green strip in half and form leaf, leaving some of strip for stem. Glue stem and leaf to flower.

Chapter 3

Stocking Stitchery

"The stockings were hung by the chimney with care, in the hopes that St. Nicholas soon would be there." For over 150 years, this line from the poem "A Visit From St. Nicholas" has perfectly expressed a child's breathless anticipation of Santa Claus. Even today's sophisticated children hardly can wait until the moment they can leap out of bed early on Christmas morning to see what Santa has left in their stockings.

You can stimulate your children's imagination and sense of adventure by creating bright and playful Christmas stockings to decorate the fireplace mantel.

Felt is probably the most widely used material for making stockings because it is easy to work with. However, it is just one of a myriad of materials you can use. Or, you can crochet or knit Christmas stockings. Whatever material you choose, be sure that you give the stockings a stamp of individuality so that each child can have fun hanging *his very own* stocking before going to bed on Christmas Eve.

On the pages that follow, you will find photos of intriguing designs, step-by-step instructions, drawings, and material requirements. This information will ensure your success in turning out Christmas stockings that will delight small children and grownups alike.

The setting pictured at the left looks as though it stepped out of the poem "A Visit From St. Nicholas," complete with "visions of sugarplums," wreath, stockings "hung by the chimney with care," and apothecary jars brimming with sweets.

Fanciful felt creations

You'll enjoy making Christmas stockings with felt; it's the easiest of all materials to work with. Because felt (a nonwoven fabric) doesn't fray or ravel, you don't have to worry about hemming or binding the seams. In addition, it's easy to stitch by machine or by hand, and you can glue decorations onto it.

Another reason for felt's popularity is that it comes in several widths and weights, and a veritable rainbow of colors. If you need only small amounts, you can also purchase it in 12-inch squares.

The captivating collection of beautifully decorated Christmas stockings shown on page 62 vary from 10 to 14 inches tall. To duplicate these one-of-a-kind designs, see the illustration below, right, and enlarge the pattern pieces to the desired size. Cut two of each pattern piece.

To make the skate stocking (far left), glue the skate blade to the edge of the stocking foot. Glue the rest of the designs to the front of the stocking. Allow the glue to dry thoroughly. Stitch the two stocking pieces together, right sides together, leaving a ¼-inch seam. Trim the points and curves, and turn the stocking right side out. Press lightly on the back of the stocking, if necessary.

The green stocking with the exaggerated turned-up toe is certainly a fanciful design.

Glue the designs to the front of the stocking, then stitch the two pieces together, right sides together, leaving a ¼-inch seam. Trim the points and turn the stocking right side out. Glue the designs to the cuff and stitch a seam down the back, with right sides turned together. Stitch the cuff to the stocking, with the wrong side of the stocking facing the right side of the cuff. Fold the cuff down at the seam line, and edge it with a row of fluffy ball fringe.

The red stocking with the pompon on the toe has a sculptured effect that separates it from the other patterns. Cut out two of each pattern piece and stitch the foot trim to the main piece, leaving a ¼-inch seam.

Glue the felt designs to the front of the stocking, and outline the designs with jumbo yarn glued on. Stitch the two stocking sections together, right sides together, leaving a ¼-inch seam. Trim the curves and points, and turn the stocking right side out. Attach a yarn pompon to the toe.

The yellow stocking almost resembles a mosaic because the surface decorations of colored felt form a carefully arranged pattern.

Glue the designs on the stocking front, and allow the glue to dry thoroughly. Stitch the two stocking pieces together, right sides together. Trim the points and curves, and turn the stocking right side out.

The stylized floral motifs on the brightly colored felt stockings shown at the top of the opposite page are a departure from the run-of-the-mill Christmas designs. After experimenting with these designs, you'll probably conjure up your own colorful versions.

You will need an 18-inch square of felt for each sock. Other materials include white glue, scraps of colored felt, and thread. From the 18-inch square, cut two stocking shapes and a loop for hanging. Stitch the two sections together on the sewing machine, leaving the top open. Cut the decorative trims from scraps of brightly colored felt.

Stylized floral motifs

L-o-n-g Christmas stockings

Socks that wiggle their toes

For the one at the far left at the top of page 65, cut the diamond shapes, heel, toe, cuff, circles, and flowers from different colors of felt, then glue them to the front of the stocking as shown in the photo.

For the middle stocking shown at the top of page 65, use bright, contrasting hues to construct the multipetal design. Make petals in four different sizes, and glue petals on petals to achieve the three-dimensional look. Then, glue completed flowers onto front of white stocking base. Cut heel, toe, cuff, and loop from blue felt; glue them in position.

The stocking at the right at the top of page 65 features tulip, daisy, and daffodil silhouettes, and leaf and stem shapes in a random pattern. Because this design covers a great portion of the stocking, the cuff, toe, and heel have purposely been omitted.

L-o-n-g Christmas stockings, such as those pictured at the bottom of page 65, are in-tended for those who are extremely optimistic about Santa's generosity. For each one of the three, you will need two 22x12-inch pieces of white felt, plus scraps of red, green, and yellow for trim. You will also need thread and glue, pinking shears, and scissors.

To make the one with the Noel greeting, first cut the two long stocking shapes from white felt. Then, sew the two sections together on the sewing machine, leaving the top edge open. Cut a red felt toe, a cuff, a loop for hanging, and two different sizes of squares with scissors. With pinking shears, cut ¼-inch-wide strips of red and green felt with pinking shears. Cut one green felt circle and one square with scissors. Glue on the red felt cuff and toe, and edge them with the narrow pinked strips of green felt.

Glue on the red and green circle and squares, alternating the colors. Cut the pinked strips of red and green felt to form the

66

ing loop from green felt. Cut the red diamonds with the pinking shears, and the petals with scissors. Glue the designs in place. For the yellow centers in the flowers, glue on a small circle of yellow felt or embroider them with yellow yarn.

Socks that wiggle their toes, such as the ones on the facing page, are a rarity unless you make them yourself. The whimsical collection shown hanging from the fireplace mantel were designed and made with every member of the family in mind. Each of these stockings measures a generous 18 inches from the top to the heel and 12 inches from the heel to the tip of the toes.

First, draw a pattern on paper, using the scale drawing on this page as a guide. Cut out both the front and back sections of the stocking at the same time to be sure that both sides match. Also, this saves cutting time. (Make sure that you have good sharp scissors for cutting so the material will have an even edge.) Use matching thread and stitch the two pieces together by machine. Keep the seam about ¼ inch from the outside edge. Cut a loop for hanging and stitch it to the top left corner of the sock.

Thumb through old books, magazines, children's coloring books, or old greeting cards for ideas for the sock designs. Select pictures and motifs that personalize the socks for each member of your family.

The sock for Dad features a humorous interpretation of the new car and lakeside cottage that are at the very top of his 'wish list.'

Little daughter's stocking, second from the left, brings back fond memories of the roly-poly snowman she had fun making during last week's snowfall. She will treasure her stocking for many years to come.

For the young man of the family, there are cutouts on his stocking that hint of the brand-new band uniform and shiny horn he'll find peeking out from under the Christmas tree.

The designs on Mom's stocking, even though they are not very glamorous items, are a glowing tribute to the successful vegetable garden she labored over last summer.

Before you hang these stockings from the fireplace mantel, stuff small amounts of cotton or crumpled tissue paper in each of the toes to give a wiggly effect. Now, you're all set for a visit by that jolly old gentleman who will stuff the stockings with goodies.

The design suggestions given above are intended only to stir your imagination. Before

letters N-O-E-L (steam press one strip of curving felt to form the letter O). Glue red letters on green background, and green letters on the red background.

The long striped stocking is simply adorned with a sprig of holly cut from felt, yet its effect is smashing.

To duplicate the design, cut the two stocking shapes from white felt. Then, stitch the two sections together on the sewing machine, leaving the top edge open. Cut the heel, toe, cuff, and a loop from red felt with scissors. Use pinking shears to cut the stripes and the inside edges of the cuff, toe, and heel. Glue all of these pieces in place.

Cut out four holly-shaped leaves from green felt. Glue them near the top of the stocking, and to make the holly more realistic, embellish the cluster of leaves with red ball fringe or felt berries.

The argyle stocking is ornamented with stylized flowers in each diamond.

To fabricate this one, cut two stocking shapes from white felt and stitch the two sections together as in the previous designs. Then, using pinking shears, cut the cuff, toe, heel, diamond shapes, 12 petals, and hang-

you embark on your stocking project, give careful thought to the interests and hobbies of each family member. Regardless of whether they're sports, music, gardening, art, fashion, cooking, reading, travel, or the stock market, you can incorporate something meaningful into the theme for your stocking designs.

After you've cut out paper patterns for the designs, transfer the motif you wish to reproduce to felt and cut out the trims and letters to scale. Position the designs on the sock in a pleasing arrangement. Glue one piece at a time, leaving the others in place.

The Christmas stockings in the pinwheel arrangement shown across the page should furnish you with some very good ideas for your own holiday stitching. These clever, attractive felt creations are actually a snap to make. All you need is some felt, matching thread, white glue, scissors and pinking shears, and a few odds and ends for special trim. Look through your sewing supplies for beads, buttons, sequins, and scraps of decorative braid, ball fringe, and rickrack to use for trimming these stockings.

Before making your stocking forms, cut out paper patterns for the two basic shapes — the customary stocking shape and the pointed, turned-up-toe version. The stockings shown here measure 18 inches long from the heel to the top of the stocking.

The instructions that follow begin with the green stocking at the bottom of the page and move in a clockwise fashion around the page.

Jack-in-the-box stocking: this jolly Jack, who is fairly bursting out of his box, is bound to win the heart of the youngster who becomes the proud owner of this stocking.

Using your paper pattern and green felt, cut two of the large stocking shapes and a loop for hanging. Stitch the two pieces together by machine. Then, sew the loop to the top. (Stitch ¼ inch from the edge of the felt, and use matching thread because the seam stitching is on the right side.)

Assemble the various pieces of the design as you cut them out. This way, you can tell if they are scaled to one another. Then, glue them in place on the front of the stocking.

Tote for T-O-Y-S: this is the simplest of all designs to make and will appeal to the 'all thumbs' hobbyist.

Use the same regular paper pattern, but cut the two large stocking shapes with your pinking shears. Stitch the two sections together, leaving the top open. Cut the T, O, Y, S, and hanging loop with shears. Arrange the felt letters (each one a different color) on the front of the stocking and glue in place. Sew a loop at the top for hanging.

Jovial jester: the mischievous-looking character on this blue stocking will bring giggles of delight from a small child.

Using the paper pattern and blue felt, cut out two of the large stocking shapes and a loop for hanging. Stitch the two pieces together, leaving the top open.

Cut out each piece of the design from felt. If you have difficulty drawing your own design pattern, trace a similar design from a child's coloring book. Position design pieces on front of stocking; glue them in place.

Tree ornaments: why not decorate some stockings that complement the ornaments on your Christmas tree?

Construct your basic stocking first, using the paper pattern as a guide. Then, using different colors of felt, cut out five pieces that resemble tree ornaments. (These will show up best on a dark background.)

Arrange the felt pieces on the stocking front and glue them in place. Glue gold baby rickrack to simulate ornament hangers. Trim felt ornaments with decorative metallic braids, sequins, and small beads, glued onto felt.

High-button boot: here's a variation of the traditional Christmas stocking — a turned-up-toe version — that will appeal especially to teen-agers and adults.

Use the turned-up-toe paper pattern, and cut out two stocking sections and the loop for hanging from felt. At the same time, cut out the scalloped trim by following the inside curve of the pattern. Stitch the two stocking sections together, stitching the blue ball fringe in the seam at the same time. Glue the scalloped border in place.

Argyle stocking: cut the two felt pieces, following the pattern, and stitch. Cut out argyle and flower designs and glue in place.

Rope-skipping figure: construct the basic stocking first, using a dark color of felt. Cut and assemble all the parts of the doll, and glue in place. Use fine gold cord for the skip rope, and attach it with glue.

Here's a kaleidoscope of eye-catching stockings ▶ that you can duplicate or adapt to your own needs. Imagine how colorful each of the stockings will look as it hangs from the fireplace mantel.

Fabric fantastics for your family

Handmade Christmas stockings, guaranteed to make Old St. Nick take a second look while he is stuffing them with small gifts and snacks, are designed for those who enjoy sewing by machine with fabrics other than felt.

The top sock (for Dad) utilizes striped knit fabric for the sock itself. Cut the cuff, heel, and toe pieces from white bonded knit fabric. (Follow the sketch below for cutting out all the pattern pieces.) Stitch backing to the front and back pieces of the stocking. (Use any non-stretch fabric for the lining.) Turn the heel

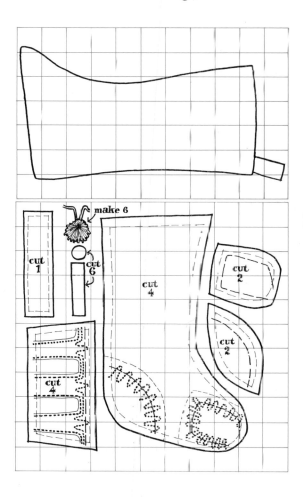

These vibrantly colored Christmas stockings are made of knit fabric, cotton duck, and red flannel. The striking stocking trims are of the applique and embroidered variety.

and toe pieces under ⅝ inch; sew in place, using thread of a contrasting color. For a humorous touch, stitch yarn and snippets of lace to the sock, following the picture for placement of the trim.

Stitch the two sock halves together (right sides together), then turn the sock right side out. Cut the top cuff pieces (you'll need four) and the hanging loop from white knit fabric. Sew two sections together to make the cuff, with right sides facing; leave the top open. In stitching the lower edge, catch in the pompons at the end of the yarn loops.

Turn the cuff right side out; stitch the facing at the top of the cuff to the sock. Fold in the outer part of the body; blindstitch. Attach the loop for hanging.

Mom's sock (top right) sports a large buckle on the toe. Fashion this of closely woven fabric. (Cotton duck is a wise choice.) To make this stocking, first cut your pattern according to the sketch at left. Make sure that you include a ¼-inch seam allowance.

Pin or baste the appliques to the front half. Set your sewing machine for full-width satin stitch, following the instructions in your sewing machine manual. Outline the motif, using contrasting mercerized thread. (The bobbin thread can be any color, as it won't show.) When the stitching is completed, trim off the excess fabric around the edges.

If you are appliqueing motifs by hand, use the satin stitch shown in the drawing at the right. Cut a bias strip 1¾ inches long for inside top facing. Make a 1¼x6-inch loop for hanging. Turn under ¼ inch at both sides of loop, stitch, and attach to stocking.

With the sock pieces placed so the right sides are facing, stitch them together, leaving the top open. With the right sides facing, sew on the bias strip. Press flat, and handstitch the inside hem of the facing.

The Santa-trimmed stocking, an excellent choice for any little boy, is made from red flannel and trimmed with yarn.

Cut out the two pieces of the stocking 18 inches long. On the front section, make Santa's face and the mitten, boot, and cap motifs from lengths of yarn crochet chains. Leave an abundance of loops around Santa's face to

Calico-lined carryalls

simulate his white beard. Complete the stitching on all of the crochet trims except the top four rows before seaming the two sections of the stocking together.

After stitching on the wrong side, turn the sock right side out, turn the top hem under one inch, and blindstitch in place. Stitch on the top four rows of white crochet chains. Attach a red flannel loop for hanging.

Big sister's 'mod' style Christmas sock, shown at the left of page 70, is fashioned of closely woven cotton fabric, the same as Mom's. Cut your pattern pieces according to the sketch on page 71, allowing a ¼-inch seam allowance. Pin or baste the applique motifs to the front of the stocking and satin-stitch by machine or by hand, following the instructions given for trimming Mom's stocking. Also, follow the previous directions given for the construction techniques.

Here's a collection of calico-lined stockings that is quick and easy to make. And, best of all, each stocking is large enough to hold a goodly assortment of small packages and Christmas goodies. All of them, except the striped one shown at the far right in the photo, are made of burlap. For the striped stocking, use any cotton or knit fabric.

To duplicate these stockings, make a paper pattern first, and then cut out two stocking shapes from burlap or striped material and two from a patterned calico fabric of matching or contrasting colors. Sew seams together on wrong sides of both sock and lining. (Use invisible thread, and you won't see stitching.)

Attach a row of ball fringe to the top part of the calico lining, repeating a color in the material. Remove every other pompon from the ball fringe and attach small gold or silver bells in their place. Next, place the wrong

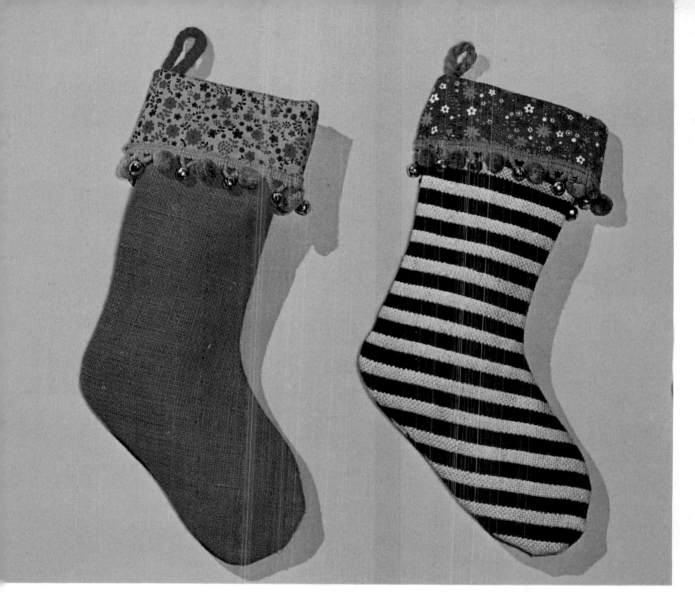

Slender striped stocking

sides of the burlap sock and the calico sock together and handstitch the seams. Add a loop.

This red and white striped stocking will sound a welcoming note as a front door decoration, or hanging from the fireplace mantel.

Cut a paper pattern 24 inches long and 13 inches from heel to toe. Cut stocking out of striped flannelette, as the picture suggests. Make the top wide enough to accommodate a large oval embroidery hoop. Stitch the two pieces together, right sides together.

Sew a wide cuff of green flannelette around the top, and edge it with red ball fringe. Handstitch oval hoop around top and underneath cuff to keep mouth of stocking open. Stuff toe of stocking with tissue paper so it will keep its shape. Fill the top of the sock with elfish toys, small, gaily wrapped packages, and sprigs of holly. Sew small sleigh bells to the toe of the stocking.

Cheery crocheted stocking

Here's a Christmas stocking that little children will love. In order to duplicate this large, colorful, handmade treasure, all you have to know about crocheting is the simple chain and single crochet stitches. And, it won't take you long to make because the stocking is made of heavy acrylic rug yarn, using a large size crochet hook.

Here's a list of materials you will need to make the crocheted Christmas stocking: acrylic rug yarn—1 skein each of scarlet, tangerine, and kelly green; 2 skeins of light purple; two 2¼-inch brass curtain rings; and a size 1 crochet hook. If you have rug yarn left over from previous projects, use it for making the stockings. (See page 35 for a list of the crochet abbreviations used in the instructions for this stocking.)

With red yarn ch 3, sl st in first ch to form ring. *Rnd 1:* ch 1, 6 sc in center of ring, sl st to first sc. *Rnd 2:* ch 1, 2 sc in same sp, 2 sc in each sc around (12), sl st to first sc. *Rnd 3:* ch 1, 1 sc in same sp. *2 sc in next sc, 1 sc in next sc. Repeat from * around ending ch 2 (18 sc). Sl st in top of first sc. *Rnd 4:* ch 1, 2 sc in same sp, * 1 sc in each of next 2 sc, 2 sc in next sc. Repeat from * around (24 sc.). Sl st to top of first sc. *Rnd 5:* repeat rnd 4 (32 sc). *Rnds 6 through 11:* ch 1, 1 sc in each sc around, sl st to first sc. Fasten off.

Rnds 12 through 14: attach purple yarn. Repeat rnd 6. *Rnd 15:* ch 1, 1 sc in each of first 15 sc, 2 sc in each of next 2 sc, 1 sc in next 15 sc, sl st to first sc. *Rnd 16:* ch 1, 1 sc in first 16 sc, 2 sc in each of next 2 sc, 1 sc in next 16 sc, sl st to first sc. *Rnd 17:* ch 1, 1 sc in first 17 sc, 2 sc in each of next 2 sc, 1 sc in 17 sc, sl st to top of first sc. *Rnd 18:* ch 1, 1 sc in first 18 sc, 2 sc in each of next 2 sc, 1 sc in 18 sc, sl st to first sc (40 st). Fasten off.

Rnd 19: count back 20 sps from end of last row, attach purple yarn, 1 sc in each sc around. Do not join row. Ch 1, turn. *Rows 20 through 30:* 1 sc in each sc across, ch 1, turn. Omit ch 1 on row 30. Fasten off. *Heel—Row 31:* attach green yarn in 6th sp down, 1 sc in each sc across to 6th sc from end (30). Ch 1, turn.

Rows 32 through 35: 1 sc in each sc across, ch 1, turn. *Row 36:* fold heel section in half, marking center of last row. 1 sc in each sc to marked center, sk 1 sc, 1 sc in each sc across, ch 1, turn. *Rows 37 through 43:* repeat row 36, decreasing 1 st at center of each row (22 st after row 43). Fasten off. Fold heel and whipstitch row 43 edge together to form back seam. *Row 44:* to complete heel, attach purple yarn to purple sc sp just above green row, 1 sc in each green row across to other side, sl st purple to side purple sc sp, ch 1, turn. *Rows 45 through 48:* 1 sc in each sc across, sl st to side, ch 1, turn. Omit ch 1 on row 48 and fasten off. *Rnds 49 and 50:* attach purple yarn to center back, *ch 1, 1 sc in each sp around, sl st to first sc.

Repeat from * for rnd 50. Fasten off. *Rnd 51:* attach orange yarn at end of purple rnd, * ch 1, 1 sc in each sc around, sl st to first sc. *Rnds 52 through 55:* repeat rnd 51. Fasten off. Fold stocking flat and mark center front for guide. *Rnd 56:* attach purple yarn at end of last rnd, 1 sc in each sc to 1 sc sp before marker, 2 sc in this sp, 1 sc in next sc, 2 sc in next sc, 1 sc in each sc around, sl st to first sc. *Rnds 57 and 58:* ch 1, 1 sc in each sc around, sl st to first sc. Fasten off after rnd 58. *Rnd 59:* attach red yarn at end of last rnd. Repeat rnd 57. *Rnd 60:* ch 1, 2 sc in next sc, 1 sc in each sc around, 2 sc in last sc, sl st to first sc. *Rnds 61 through 65:* repeat rnd 57. Fasten off after rnd 65.

Rnds 66 through 69: attach purple yarn, and repeat rnd 57. Fasten off after rnd 69. *Rnds 70 through 75:* attach green yarn, and repeat rnd 57. Fasten off after rnd 75. *Rnd 76:* attach purple yarn, 1 sc in each sc around. Sl st to first sc. Fasten off. *Rnd 77:* attach red yard, 1 sc in each sc around, fastening in brass rings, one inside center back, and one inside center front, by crocheting through them. Sl st to first sc. *Rnd 78:* work 1 sl st in each sc around. Fasten off.

Hanging strap: attach red rug yarn to one of the brass curtain rings, then ch 50, and attach the chain to the other brass ring with sc. Make 1 sl st through the back loop of each ch across to the first ch. Fasten off.

Crocheted stockings in bright and cheerful colors are just as popular today as they were in Grandmother's time. And, because of their stretchiness, they have room for many small treasures. ▶

Chapter 4

Focus on Your Fireplace

There's nothing quite like a fireplace to create a storybook setting for the holiday festivities. It has long been the custom to deck the mantel with branches of greenery and candles and hang Christmas stockings there. Another favorite that's rich with the symbolism of Christmas is the Nativity scene. Christmas carols, either religious or secular, offer an almost endless supply of decorating ideas, too. Other signs of the season that should inspire you to create fanciful decorations are angels, bells, and stars.

Some Christmas symbols, although steeped in tradition, are whimsical, too. These include striped peppermint candy canes, gingerbread men, and Santa Claus.

But don't restrict yourself to these traditional decorations. Make unconventional and dazzling mantel trimmings from tucked-away family heirlooms, art objects, and pieces of sculpture. Or, create simple but charming ornaments from pine cones, greenery, driftwood, flowers, and fruit. When combined with shiny glass balls, velvet or satin ribbons, and candles, natural materials often become the feature attraction in a room.

Unleash your inventiveness and display your skill by fashioning some of the projects presented in this chapter. They will transform your fireplace into a cozy focal point for your family's Christmastime activities.

The fireplace decorations in the room at the left follow the traditional theme established by the Christmas tree nearby. Antlers, jars of sweets and snacks, clusters and garlands of greenery, and red bows are artfully arranged.

With a little help from nature

A fireplace always adds a welcoming touch to any room, but when you deck it with holiday decorations made of natural materials, it fairly radiates warmth and conviviality. Regardless of whether there is a roaring and crackling of flames, a few glowing embers, or freshly cut logs resting on the andirons, the fireplace is the focal point of a room.

Use wreaths, sprays, and garlands made of greens, berries, pods, pine cones, fruit, and grasses to adorn the mantel and the wall above the fireplace. Then, strengthen your theme by concocting decorations of the same materials for the fireplace hearth.

The horseshoe tree shown at the upper left of the opposite page is inspired by the ranch-style setting. The massive fieldstone fireplace provides the perfect backdrop for this rugged decoration.

To make this one, first construct the tree shape from plywood and finish it with walnut stain. Arrange the horseshoes in rows on the plywood branches and nail them in place. To add fullness and to relieve the starkness of the tree, wire green silk tree ornaments and sprigs of holly to it. Mount the decoration securely on the fireplace wall.

The hearth decorations are equally interesting. Instead of the usual Christmas stockings hanging from the fireplace mantel, riding boots are lined up on the hearth to hold the traditional 'stuffer' gifts. On the opposite side of the hearth rests a bowl of fruit and a basket of freshly cut logs.

Magnolia leaves and apples, simply arranged between wall lanterns, provide the mantel decoration for this tombstone marble fireplace (shown at the upper right of the opposite page). This formally balanced mantel decoration is well suited to the furnishings and architecture of any colonial-style home.

To duplicate this mantel decoration, first attach a block of floral foam to the wall with florist clay. With floral picks, anchor the magnolia leaves and apples in a symmetrical arrangement to the block of foam. Make two small matching decorations of the same materials and place them at either end of the mantel beneath the wall sconces.

The wall sconces are reproductions of eighteenth-century exterior lanterns. The small pine-cone tree that rests on the table in front of the fireplace re-emphasizes the natural theme and also is a handmade decoration.

Holly, boxwood, and magnolia leaves are used to create the mantel decoration shown at the lower left of the opposite page. The natural woodtones of the fireplace and the paneling above it provide background for decorations of natural materials.

To make this large wreath, use a plastic foam wreath for the base, or make a wire wreath base. Cover the form with greens, add clusters of red berries, and tie a huge red velvet bow for the final festive touch.

Arrange more greens and clusters of red berries at either end of the mantel to enhance the gleam of old pewter and the glow of candlelight. The total effect is one that conveys the traditional holiday spirit.

A gracefully curved cedar branch provides the base for the fireplace decorations shown at the lower right of the opposite page. The wall hanging of natural materials, casually arranged, complements the red brick corner fireplace of contemporary design.

Make this stunning decoration by first studding the branch with fresh green Chinese holly. Then, add coppery bronze ribbon streamers. Next, slice pine cones horizontally with a power saw and spray them with copper-color paint; wire the cones to the branch. To form the centers, use copper-color wire mesh pot scrubbers, shaped to form buds or pressed flat, and glue one to the center of each pine cone with white glue.

The raised hearth features a tall arrangement that rests in an antique French copper milk pail filled with water-soaked floral foam. Actually, you can use any water-holding vessel for this arrangement. Insert stems of tropical palm boots, glycerin-processed loquat leaves, and fresh Jeffrey pine into the floral foam. Use long, rigid wires to hold cones that have been sliced with a power saw to the floral foam. Center the pine cones with glued-on curly metal pot scrapers.

To process the loquat leaves, first mix a solution of one part glycerin to two parts boiling water. Then, split the ends of the branches. Soak the stems in the solution for two weeks in a dark room.

Horseshoe tree

Holly, boxwood, and magnolia

Magnolia leaves and apples

Curved cedar branch

Old-fashioned bird cage

Expanded aluminum

Good-to-eat mantel decorations

Flower-covered tissue boxes

Natural materials plus

When you team natural materials with man-made items, there's no limit to the kinds of decorations you can create for your fireplace mantel. Combine greens, flowers, seeds, branches, and pods with metal, plastic, glass, and paper. You'll be amazed by the results.

The photos shown on the opposite page are only a small sampling of mantel decoration possibilities. Dream up some of your own, too. If, for example, you have a handsome painting hanging over the mantel, highlight it with garlands of greens and holly. Combine candles and candleholders in assorted sizes with a floral arrangement. Or, if you have a mirror over the mantel, create a kaleidoscope of color with dried marigolds, zinnias, dahlias, and bachelor's buttons bordering the mirror frame.

An old-fashioned bird cage, reminiscent of the old song, "I'm Only a Bird in a Gilded Cage," takes on new splendor when it houses red carnations atop a fireplace mantel.

If you don't have one of these cages tucked away in your attic or basement, you shouldn't have too much difficulty locating one. Just go to a few white elephant or garage sales.

Don't be discouraged if the finish is in bad repair. All you have to do is scrape it with a wire brush to remove the old finish, then apply a fresh coat of gold spray paint.

Insert a needlepoint cup on the floor of the bird cage to secure stems of fresh mugho pine sprays and red carnations of varying stem lengths. Let some of them burst out of the open cage door. Top off the mantel decoration with a flowing six-loop streamer bow (made of three-inch-wide velvet ribbon) wired securely in place.

Expanded aluminum may seem like a strange material to use for an arrangement, yet here it encases a sheaf of holly and greens for a striking decorative effect.

You'll marvel at the ease with which you can convert these sheets of metal into a myriad of holiday decorations. (Purchase it at hardware stores, in either gold or silver.) You can cut it into triangles, rectangles, or squares easily with tin snips or kitchen shears. To make folds, pleat the mesh with your fingers, then use the sharp edge of a countertop to make the creases sharp.

To make the spiral mantel decoration, begin with a piece of metal mesh that measures 24x 12 inches. Starting at one corner, cut toward the diagonal corner; stop about 11 inches from the edge. Roll the mesh around a cylinder to form the spiral. Secure the spiral piece of expanded metal onto a painted wood block that measures 4½x4½x3½ inches. Arrange the holly and greens artfully, and hang a shiny red Christmas ball from the gracefully arched strip of metal mesh.

Here's a good-to-eat mantel decoration that is bound to attract attention. It combines garlands of greens, a wall-hung cookie tree, and a lineup of apothecary jars, each one brimful of cookies and snacks.

For the center of the mantel, cover a clay flowerpot with green burlap, then anchor a small artificial tree in place. Load the branches with red and white striped candy canes and cutout cookie characters decorated with icing and colored sugar. Drape swags of greens at either side of the tree. For a touch of bright, shining holiday red, wrap lengths of satin ribbon around the tops of the apothecary jars. Fill the jars with a mouth-watering selection of cookies and snacks.

As the big day approaches, and your taste-tempting assortment of goodies has dwindled, pick up a new supply at the bakery.

Flower-covered tissue boxes, stacked in an artistic grouping, are so cleverly disguised that you'd never guess their origin.

Use the flower-patterned tissue boxes as containers for shiny Christmas tree balls and fresh maidenhair fern. (If your tissue boxes are not patterned, cover them with gift wrapping paper.) Insert the ferns into containers and fill them with water to keep them fresh and green. (If fern is not readily available, substitute greens cut from the lower branches of a too-tall Christmas tree.) Team this inexpensive array of casually arranged decorations with candles of any color to harmonize with the flower-covered boxes. To prevent the candles from falling off the boxes, anchor them to the top of the boxes with florist's clay.

Attach clusters of assorted sizes of gold Christmas balls to the boxes with fine wire. Arrange the entire grouping toward one end of the fireplace mantel.

Captivating mantel decorations

It's always fun to make exciting decorations out of unlikely materials, especially when the results are as gratifying as the pictures on the opposite page indicate. Even though a fireplace always is inviting, any one of these three will intensify the holiday spirit.

Contemporary fireplaces deserve lively, contemporary decorations for the Yuletide season. The starkly severe fireplace here, in its modern setting, is accented by vertical panels embellished with brightly covered ribbon balls.

To duplicate these panels, cut two lengths of plywood, and cover them with burlap to add texture. Using balloons of different sizes and shapes as forms, make balls by wrapping narrow strips of self-adhesive ribbon around the balloons. Moisten and attach ribbon with each loop until a network is formed. Then, prick ballons with a needle; remove them.

Cut leaves from wide ribbon and curl them. Attach the balls and leaves with staples or glue until the panels are covered.

Convert discarded bowling pins into a jovial Mr. and Mrs. Santa Claus and display them, nestled in greens, on your mantel.

To make the figures, simply tack on wooden or plastic spoons for arms and hands. (If you use plastic spoons, rough them up with steel wool or sandpaper so paint will adhere.)

To dress Mrs. Santa, fashion her apron and cuffs from cotton remnants and dip them in a solution of one part white glue and one part water. Wring out the excess and apply to body, tying the apron with a bow in the back. Dip cotton fringe in the glue solution to form the décolletage, and glue on a discarded brooch to ornament it. For her hair, dip yarn in white glue and arrange it on top of the bowling pin. Glue a small toy over her apron between the hands. Allow to dry thoroughly.

To outfit Mr. Santa, use strips of turkish toweling for the collar, cuffs, and jacket trim. Dip yarn in white glue and adhere for hair, beard, and moustache. For Santa's hat, roll a 4-inch square of red felt dipped in the glue solution into a cone and trim it with a band of terry toweling. Fashion Santa's pack from a 9-inch red felt square, and attach it to body with cotton cord dipped in glue solution. Allow figure to dry.

To finish both figures, apply two coats of gesso, drying 12 hours between each coat. Paint the figures with tempera paints, omitting facial features. Then, apply one generous coat of varnish. When it is dry (about 36 hours), paint in a hint of facial features with India ink. Then, apply a glaze solution. Wipe off the excess glaze, and let dry.

This handmade Madonna and Child creation will beautify any mantel, chest, or table.

To reproduce this eternal Christmas symbol, nail and glue a cardboard mailing tube (3 inches in diameter, 24 inches long) to a wooden base. (Here, an inverted wooden salad bowl is used.) For the Madonna's arms, cut wood paint-mixing paddles and affix to the top of the tube with small screws and nuts.

Cut a 3-inch diameter plastic foam ball in half for the shoulders, and pierce the top with a section of a small paper tube. Glue an egg-shaped foam ball to the top of the tube to form the neck and head. Tilt the head slightly when securing it to the neck. Glue the head and shoulder ensemble to the top of the tube. Insert pins through the foam into the mailing tube for added strength. Brush several coats of gesso on the head and shoulders; let dry.

Form the Child from a short length of wooden dowel and small wooden beads. Coat several times with gesso and let dry.

Dip strands of thin cotton yarn in white glue and arrange it for hair on the figures. For the robe, dip muslin or sheeting in a solution of one part white glue and one part water and drape around the shoulder. Use straight pins to secure the draping and pleats until the fabric is dry. Dip another length of fabric in the glue solution and drape it as a mantle over the Madonna's head. Use a third piece to wrap the Child. Position the Child in the Madonna's left arm.

When dry, glue a 3-inch circle of cardboard to the Madonna's head and a 2-inch circle to the Child's head for halos. Paint all with three coats of gesso. When dry, color with tempera paints, using flesh tones for the skin.

Brush on two coats of satin varnish. If you like, antique the figures with a solution of one part varnish, one part thinner, and burnt umber, rubbing off excess with a soft cloth to achieve the desired antique-like finish.

Wall panels

Madonna and Child

Converted bowling pins

Chapter 5

Tabletop Magic

Set the stage for your holiday festivities by adding table decorations that depict the joys of the season. Choose a theme and colors that harmonize with your other Christmas decorations, and create your own tabletop magic.

Take a close look at all of your tables to see which ones will lend themselves to holiday adornment. The dining table is a natural, because much of the entertaining takes place there. But don't stop there. Coffee or cocktail tables, end tables, console tables, and occasional tables are all likely candidates for special consideration.

If you have a small table in an entrance hall, be sure to decorate it to provide an extra note of welcome to anyone who enters. And the breakfast table—what better way to start the day than by viewing colorful table appointments while you're eating your breakfast and planning the day's activities. Also, don't forget the children's rooms. Just think of how much fun it will be for them to wake up each morning during the Christmas season and see a cheery holiday decoration of their very own.

In order to avoid a cluttered appearance, remove some of the year-round decorative table accessories when you add the holiday decorations.

On the following pages you'll find many eye-appealing tabletoppers and instructions for making them.

The Three Wise Men at the left, perched on a table in the foyer, are a reminder of the Wise Men who trekked across the Eastern sands bearing gifts for the Christ Child. Instructions for making this trio of religious figures are found on page 86

Familiar Christmas scenes

Although new designs, new materials, and new color combinations emerge each year as the holiday season rolls around, the themes of Christmas remain the same. The beloved Nativity scene. Christmas carolers, and holiday pixies and elves, which are so deeply steeped in tradition, always receive a warm welcome. And when you make these figures yourself, they have even more appeal.

In order to display any of these scenes to the best advantage, remove the rest-of-the-year table accessories first, then arrange your grouping in an attractive fashion.

Nativity scenes

Although nearly two thousand years have elapsed since the Nativity scene was played with its original cast, the drama and beauty of the event are relived through the display of creches each Christmas. You can create time-honored creches of many different materials in designs that range from pure traditional to contemporary versions.

The Three Wise Men bearing gifts (pictured on page 84) are stylistic in design. Actually, they are created from wooden table legs in three heights—8½, 10, and 12 inches.

Mount the table leg bodies onto the wooden bases that measure 2¾ inches square by ⅞ inches thick. Remove the glides from the table legs and attach each leg to a base, using either a screw or glue to fasten them securely. Give the figures a coat of gesso, then paint them with acrylics.

Cut the facial features, the gift chests they are holding, and the trim on their cloaks from balsa wood. To form the arms, use tongue depressors or blades cut from a louvered window shutter. For the crowns, utilize wooden beads or a cone-shaped creation that you make from wood or cardboard. For a distinctive touch of elegance, glue on a band of tiny gold beads to rim the crowns. Arrange the trio on a small table or on a fireplace mantel.

The entrancing paper-cylinder creche figures pictured at the top of the opposite page are arranged on a table under the sweeping branches of palm fronds. This is appropriate because the fronds portray symbolic protectiveness. To make this handsome collection,

you will need 2-inch mailing tubes, gift and brown wrapping paper, felt-tip pens, and a small copper scouring pad.

For the figures of the Wise Men and the shepherds, cut a mailing tube into lengths that vary from 6 to 8 inches long; for Mary, cut a 5-inch length.

To make the colorful robes, use ornately designed gift wrapping paper, backed with construction paper to add firmness. Glue the paper into folds on either side of the tube bodies. For the shepherds' robes, use ordinary brown wrapping paper.

Use felt-tip pens to draw on the faces, and make the hair of cotton or yarn. Use a small copper scouring pad to make the turban for the Wise Men, and small gold paper medallions to make the crown and the halos.

The creche shown at the bottom of the opposite page is a natural for wool gatherers, and you don't even need a knitting needle or a crochet hook to construct it. You can make all of these quaint and lovely figures easily by mastering two easy-to-do techniques—making yarn tassels for the bodies of the

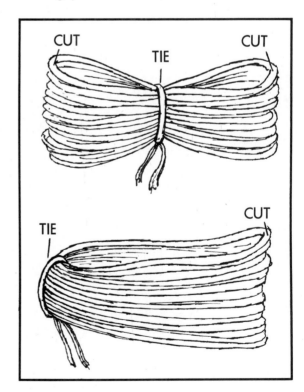

Paper tube creche figures

Creche for wool gatherers

Humble cornhusks

Dickens carolers

figures, and pompons for the heads and bodies of the animals. The triptych that serves as a background for the grouping is cut out of artist's board. Paper doilies spray-painted in a stained glass effect are glued into the three openings.

To make the figure of Mary, start with the face by winding pale pink yarn around a 2-inch-wide piece of cardboard 100 times. Slip out the cardboard, and tie the yarn in the center to form a pompon. (See the drawing at the bottom of page 86.) Clip the pompon to about 1¼ inches in diameter.

To make the hair, wind light brown wool around a 2-inch-wide card 50 times. Slip out the card, tie one end of the yarn, and clip the other end. Tie the yarn to the pink pompon head, and clip it to a length that measures slightly longer than the face.

For Mary's robe and body, make large tassels. Wind white wool yarn around a 6-inch-wide piece of cardboard 100 times. Make a second tassel the same way with turquoise yarn. With a short length of white yarn, encircle the white tassel and half of the turquoise tassel and tie. (These ties form the waistline.) Fluff the remainder of the turquoise tassel out at the back to form the cape. Attach the pompon head for the tassels. Make the eyes of blue sequins, and the halo of gold lace ribbon, slightly gathered.

Make all of the other figures in the same manner, using other colors of yarn. Increase the length of the tassels by one inch so the figures will be taller than Mary.

Make the animals from various sizes of pompons tied together and shaped with scissors to form the head and body. For a spotted effect, combine black and white yarn during the winding. Make the animal legs from chenille stems wrapped with yarn.

Humble cornhusks are the principal ingredients in the replica of the manger scene at the top of the opposite page. All of the figures are made of cornhusks, either natural or dyed. Anyone who enjoys converting natural materials into decorative accessories will have fun making this creche and take pleasure in displaying it for many holiday seasons to come.

To duplicate this masterpiece, select sturdy, well-dried cornhusks, and fashion each figure out of four ¾-inch-wide plain husks. Place one strip on top of another, and fold down the ends of all four layers ¾ inch from the top. Fold down the ends again, hold them in place securely, then wrap another ¾-inch-wide husk around and around this fold. Cover this roll with a 3-inch-wide smooth husk; fold it around and over the roll, leaving two inches of the husk sticking up at the top. Twist and fold this 2-inch piece of husk down behind the covered roll. Tie at the bottom of the roll, directly under and ¼ inch down, to form the neck.

To fashion arms and legs, push wires up into the neck. Wrap cornhusks around arm wires, layer upon layer, to form arms and hands, and tie off. Wrap wires with cornhusks to form feet and legs. Tie at waist.

For the men's noses, twist ½-inch-long pieces of husks and tie them on the faces with thread. Place a brown or black husk over nose to simulate a beard and eyebrows and to cover thread used to tie on nose. Shape faces from cornhusks; shape them over and around brown or black husks used for beard and eyebrows and tie around back of head.

Vary the sizes, shapes, and colors of all of the figures. Bend some into a kneeling position. Clothe the figures with garments fashioned of cornhusks dyed with fabric dye. Paint facial features with black India ink. Use red poster paint to color lips and cheeks.

To construct camels, shape the bodies of wire first, then wrap the entire wire frame with cornhusks tied or wired in place. Build the shelter from cornstalk strips or wood dowels. Make the crib from wood dowels laced with strips of cornhusks.

Arrange the entire grouping in a pleasing composition on the top of a small table.

The family of carolers, suggestive of the Dickens era, is the intriguing assemblage at the bottom of the opposite page. Ever since the heavenly host celebrated the coming of the Saviour with song on that first Christmas morning, carols have been an intrinsic part of the Christmas season. With this rich heritage, it's no wonder that carols declare the good tidings of great joy each year.

It's hard to believe that this group of figures, gaily attired in holiday finery, started out as ordinary plastic bottles, which often are cast away without a thought for their recycling possibilities.

To make these carolers, first select plastic bottles—preferably each one a different size. Place a small amount of sand or plaster in the bottom of each bottle for stability. To make the heads, select plastic foam oval shapes in sizes that are compatible with the various bottles. Rout out one end of the oval foam egg so that the head will fit over the neck of the bottle.

Paint the facial features and the bodies with enamel paints. Run pipe cleaner arms through small holes in shoulders, and glue on hair made from yarn or a metal pot scrubber. Use brightly colored fabric scraps to make the scarves, bonnets, and caps. Make miniature song books for each caroler and attach them to the outstretched arms.

Pixies unloading a heap of petite gift packages are the center of attention in the bewitching table centerpiece scene pictured at the top of the opposite page. Make this assemblage of lively sprites and their trappings for a buffet table, end table tableau, or an under-the-tree surprise.

But don't let the pixie scene be the only surprise. Wrap tiny gifts—ring, cuff links, coins, or a charm—to pop into the burlap bag. Or make a slit in the top of the mushrooms and give them to guests as party favors to take home and use for banks.

Use a balloon to form the large mushroom cap. Blow it up and cover it with plastic wrap, taping the ends. Dip torn bits of paper 1½ inches square in a mixture of one part water to two parts glue and apply to coat the balloon. Overlap each piece about ¼ inch. Use five or six coats of papier mâché to give the balloon added strength.

When the mushroom cap is dry, cut the balloon in half, then, trace a circle the same size as the cap edge on cardboard. Center an oatmeal box in the circle and draw around it. Cut out the doughnut shape with the inner circle slightly smaller than the circle you drew. Set the ring on top of the oatmeal box, and secure it with tape and two layers of papier mâché. Attach the half-sphere in the same way on top of the doughnut. For the stovepipe that protrudes from the roof, bend a piece of wire and add desired thickness with glued paper. Make the cone stovepipe top from a cardboard circle with a 1-inch radius. Dip a small piece of cotton in glue to attach the cone to the stovepipe.

Next, add a layer of paper to the oatmeal box. Outline the door and window by dipping fat string into the glue and placing it on the box. Then, paint the entire house with a coat of undiluted glue and let it dry. (You can put it into a low oven to speed up the drying process.) Finish with a coat of gesso and paint in appropriate colors. You can make many sizes of extra mushrooms, depending how large you want your centerpiece to be. Cut the stems from cardboard tubing, adding ¼ inch to attach the stems to the top. Glue a covering of white felt in place on the stems. Center the stem on a halved foam ball, and cut out a hole in the ball in which to fit the stem. Cut out four red felt top pieces and glue them to the mushroom caps. Slide a white felt circle up around the stem to cover the underside of the mushroom.

To construct each pixie, you will need two 12-inch white chenille stems; 26 inches of moss green velvet tubing cut into two 7-inch lengths, two 3½-inch lengths, and a 5-inch length; one foam egg 2 inches in diameter; a red flower pip; one chenille bump (sold by the yard in hobby shops); white, red, and green felt; and two drapery weights.

Begin the assembly by threading 7 inches of tubing on a 12-inch white chenille pipe cleaner stem. Center the tubing and bend the stem into a U-shape. (See figure A.) Twist the uncovered ends into circle feet. Then, glue felt soles to the bottom of the chenille-stem feet. Place a drapery weight on each foot and glue the top of the shoe over it. For the arms, slide 3½ inches of tubing on a 6-inch stem. Center the tubing, and loop the hands. The body has 5 inches of tubing on a 6-inch stem. Bend the body into a U-shape.

Assemble pixie by slipping body piece over legs. Twist the body on itself up about 1½ inches. (See figure B.) Slide arms through stem ends and twist again. (See figure C.) The eggs fit onto the body stem. Use chenille bump for beard and flower pip for nose. The pattern for the eyes is shown on the drawing. Cut out the coat as shown in the drawing, dress the figure, and glue on the button. Glue the edges of the hat together, turn up the brim, and pin to head. Add a felt hat band.

Make a small drawstring bag of green burlap to hold the miniature gift packages. String a green cord through the casing.

Finally, arrange your scene according to your tabletop space. Place the large mushroom house on scraps of green burlap that have been fringed to simulate a grassy slope. Arrange the wee gift packages so they appear to be tumbling out of the green burlap sack. You can balance the elves in almost any position—sitting, standing, or reclining—because of the drapery weights in the feet. Now, the industrious little elves are all set to join the holiday festivities.

90

Pixies star in centerpiece scene

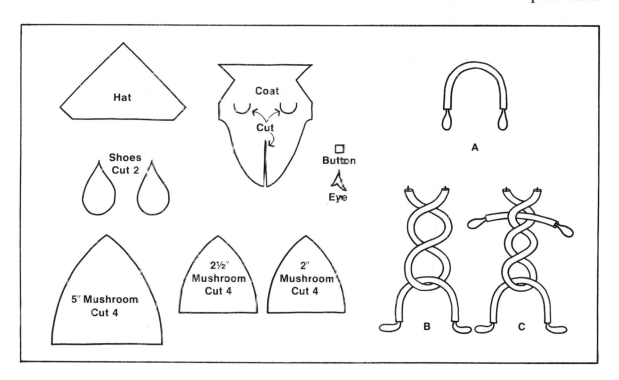

Expanded aluminum extravaganza

Handy kitchen gadgets

Yarn-wrapped angels

Kitchen grater shrine

Enchanting tabletoppers

If your tastes lean toward the contemporary and you need a touch of originality on a table or a desk, try your hand at one or more of these delightful holiday decorations. Even with close scrutiny, it's hard to detect the materials from which they're made.

The expanded aluminum tree shown at the upper left of the opposite page is worthy of a place of honor at holiday get-togethers.

To make this magnificent tree, cut a triangle measuring 33x33x24 inches from a 24x48-inch sheet of expanded aluminum metal mesh. Fold at intervals. To make the folds, pleat the mesh with your fingers, then use the edge of a countertop to make the creases sharp. Nail bottom section to wood block.

Add small round mirrors, arranged from peak to base; hold them in place with double-faced tape. Hang shiny red Christmas balls with ornament hooks along the folds.

You'll marvel at the ease with which you can create eleventh-hour decorations with this metal mesh material, which you can purchase in hardware stores. It comes in holiday colors—gold and silver. Cut it into triangles, rectangles, or squares with tin snips or shears.

Handy kitchen gadgets provide the makings for the sprightly tabletop decoration at the upper right of the opposite page. This type of tabletop decoration is equally attractive whether it is lighted or unlighted. And the best part of all is that there is nothing to pack away after you've enjoyed it.

To fabricate this humorous centerpiece, glue ordinary plastic drinking glasses to the palm side of chintz hot pad mittens to act as candle cups. Use a bright orange lacquered tray for each mitt and candle ensemble.

Arrange beeswax candles in the candle cups, cheese and crackers on a cutting board, an ark full of stuffed figs, and some fresh fir cuttings to add color.

Angels that virtually sing their greetings from a field of evergreen boughs are pictured at the lower left of the opposite page. These yarn-wrapped contemporary angels are bound to add excitement to any tabletop.

For each figure, cut a 2-inch diameter cardboard mailing tube 12 inches long, and glue a cardboard disk to the bottom. Place beans or pebbles in the bottom of the tube to weight it down. Pinch the top of the tube flat. Insert a 1/8-inch dowel, sharpened on the upper end, up through length of tube, allowing one inch to protrude from the body. (Head will be impaled on this dowel.) Glue heavily and hold pinched top of tube flat with staples. When dry, trim shoulder line. Wrap tube with rug yarn, starting at base of neck. When you begin wrapping, start 36 inches in from end of yarn, so this will hang free at neckline. Glue yarn lightly and pin until glue dries.

For arms, cut two 1¼x6-inch pieces of cardboard. Tape a length of light wire along the center of each arm, and wrap them with two layers of yarn. Glue them to the back of the angel, following the shoulder line.

Paint a flesh-colored face on a 2-inch satin ball and impale it on the dowel neck. Glue a layer of corrugated paper around dowel, then wrap it with end of yarn which was left. Continue wrapping to form a cowl, covering the shoulder. Glue lightly; pin till dry.

Make wings of four layers of felt. Use shades to coordinate with angel bodies. Stitch a deep 'V' on longest wing piece to simulate feather line. Lay next shorter piece on first piece and stitch through centers of each division, curving to center back point. Using this same method, add the other two layers of wings to back of angel, covering attachment of arms. Bend arms in position.

An ordinary kitchen grater is the attractive shrine for the sculptured Madonna shown at the lower right of the opposite page. To reproduce this setting, paint a wooden pedestal base (the one shown here is the cake-stand type) and an old cheese or lemon grater with flat black spray paint. With pinking shears, cut a circle of red felt two inches less in diameter than the pedestal top, and place it on the tabletop pedestal for color separation between base and grater. Unless the Madonna will stand without support, insert a thin dowel into the hollow in the bottom of the figure, and secure the dowel in a small square of plastic foam sprayed black. Place Madonna in front of grater shrine.

Fill a needlepoint cup with holly, rosemary, and red candy balls, and position it at the base and to the side of the Madonna; place a candle behind the grater shrine.

Tables for entertaining

A beautifully decorated dining table makes any meal look more appetizing. And, at Christmastime, when almost everyone entertains loved ones, you can apply a multitude of decorating ideas to making centerpieces that will suit any festive occasion.

Greens provide the backdrop for the table setting shown at the top of the opposite page. If you live in a year-round warm climate, this will be the hit of any patio party. If not, this distinctive and flamboyant design will be equally at home indoors in front of a fireplace with a roaring fire.

To duplicate this setting, crisscross two runners of bright red fabric, bordered with fringe. Then, balance the whole arrangement with polka-dotted fake mushrooms in assorted sizes, various sizes and shapes of rocks painted flat black, and a pair of humorous pixie characters. Highlight this assemblage with a grouping of candles set high enough so it won't interfere with table conversation.

Make napkin rings of cardboard mailing tubes cut in 2-inch pieces, covered with colored paper and trimmed with ribbon bows.

Greens and shiny red apples used together, as in the candlelight setting at the lower left of the opposite page, signify hope for the forthcoming spring.

In Austria, where this custom originated, the family gathers on Christmas Eve and sings carols. Father lights the first candle, and Christmas dinner is served. The second candle is lit on Christmas Day; the third on New Year's Day; and the last on Epiphany.

To build this triangular-shaped tree, use ½-inch-square wood sticks for the base. Cut three pieces 16 inches long and three pieces 11 inches long. Starting at one end, carve ¼-inch-deep notches on three sides of all six pieces with a sharp knife, as shown in the drawing at the right. Stagger the placement of notches.

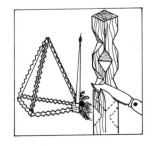

Paint all of the pieces with three different shades of poster paint. When the paint is dry, glue the 16-inch pieces to the triangular base, which is made from three 11-inch pieces. Set the triangle on a round place mat that is 16 inches in diameter.

Cut a notch halfway through three apples and fit them into base at corners. Cut out a triangular piece from the blossom end of one apple and set the apple on top of the decoration. Cut a circular chunk out of the center of all the apples; put small candles in the holes. Decorate the tree with small pieces of evergreen branches and gilded nuts.

The pyramidal-shaped centerpiece pictured at the lower right of the opposite page has red carnations peeking out from each side. This statuesque arrangement is intended for use on a table that is pushed against the wall so its height will not interfere with across-the-table conversation.

To fabricate the tree, cut out four identical triangles, 15½ inches on each side and 6 inches at the base, from construction board. Within these triangles, cut 13½x5-inch triangles, leaving a 1-inch border. For the base, cut a 6-inch square of construction board, leaving a hole in the center large enough to accommodate a cardboard-cylinder trunk.

Cover all the cutouts with adhesive-backed green velour paper; assemble the sections to form a pyramid. Trim the sides and base with a narrow edging of silver cord, and wind silver cord around the tree base to cover it completely. Let a spiky silver tassel act as a treetop ornament, and dangle silver cords.

Place a casual arrangement of red carnations and foliage in a bowl that fits into the pyramid. Cluster small crystal pyramids, each with a glittering, many-faceted stone suspended in the center, around it.

Bright red oilcloth and a cluster of glowing lanterns are the focal point of the delightful holiday table setting shown at the top of page 96. The lanterns actually are food and beverage cans that you punch with nails in all kinds of rows and curlicues. Place candles inside the cans so flames will flicker through punched patterns. Use funnels to top the cans, and attach the two with liquid steel. (You can find this product in tubes at hardware stores.) Cut off ends of some of the funnels; clip others with tin snips and curl down strips with long-nosed pliers.

Greens provide the backdrop

Greens and apples signify hope

Pyramid of red carnations

Red oilcloth and glowing lanterns

Mistletoe ball

Santa centerpiece

Spray-paint lanterns with colorful enamel for a glossy finish, or matte finish paint for a dull finish. If you like the looks of shiny, unpainted cans, leave them as they are. Group lanterns, then scatter pine cones painted gold or silver to add interest to the arrangement. For an extra Christmasy touch, place a poinsettia or fresh greens close by.

The holiday mistletoe ball shown at the lower left of the opposite page is suspended from a brass chandelier and adds just the right festive touch to a holiday luncheon, brunch, tea, dinner, or cocktail party.

To duplicate this beguiling beauty, begin by dampening a 10-inch plastic foam ball. Insert stem ends of enough fresh mistletoe to cover ball completely. Drill two small holes in top of ball, and thread a sturdy wire through holes. Hang kissing ball from a ceiling fixture, centered over dining table.

Using 2-inch-wide red weatherproof florist's ribbon, tie lavish bows to cover the wire. Center a big bow under the mistletoe ball and drape ribbon streamers toward the four corners of table. Finish each streamer with a corsage of fresh English holly and berries.

The Santa centerpiece shown at the bottom right of the opposite page is bound to make both children and adults chuckle.

To make this needlepoint version of St. Nick, you will need a size 13 tapestry needle; 6 skeins black and 2 skeins flesh Persian needlepoint yarn; 2 skeins each red and white 4-ply knitting worsted; and ½ yard 5-mesh-to-the-inch needlepoint canvas.

Before you take a stitch, cover all edges of canvas with masking tape to keep them from fraying. Draw Santa's face and other features onto the canvas with a waterproof pen, allowing a 1½-inch allowance on all sides for turning under later. Be sure to draw patterns so stitches can be worked crosswise on Santa's face When completed, put right sides of canvas together and stitch along side to make a back seam. Cut excess canvas and turn right side out, forming a cone. Cover a circle of cardboard with white felt to fit bottom, then glue so Santa will stand.

Basket weave stitch: use this stitch (see the sketches below) as a filler for hat and for white on backside of Santa.

Continental stitch: use this stitch for moustache, nose, and mouth. Work from right to left, as shown in sketch. Turn canvas around as you work from row to row.

Turkey stitch: use this stitch for making Santa's beard and hat trim, following the numbered sketches below.

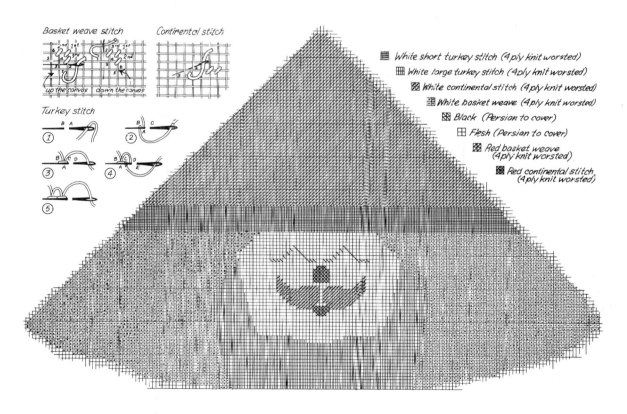

Basket weave stitch   Continental stitch

up the canvas | down the canvas

Turkey stitch
① ② ③ ④ ⑤

White short turkey stitch (4 ply knit worsted)
White large turkey stitch (4 ply knit worsted)
White continental stitch (4 ply knit worsted)
White basket weave (4 ply knit worsted)
Black (Persian to cover)
Flesh (Persian to cover)
Red basket weave (4 ply knit worsted)
Red continental stitch (4 ply knit worsted)

97

Live and lively table decorations

If you're given to nostalgia during the Christmas season, you're bound to want some live table decorations for your Yuletide festivities. There's nothing available yet in the way of man-made materials that can replace the color, form, and texture of nature's handiwork.

The Arctic scene at the upper left of the opposite page is an updated version of the chemical gardens of a generation ago. You'll witness one of nature's most mysterious spectacles when you see the chemical reaction on this unusual table centerpiece.

To duplicate this scene, line a ceramic tray or platter (do not use metal) with a ½-inch layer of white foam. Then, glue inverted plastic bowls in place. Landscape the scene with pine cones and bare branches.

The next step is to combine the following ingredients in a jar or bowl: 6 tablespoons each of salt, bluing, and water; and 1 tablespoon household ammonia. Mix well, and pour the mixture slowly over the bowls, branches, and pine cones, which you first moisten with water. Within a few hours, 'snowflakes' will begin to appear. The fragile growth will continue for several days. (The foam base soaks up much of the mixture.) Should bare areas appear after the arrangement starts growing, drip more of the solution over these spots. If additional color is desired, apply food coloring or liquid fabric dye in a medicine dropper sparingly on the arrangement. Finally, arrange tiny wooden figures in place.

It's fun to watch a mini-forest grow right before your eyes. The one at the top right of the opposite page measures 12x20 inches.

To start this project, first anchor five or more white foam cones to a waterproof tray with glue. Layer cotton batting on the tray base; cover batting with potting soil and another layer of cotton batting.

Then, sow rye seed in the soil; keep the soil moist and in about a week the grass will be from 1 to 1½ inches high. Next, spray cotton-covered cones with water. Plant parsley, watercress, or mustard seed (from the health store) in the cotton. In a few days, the garnishes will start to germinate. Perch tiny bird ornaments on the trees if you desire; attach them with floral picks or pins.

The Christmas cactus is a sensational plant when it is in bloom, but it takes a little 'inside' know-how to get it to bloom. First of all, the Christmas cactus resents too much direct sunlight. If you place it in a south or west window, shade it with glass curtains. No diffusion is needed on a north or east exposure. Water it regularly during most of the year. And be sure the soil remains porous.

A well-tended Christmas cactus grows fast. When you want to propagate it, simply cut shoots back from tips at the second joint. Then, stick the cuttings into a moist, perlite-peat medium. Water sparingly at first or you'll rot the succulent stems. After two or three weeks, water as you would any other cutting. When the cuttings all seem to be well rooted, pot them in a very loose, porous mix in a clay pot or ceramic bowl.

The single dwarf poinsettia shown at the bottom right of the opposite page is housed in a globular glass bowl and surrounded by variegated holly sprigs. Both the poinsettia and the holly thrive in the close, moist atmosphere of the glass bowl.

The dwarf poinsettia has a unique beauty, and costs little more than the standard varieties. These small plants, which have been dwarfed chemically, give near-normal-size blooms on very short stems, allowing versatility in holiday arrangements.

Another way to enjoy poinsettias at holiday time is to fill a hanging basket with one poinsettia plant and surround it with evergreen sprigs. To keep the evergreen needles fresh and green, spray them with a plastic film (made especially for plants), and wrap the cut ends of the stems with wet paper towels before inserting them in plastic sandwich bags. Soak the poinsettia plant pot, place it in a plastic bag, and close the bag around the base of the stems.

Place the pot in a hanging basket. Distribute the evergreen branches to completely hide the pot and to set off the bright red poinsettia blooms. Hang the basket from the ceiling or on a wall bracket.

To raise healthy poinsettias, keep the soil evenly moist and display them where they are protected from cold drafts. Move them into a rather cool location during the night.

Arctic centerpiece

Mini-forest tabletopper

Christmas cactus

Dwarf poinsettia

Chapter 6

Wonderful Ways with Walls

The holiday season is a wonderful time, when family and friends share in the excitement of Christmas. Why not harness this seemingly boundless enthusiasm some evening? Gather the family together and have everyone join in making a wall decoration or two. All of the wall decorations in this chapter are easy to make and will raise holiday spirits to an even higher level.

Make wall decorations of paper, straw, felt, fabric, or natural materials. They can be large or small, or in between, depending on the size of your rooms and the area you wish to decorate. There might be one area where you feel a massive wall hanging is just right; another space might be perfect for a simple wreath. Decide what materials and size best complement your decor, and choose colors that harmonize with your furnishings and other Yuletide decorations you may have.

If your idea of Christmas decorations follows along the traditional lines, create your wall decorations in the same sentimental vein. If, however, your tastes lean more toward the contemporary styles, adapt the same holiday spirit to sophisticated modern designs. The choice is up to you, and most likely you will be influenced by your own life-style and the particular mood that is reflected in your style of decorating.

The foil collage at the left projects a cathedral-like effect. The open Bible, with an arrangement of roses behind it and the grouping of lighted tapers in a variety of sizes and designs of brass candlesticks, adds to the feeling of reverence.

Imaginative wall hangings

Display the holiday spirit in your home by making an assortment of one-of-a-kind wall hangings. On the pages that follow, you will find illustrations and instructions for hangings made of metallic paper, straw, felt, fabric, and an assortment of natural materials.

Metallic paper magic

Wall decorations made of metallic paper have a regal appearance, yet their origin is humble. It takes only a small amount of material, and some time and patience, to duplicate those described on these pages.

The arched foil collage shown on page 100, with the lighted tapers in front of it, glorifies the Christmas story, symbolized by the Bible opened on a lectern. Here, the archway is free-standing and held in place by the small chest.

To make this beauty, first cut plywood in the shape of an archway. Then, prepare the gold foil in this manner: from a roll of paper-backed foil, tear off about two feet. Crush it into a tight ball until the entire surface is wrinkled. Open it up and spread it out flat with the palms of your hands. Spray a puddle of quick-drying enamel into the foil. Moisten a cloth with turpentine to rub paint over the foil. Apply pressure while rubbing to produce the rich texture of darks contrasting with the golds. Tear the foil into random sizes and shapes and apply the pieces to the plywood backing with white glue. Arrange the size and shape of the torn portions for a pleasing effect. After you've glued the pieces over the entire surface, you may notice that some torn white edges show. If so, stain these dark by wiping a thinned solution of the same paint used before. When the paint is dry, finish with a coat of liquid plastic.

The Madonna foil collage shown at the top of the opposite page, with its subdued glow, captures the reverent spirit of the holiday season. The only materials needed are a piece of plywood, some paper-backed gold foil, and a small amount of cord.

To make this collage, trace the outlines of the pattern shown here onto the piece of plywood. Then, crumple a sheet of paper-backed foil. Flatten it out, taking care to pull it apart gently so that the foil does not tear.

Spray the foil with flat black paint. Next, moisten a cloth with paint thinner or turpentine and wipe over the surface in a circular motion. Tear the treated foil into random shapes and paste them to the plywood background with any white glue. The amount of paper you'll need will be about one and a half times the area to be covered.

For the inner part, trace the outline on the paper side of the gold foil, reversing the pattern. Cut out and paste foil to conform to the design. Trace the cord pattern on the collage. With heavy glue, make a small bead along the traced cord lines. Lay cord along the glue, cutting at the corners. When the paper and cord are both thoroughly dry, coat the entire surface with liquid plastic.

For the Wise Men plaque shown at the bottom left of the opposite page, you will need one sheet of gold cardboard, a roll of gold paper, a roll of red paper, one package of printed paper, four metal pot scrapers, gold braid trims, and velvet ribbon.

To duplicate this plaque, cover ¾ of three narrow boxes (in three sizes) with red wrapping paper and the remaining ¼ with gold paper. With a black marking pencil, draw on the facial features.

To make the capes, cut the patterned wrapping paper to fit around the boxes, making the bottom wider than the top. Trim the edges with gold foil tape and attach to boxes. Trim bottoms of boxes with gold tape.

For the beards, use metal pot scrapers stretched and shaped to fit over the box fronts. Cut the crowns from gold cardboard and add gold foil trims for the crown jewels. Finish by mounting the boxes onto a wooden picture frame. Tack or glue the largest box directly to the frame. Insert dowels or attach large spools to the backside of the remaining Wise Men; glue the other side of the spools to the larger Wise Man. From the back of the frame, pound nails into the dowels or spools.

Straw wall hangings

There are a multitude of ways to use wicker, straw mats, and woven baskets to concoct unusual wall hangings. The materials used are inexpensive and fun to work with.

Madonna foil collage

Wise Men plaque

Santa wall piece

Holy Family wall hanging

Angel wall hanging

Banner with buttons

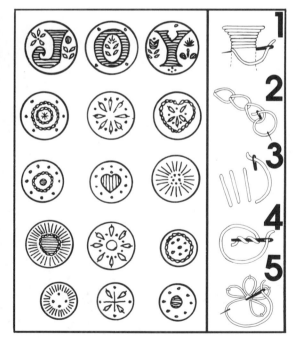

This Santa wall piece (shown on page 103) has a unique, contemporary appearance. In his own droopy-eyed, easygoing manner, he'll delight all who pause to greet him.

To make this distinctive hanging, first draw patterns on ¼-inch plywood for the hair, beard, and eyelashes. Soak wicker in water until it is pliable. Then, shape the strips of wicker to the patterns and secure them to the board by putting in the nails at an angle on each side of the wicker strands. Don't drive the nails through the wicker, as this will cause it to split. Allow the wicker strands to dry completely.

Next, permanently fasten the ends of the wicker loops together, using wire and glue. Then, wire the loops for the hair and beard together to form separate units. (These make Santa's hair and beard when assembled.)

Roll one woven place mat into a cylinder so that it fits into a large wicker cornucopia that has been spray-painted red. Wire the cylinder together. Then, wire it to the cornucopia, forming the face and hat.

Wire the wicker beard and hair units to the head assembly. Wire the eyelashes (wicker strips) to two small wicker cornucopia eye sockets, then wire the sockets to the face mat. Roll yarn into small balls—a red one for the nose and two blue ones for the eyes. Wire the trim into place. Trim the peak and the brim of Santa's hat with frayed ropes, as shown here, or with white excelsior.

Next, wire the entire head assembly to a rectangle of hardware cloth. Tuck sprays of evergreen into the hardware cloth to form a background for the face. Sew three woven place mats together with wire or string, going through every other loop at the edges. (This will conceal the stitching.)

Finally, wire this triple-thick mat to the hardware cloth backing the Santa face, and add a loop for hanging the decoration.

Felt and fabric backdrops

Here and on the next few pages are a variety of familiar greetings of the Yuletide season. Some of these wall hangings are of traditional designs; others are contemporary versions. They lend themselves to a host of backgrounds, both indoors or out. Also, they make wonderful gifts for the special people on your Christmas list. Before you shop for materials for these wall hangings, make an exhaustive search of your sewing supplies for odds and ends of fabric and felt you can use to create these ingenious decorations.

The Holy Family is depicted on this large-scale fabric wall hanging, which has a Spanish feeling in colors and lines.

To make the hanging, first cut a large panel of red felt for the wall panel, and mount it on a wooden dowel for hanging. Next, cut out the figures and features of Mary, Joseph, the Baby Jesus, and the donkey, and applique them to the felt background. Use colored yarn for Mary's hair, folds on Joseph's cloak, and the reins of the donkey. Attach the yarn with either glue or thread.

This banner with buttons is a holiday hang-up that will delight needlework enthusiasts. And, the materials you'll need are inexpensive and easy to find.

To make the hanging, embroider the buttons first. Buy the uncovered kind. You'll need 3 size 100 (2½ inches), 8 size 60 (1½ inches), and 22 size 36 (⅞ inch).

Following the sketches at left, pencil the designs on appropriate colored fabrics. The fabrics used here are lightweight cottons in violet, magenta, orange, and red—enough for two 3½-inch circles and two 2-inch circles of each color. You'll need enough natural linen for a 12x7½-inch rectangle, three 4½-inch circles, and fourteen 3-inch circles.

Embroider the designs with lightweight yarn in violet, magenta, green, orange, and red. (Follow the photograph for stitches and colors to use. Follow the sketches below the photograph when embroidering the designs. The stitches used for the various designs are at the right of the designs. The directions for doing these stitches are on page 106.) When the embroidery is completed, cut out circles of fabric and cover the buttons according to the manufacturer's instructions.

For the background, fold a 36x15-inch piece of magenta felt in half. (When used double, the hanging will have more strength to support the weight of the buttons.) Make sure the folded edge of the felt is at the top of the banner. Stitch a one-inch seam at the top to slide a brass rod through.

Crease the edges of the neutral linen rectangle to measure 10¾x6 inches. Press the edges and pin the piece into position on the felt background. Pin or baste the rickrack trims in rows, using the photo as a guide. Stitch the rectangle and rickrack trims in place. Sew the buttons onto the background and stitch the side edges together. Cut fringe along the bottom edge, making the cuts about ¼ inch apart. Insert a 16-inch brass cafe curtain rod through the top. Or, if you prefer, make four or five felt loops at the top and thread the rod through the loops.

Directions for making embroidery stitches:

1. *Satin stitch:* to make this stitch, keep straight stitches close together, leaving no space between stitches. Keep an even tension on the needle and thread.

2. *Chain stitch:* bring needle up through right side of fabric. Hold yarn to form a loop with your thumb. Pass needle through the same place again and bring it out ⅛ inch in front of the previous stitch.

3. *Straight stitch:* this is probably the easiest one to master. Make each stitch in a straight line the same length, and separate one from the other.

4. *French knot:* bring the needle out to the right side of the fabric. Hold yarn with your left hand and wind it around the needle twice. Pull yarn until tight. Then, put needle back close to where the yarn came out. Loosen knot enough to push the needle through to the wrong side. Pull the yarn to form a knot. The size of the finished knot will depend on the weight of the yarn, or, if you are using embroidery floss, it will depend on the number of strands you use.

5. *Lazy daisy:* make loops as for chain stitch above. After each loop is completed, make a small stitch to secure it in place.

The stylized angel shown at the bottom of page 104 is worthy of display in the most elegant contemporary home. This large-scale wall hanging is perfect for a vast expanse of wall space. The colors of the hanging are rather subdued and do not detract from the beauty of the textured grass cloth wall covering in the background.

For the background, cut a length of coal black felt and make a 2-inch hem at both the top and the bottom.

Trace the pattern for the angel design with sewing chalk or a white pencil. Cut out the felt pieces and assemble them in mosaic fashion. Glue the pieces in place after the pattern has been established. Insert brass cafe curtain rods in both hems to support the top and to give weight to the bottom.

You could also use this as a room divider if you repeat the design on the opposite side of the felt scroll.

The royal blue banner shown at the upper left of the opposite page hangs next to a fireplace, where its blue background reiterates the blue of the holiday candle standing on the mantel. For this banner, you will need felt, glue, and a brass cafe curtain rod.

For the background, cut a piece of royal blue felt that measures 36x45 inches. Cut 60 harlequin-shaped leaves from kelly green felt, and stitch them to the banner background into a tree shape. Start five inches from the top and eight inches from the bottom.

Trim the tree with eleven gold felt horns and ten 4-inch and eight 2½-inch circles cut from hot pink felt; glue them in place. Top the tree with two gold stars.

For the scallops on the border, use half circles of felt that are 6 inches in diameter. Stitch them to the banner, then cover the hem with decorative trims. Fold five 5-inch squares of blue felt in half for the dowel casing and stitch to the top of the banner. Arrange the felt letters that spell out the greeting on the bottom of the banner, and glue them in place. Mount the wall hanging on a decorative brass cafe curtain rod.

This Noel greeting can help to carry out your Christmas color scheme. Cut the letters freehand from white felt, then glue or sew them to the background material. (Felt was used in this one, but you can use any firm fabric that you wish.)

To make the border, use the outside strip of bulky yarn in the same color as the background. (When you are stitching the yarn to the fabric by hand, conceal the thread inside the yarn.) Glue the remaining two lengths of yarn to the felt. Use a second color of yarn around the edge and the U-shaped center. Attach a third color of yarn down the sides and to outline the letters. Where the ends of yarn are to be mitered and then glued together, cut the yarn on the diagonal.

Hem the top of the banner, and attach bells at varying lengths to the yarn. Insert a brass curtain rod inside the hem, or substitute a wooden dowel painted or stained in a harmonious color.

This burlap wall hanging (it also can be used as a room divider) will set a festive mood for the holiday season year after year, no matter where you display it.

To make this wall hanging, start with a 1¾-yard length of 36-inch-wide green burlap. Turn under two inches at the top edge and stitch an open fold to hold a curtain rod. Sew a close, running stitch seven inches up from the bottom the width of the burlap piece.

Christmas slogan banner

Noel greeting

Burlap tapestry hanging

Next, sew the outline of a tree, trunk, and tree container with close running stitches. For the tree, sew a triangle outline 27 inches wide at the base and 31½ inches high from the center of the base to the point. The 7-inch-tall tree container should measure approximately 9½ inches wide at the top and taper to a 5-inch-wide bottom.

Within the tree triangle, clip the horizontal threads of burlap and pull them out. Interweave lengths of jumbo wool yarn, metallic rickrack, gold middy braid, novelty gold trims, and ripple trims in the vertical threads that remain in the design. (For ease in handling, start at the bottom of the triangle and clip out only enough threads to accommodate the width of the trim that is to be woven each time.) Leave a horizontal thread unclipped between each trim. Clip all trims evenly at the sides, and tip ends with all-purpose glue.

For the tree container, interweave a 1½-inch-wide gold ribbon, leaving several folds at one side for the fluffy trim effect. Catch folds in place with thread. Interweave the rest of the container with white yarn, alternating the interweaving from row to row (two

threads over and two under on one row, then two under and two over on next row).

For the tree trunk, remove the vertical threads of burlap so the gold ribbon can be interlaced within the area. Catch the ribbon with thread to hold it in place. Use white yarn for the star on the treetop.

At the bottom of the hanging, interweave three rows of yarn above the stitched line. Draw out horizontal threads for fringe.

Insert a dowel and small brass hooks at the ends at the top for hanging.

Make the burlap wall hangings pictured here any size you want. Cut the burlap to the desired size, then stitch under two inches at the top width and stitch an open fold to hold a curtain rod or wood dowel.

Cut the felt pieces according to the patterns shown here, and glue them to the burlap. Use liquid gold from a tube to draw the angels. Add other trims to the felt and attach them with glue; use gold paper doilies for the

angels' halos. Trim the gown with large and small sequins, gold braid, and yarn.

At the bottom of the burlap hanging, sew a close running stitch the width of the burlap, seven inches up from the bottom edge. Interweave three rows of yarn above the stitched line. Draw out the horizontal threads for a fringed border. At the top, insert a rod and a small brass hook for hanging.

The beribboned sleigh-bell banner shown on page 111 at upper left, fashioned from felt and suspended from a 15-inch dowel rod, will bring added punch to any wall in your home.

To duplicate this wall hanging, you'll need a piece of red felt that measures 12x38 inches. Trim this felt panel with ¼-inch ribbon cut in varying lengths and glued to the background. At bottom, hang a bell from each side and from point. At top, hang a bell at each end of rod; attach holly to picture hanger.

The four-section holiday tree shown on page 111 at upper right—the home-grown variety—is displayed in a 25x32-inch picture frame. The overall height of the tree measures 22 inches; the width, 14 inches at the base.

To make the four tree sections, laminate silk wallpaper to paper for added body and cut sections varying from 4¼ inches to 5 inches high. For strong vertical lines, cut the tips from fireside matches, paint the wood red, and glue them to the tree. To give the wall plaque a bit of dimension, glue a couple of wood blocks to the back of each section. Next, cut and score birds from foil; glue gold doilies and beads in place. Flank tree with strands of ribbon tacked to frame backing.

The pre-Christmas patchwork hanging shown on page 111 at the lower left helps count off the days of Advent. Buttoned-down, numbered triangles reveal the symbols of the season—one for each day of Advent.

You'll need one yard of 45-inch-wide red sailcloth for the background and the loops at the top. Cut two pieces that measure 21x36 inches—one for the background and one for the lining. Following the pattern shown on page 110, cut a tree triangle that measures 24x24x17 inches from red and green striped sailcloth. (This piece will not show in the finished hanging, but it accommodates the buttoned-down triangles.) Bond this piece to the 21x36-inch red background with permanent fabric bonding film, following manufacturer's direction for fusing pieces together.

Cut the tree trunk from a scrap of fabric, and fuse it to the background fabric as you

◀ **Burlap and felt** are a hard-to-beat combination for making wall decorations. To make the trio shown at the left, all you have to do is cut, hem, stitch, glue, and fringe the fabrics.

did for the tree. To make the star that goes on the tip of the tree, cut eight small diamond shapes and a circle from fabric snippets. Follow the same bonding procedure and position the star.

Using white thread, machine-stitch a ¼-inch seam inside the tree shape, star, and trunk. Embroider decorative swirl designs on both sides of the tree.

Next, cut 24 triangular and diamond-shaped pieces from felt. (Here, three shades of green were used—olive, kelly, and apple.) These pieces are the ones that will show when the patchwork triangles are reversed.

Apply fusing material to each felt piece. Set these pieces aside, then cut the same number of pieces from cotton or calico; apply bonding material to the back and fuse the felt and fabric together. Machine-stitch ¼ inch inside the edges. On all pieces, cut buttonhole openings. Set aside until later.

For the loops at the top, cut three 8x9-inch pieces from red background fabric. Fold over the 9-inch side and stitch a seam ½ inch from the edge. Turn right side out and press flat. Fold each loop in half, stitch the raw edges together, ¼ inch from the bottom. Pin and stitch to the hanging.

For the lining, cut a piece of fabric 21x36 inches. Place the right side of the lining and the red background together. Pin and stitch on three sides, leaving the bottom edge open. Turn the hanging right side out and press. Topstitch ½ inch from the edges on the sewn sides. Using red thread, sew across the bottom with the zigzag stitch on your sewing machine. Stitch red fringe across the bottom, or make your own fringe.

Place all of the triangles on top of the tree shape; mark button placement. Remove the shapes and sew on buttons. Use ¾-inch-size buttons on triangles and ¼-inch size for the star and swirls.

Stick gummed gold foil numbers in place (1-inch size on patchwork side; ½-inch size for the felt sides). Glue pictures pertaining to the season onto the felt sides so they will be ready to make their appearance as their particular day arrives. Button all of the shapes to their corresponding number.

Stain a 1x22-inch dowel and doorknob finials in a walnut finish. When the stain is dry, glue the knobs to the ends of the dowel. For added luster, apply a coat of satin-finish varnish. Thread the rod through the three loops at the top of the hanging.

Utensils from a kitchen cupboard, shown at the lower right of the opposite page, will bring rave notices to the homemaker who uses them in a holiday hang-up. Display the fanciful creation over a kitchen desk or a breakfast counter, or present it to a gourmet friend who collects cooking utensils.

This hanging features a wire whisk, a wooden spoon (cut off the handle and use the bowl for a head), tart pans, a wire basket, and a variety of salad molds. But you can use almost any utensils you desire.

To make this hanging, cover a 15x30-inch piece of plywood with red burlap, bringing the fabric around to the back of the board. Make two loops over the top to fit the dowel.

Assemble the gadgets to resemble a picture of the Madonna. Glue the flat pieces to the background. Attach others, such as wire whisks and salad molds, by drilling tiny holes in the board and then slipping a small wire from the backside through the hole and the utensil. Work the wire back to the reverse side and twist the ends together tight to hold the utensils in place. Alternate large red and green yarn tassels across the bottom and attach them with tacks.

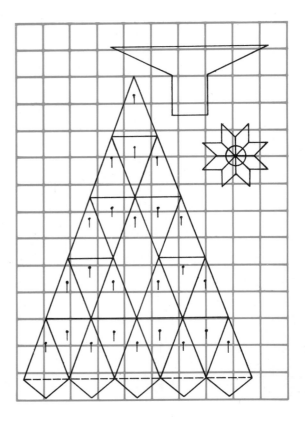

Ribbons and sleigh bells

Patchwork wall hanging

Four-section holiday tree

Angelic utensils

Sheaf of grain

Driftwood wall plaque

Driftwood sculpture

Gourds and straw

Naturally nice

There's nothing more pleasing to the eye than holiday trimmings made with natural materials. Besides being good looking, they are inexpensive to make because you can collect most of the materials needed while you are on treks through wooded areas or around lakes. Branches, pods, berries, driftwood, stalks of grain and grasses, and many other natural materials abound in most areas of the country. If you have difficulty finding what you want, you can always fall back on your local florist for supplies.

A sheaf of stalks of grain adjacent to an Early American pine secretary makes a handsome wall decoration (upper left on the opposite page). If you don't have the materials on hand, you need look no further than your florist shop and a sewing notions department.

Lash a sheaf of wheat, barley, rye, or any other grain together with thin wire. Cover the wire with dried grain heads. To make the leaves and stems more supple, slightly dampen them.

Wire on commercial pincushions so that they create a color mass where the sheaf is tied. Spread out the beards and heads at the top. Insert two or three sprigs of pine, positioning them to set off the grasses and to unify the pincushions with the total cluster.

Driftwood provides the focal point for the wall plaque shown at the upper right of the opposite page. Collect pieces of driftwood from beaches and river banks. Let them dry thoroughly, then brush and clean them. If you hesitate about creating your own designs, use designs on Christmas cards or gift wrapping paper as patterns. Paint the designs on the raw wood with acrylic paints. When the paint is thoroughly dry, spray the surface with clear lacquer.

Next, cover a rectangle of ⅜-inch plywood with shocking pink velvet, sized slightly larger than the sheet of plywood itself. After mitering the material around the corners, secure it to the back of the plywood with 'non-creeping' glue.

Arrange the pieces of driftwood on the sheet of covered plywood in a pleasing composition, and hold them in place with small screws set in from the backside of the plywood plaque. Frame the plaque with twisted pink package yarn, looped in each corner and tied in a simple bow at the bottom. Use glue to secure the yarn to the edges of the plaque.

Beachcombers, be on the alert! You, too, may find a shapely log (see the one shown at left, below) that has been weathered by the sands of time. Driftwood pieces can provide inspiration for wall hangings and become the paramount element of the design.

Drill two holes near the center of the wood with a power drill, and run an 18-inch length of florist's wire from the front to the back in a U shape. Wire short lengths of mugho pine branches to the center. Wire cedar and deodar cones individually, then into clusters of two or three, leaving a single wire 'stem.' Wire the clusters to the U-shaped wire. (If you can't locate these materials, use locally available pine branches and cones instead.

Wire small, dark brown, plastic seed pods (from a variety store, import shop, or florist supply outlet) individually, and secure them between the cone clusters. Wire loops of red satin-backed velveteen ribbon and tuck them into the arrangement under the cones. Place a large screw eye at the top back of the driftwood to serve as a wall hanger.

Straw mats and ornamental gourds are the natural materials that dominate this novel wall hanging. To duplicate this design, you'll need two 16-inch diameter natural straw mats; dried gourds from your garden supply, grocery store, or variety store; spray paints; antiquing glaze; about 2½ yards of 2-inch-wide dark turquoise grosgrain ribbon; 22-gauge wire; a brass curtain ring; and branches of variegated ivy.

Make a hanger by looping ribbon through the brass curtain ring and wiring loose ribbon ends to the center front of one straw mat. Remove the outer two rows from the second straw mat, making it about 13 inches in diameter. Form a hairpin hook from a short length of wire, push both ends through the centers of both mats, and wire together at back.

Spray scrubbed and dried gourds with turquoise, gold, and orange paints (or any colors that harmonize with your decor). When the paint is dry, spray the gourds with antiquing glaze and wipe off the excess. Push an ice pick through the gourds just below the stem, and string with wire. Mass the gourds in a suitable arrangement and push wires through centers of mats, fastening at back.

Wire loops of turquoise grosgrain ribbon and fasten with wire to the mats. Highlight the arrangement with short lengths of variegated English ivy. The ivy will retain its freshness for about 10 days.

Roundup of holiday wreaths

The Christmas wreath is a hallmark of the holidays, and will always be a favorite wall embellishment. Wreaths traditionally are made of greens attached to a circular frame and trimmed with berries, pine cones, pods, and/or tiny baubles. Usually, a dramatic satin or velvet bow adds the final elegant note to the holiday wreath.

Although the old familiar wreath reappears each year, new traditions, which are as much a part of the holiday feeling as the timeless fireplace mantel wreath of greens, are established every Christmas season.

You can make wreaths of burlap, gingham, felt, paper, and a host of unlikely materials. If you want a wreath that's decidedly different, yet striking in every way, you'll appreciate the ones that are shown on the following pages. Some of them feature natural materials; the others are constructed of man-made materials. All of them will make your walls come alive during the holiday season.

A bonus from Mother Nature

Wreaths made of natural materials are a joy to behold and give forth a subtle fragrance that is immediately identifiable with the holiday season.

The boxwood wreath adorned with colorful fruit (shown at the top of the opposite page) is a centuries-old holiday decoration. The ancient Greeks and Romans wore head wreaths made of fruit, leaves, and lotus blossoms for festive occasions. The Italian sculptor, Luca della Robbia, and his family decorated their sculptured wreaths with colorfully enameled fruit. Today, besides serving as handsome wall decorations, Della Robbia wreaths often grace a fireplace mantel or a front door, too.

In the tradition of the famous sculptor, colorful fruit was added to the wreath shown here. To make it, use a plastic foam wreath for the base. Then, add sprigs of boxwood and other evergreens, fresh fruit on floral picks, and pine cones to fill out the design.

The wreath of dried herbs that appears at the bottom left of the opposite page affords a potpourri of fragrance—not only during the holiday season, but long afterward, too.

Assemble your materials first—a plastic foam wreath base, brown or green floral tape, sequin pins, and a variety of spices.

Cover the plastic foam wreath base with either green or brown floral tape. Use borders of bay leaves in three overlapping rows as the main interest, and fasten them to the base with sequin pins. Arrange the other spices in pleasing designs. The ones used in this wreath are star anise, nutmeg, stick cinnamon, blade mace, cardamom, coriander, gingerroot, allspice, red peppers, juniper berries, white and black peppercorns, cloves, fennel, caraway seeds, vanilla and coffee beans, and small round chilies (to add spots of color). But you can use any combination you wish.

Cornhusks are back in fashion for many decorative accessories, and the wreath shown at the bottom right of the opposite page is reminiscent of those that were made years ago by the American colonists. In addition to the cornhusks, you will need a plastic foam wreath base, florist picks, small decorations, and ribbon for a bow.

Soak the cornhusks in water until they become pliable, then cut them into 2x5-inch strips. Fold them into loops and attach them to the plastic foam wreath base with florist picks. To provide accent, add small sprigs of greens, red berries, and small Christmas figures that make up the Nativity scene at the bottom of the wreath. At the top, place a bright red bow nested in a cluster of greens.

Wreaths of man-made materials

Do you restlessly anticipate Christmas long before the calendar rolls around to December? Do your fingers itch to create something dazzling and unique for your home before you're swamped with Christmas shopping and holiday parties? Then wreaths fashioned of man-made materials are for you—they won't wilt or decay, and they'll serve you well for years.

The burlap wreaths shown on page 116 all start with the same basic design. First, cut six-inch-wide strips of burlap (4½ widths of 36-inch material or three widths of 54-inch material). Pull two threads in center of each strip, and ravel one inch on edges of strips.

Della Robbia boxwood wreath

Dried herb wreath

Cornhusk wreath

Bend an opened coat hanger into a circle, leaving the last few inches of one end straight. With pliers, bend the other end into a small loop. Gather the burlap on the wire with tiny stitches. When the wire is completely covered, put the straight end through the small loop and bend it over. Arrange burlap in even gathers, and add a loop for hanging.

For the tin star wreath shown at the top of the opposite page, you will need burlap, felt, can lids, small tree ornaments, and a coat hanger wreath frame. Make an aqua-colored burlap wreath according to the directions given above. Cut a felt strip 1½ inches wide and approximately 40 inches long. Fold it into a tube and baste. Catchstitch the basted edge around the center of the coat-hanger wreath.

To make each of the stars, punch a hole in the center of a can lid. From paper, cut a five-pointed star pattern to fit the lid size. Cut into the lid between the star points (diagram 1). Bend the star shapes with a snipe-nose pliers, with the shaded areas to the back and the clear areas to the front (diagram 2). With tin snips, cut strips ¹⁄₁₆ inch wide, as shown in diagram 3. (Strips will curve over the arms.) Bend over the remaining tin to form the star design (diagram 4).

Remove the hanging wire from small tree ornaments. Put the loop through the hole in

the center of the star; reinsert the ornament. Put wire through the loop on the back of the star and attach it to the wreath.

Make a double bow from two burlap loops; staple it at the center and wrap a 'belt' around the middle. Trim the wreath with red felt ribbon, wiring it to the wreath sideways.

The Mexican fruit wreath shown at the upper left of the opposite page is actually two wreaths in one. Make the basic burlap wreath first, then make a smaller burlap wreath that has been cut three inches wide. Wire the smaller wreath on top of the larger one. Purchase an assortment of Mexican silk fruit—you will find these at a Mexican import shop, a party supply shop, or a florist shop. Wire the fruit through both wreaths.

For the rope wreath shown at the lower right of the opposite page, you will need natural hemp, a double wire frame, green hemp, artificial fruit, coasters, and a mat.

Cut the natural hemp into 9-inch pieces. Use the sales ticket knot (lark's head knot) to attach the rope strips to the inside wire of a double wire frame about 15 inches in diameter. Fill in the inner wreath with rope. Fray the open ends.

Cut the green hemp into 12-inch lengths and attach them to the outer ring in the same knot. Do not fray. Wire the fruit in pairs. Then, attach them evenly to the wreath with wire in between green Mexican fiber coasters. Wire the entire wreath to a green straw table mat about 19 inches in diameter.

The Santa Claus wreath at the bottom of the opposite page requires burlap, paper, paste, wire, velvet, felt, gesso, a plastic foam ball, and paint.

Start with a green burlap wreath, made according to the instructions above. To make the leaves, glue together three sheets of newspaper, ¼-page size, using ordinary wallpaper paste. Draw on the holly leaf pattern and cut out the leaves, following the drawing shown at the bottom of the page.

Cut the wire stems 9 inches long, glue them to the holly leaves, placing the wire from the center of the leaves to the bottom. Leave lengthy stems. With wallpaper paste, add three more layers of paper cut in leaf shapes over the stems. When the leaves are partially dry, shape the center vein and points. Allow the leaves to dry completely, and finish with either a coat of gesso and two coats of green lacquer or with green poster paint and two coats of shellac.

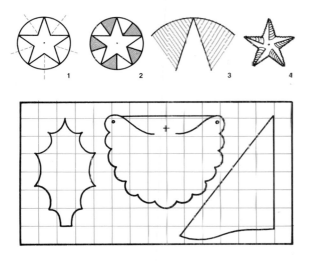

◀ **Sturdy burlap in Christmas colors** provides the background material for this collection of holiday wreaths. Fringe the edges, add some trim, and you'll be amazed at the results.

For the Santa head, which is the focal point of this burlap wreath, the construction is much simpler than it appears.

Cut the hat according to the pattern shown on page 117. Make the hat either of red velvet or felt. Tie a knot in white velvet tubing; tack the tubing to the top of the hat to simulate a miniature tassel. Stitch the back seam.

Cut a flowing beard and moustache from white felt, following the pattern on page 117, and pin them to the plastic foam head. Use a small red ball for the nose. Stick it through a slit in the moustache and fasten it to the foam base. Add a strip of white velvet tubing to form a band on the hat. Wire the head to the wreath, positioning it directly over a matching red velvet or felt bow.

Petals cut from felt combine to make the smartly tailored wreath shown at the upper left of the opposite page. In addition to the wire wreath base, you will need two colors of felt for the petals, black felt, No. 20 wire, and ribbon for the bow.

Cut five petals from one color and five slightly smaller of another color for each flower. Vary the sizes from 1½x3 inches to 2½x5 inches. Lay a larger-size petal on one of the smaller petals; machine-stitch lengthwise close to the center. Next, lay a piece of No. 20 wire close to the stitching line between the two layers of felt. Make another row of machine stitching on the other side of the wire. Bend the wire at right angles to the petal; cut the wire, leaving about 2 inches for joining the petals.

For the center of each flower, glue a 2-inch length of 1-inch-wide black felt around a stem ornament; fringe the felt and attach it to the center of the flower. Tape each five-petaled flower to a wire wreath base, and finish with a graceful ribbon bow.

The cheerful red and white checked gingham wreath shown at the upper right of the opposite page evokes a spirit of nostalgia that makes it completely at home in country-style settings. In addition, making the wreath gives you a chance to use leftover fabric from home sewing projects. To make it, you'll need gingham, corrugated cardboard, cotton for padding, glue, red flannel for berries, velvet or felt for bow, and needle and thread.

Start the wreath by cutting two 25-inch circles from corrugated cardboard. Measure three inches in from the outside circumference, then cut a second circle, leaving a ring. Glue the two large circles together.

Cut the leaves from cardboard first, then cut the same number from gingham; allow a ½-inch overlap to turn under on the backside of the cardboard. (The wreath shown here has twelve 8-inch leaves, twelve 7-inch ones, fifteen 6-inch ones, twelve 5-inch ones, ten 4-inch ones, and fifteen 3-inch ones.

Add a small amount of cotton to the topside of each of the cardboard leaves for padding. Glue the gingham to the cardboard, pulling the fabric smoothly and tightly around the leaf shape, and at the same time, pressing it firmly into the glue that has been applied to the edges and back of each leaf.

Glue the leaves to the cardboard wreath base, starting from the center top and down each side. (This is important because it makes the leaves on both sides go in the same direction and meet at the bottom.) Mix the gingham checks and the sizes and shapes of the leaves as you go. Fill in any bare spots.

Make about 30 red berries to accent the plaids and checks. To do this, cut 3- and 4-inch circles of plain red cotton flannel. Make a hard ball of cotton, put it into the center of the circle, pull the fabric tightly around the ball of cotton, and catch underneath with a needle and thread. Cut off any excess fabric, and glue berry in place.

Tie a very lavish red felt or velvet bow for the top and secure it in place.

This same wreath pattern adapts well to calico or any other fabric that appeals to you.

The Yo-Yo wreath shown at the bottom of the opposite page is one that's bound to bring to mind the oft-repeated tales of Grandmother's quilting days. You'll need scraps of calico, gingham checks, or small plaids, in various shades of red; a plastic flower loom; green yarn; heavy-duty thread; green felt; embroidery floss; a plastic foam wreath base; and a needle and thread.

To duplicate this wreath, cut thirteen 7-inch circles and sixteen 8-inch circles from your fabric scraps. You can gather the circles by hand, but the process goes much faster if you use your sewing machine to help. Using the all-purpose stitching foot, adjust the stitch length for basting and loosen the tension knob. Stitch around the circles with red thread, about ⅛ inch from the edge. Stop just as you reach the point where the stitching began; don't let these points overlap. Leave long 'tail' threads, then pull the two end threads on top of circle tightly; tie knot. (Top of Yo-Yo is the side with the gathers.)

Felt petal wreath

Gingham checked wreath

Yo-Yo wreath

Following the directions that come with your plastic flower loom, make 29 green yarn flowers with petals three loops deep.

Finish off as directed. Before attaching the Yo-Yos and flowers to the wreath base, arrange them in an attractive color sequence. Thread a needle with heavy-duty thread; make a loop once around the wreath. Form and knot the thread on itself. Place the needle through the center of the large-size Yo-Yo, then through the center of the yarn flower and back through the Yo-Yo. Place the large-size Yo-Yos on the outer rim of the wreath. Next, insert needle through a small Yo-Yo, through a yarn flower, and back through small Yo-Yo. (These small-size motifs should rest on inside rim of the wreath.) Repeat this same process until all of the circular designs are in place. Each Yo-Yo should overlap another slightly, but always in the same direction.

Cut 16 green felt leaves and vein them with green embroidery floss, using the simple stem or crewel stitch. Glue the leaves onto the back of the wreath in pairs around the outer edge. Cover the backside of the wreath with a circle of felt for a neat, finished look.

Chapter 7

Candles and Candleholders

Candles are symbols of worship as they glow in our churches, and they serve to highlight splendid holiday decorations at home. Lighting candles on Christmas Eve and on the twelve days following Christmas Eve is a time-honored tradition that sprang from the lovely notion that the Christ Child might be guided through the darkness to the house if a lighted candle were kept in the window. In medieval times, no stranger was ever turned away from the door, for who knew when Christ might come again?

With this rich heritage, it's no wonder candles are such a vital part of our life-style today. In most homes, you will find that candles share in the decorating scheme. This is especially true when it comes to entertaining.

Along with this interest in candles, it's only natural that making candles has taken a prominent place in the wonderful world of hobbies and crafts.

You need only two ingredients to make candles—a suitable wax and the proper-size wick. And the only essential equipment is a heat source, a melting pot, a mold, and a thermometer. Add some enthusiasm, and you're on your way to becoming a master at candlecraft.

As you develop your skills at candlemaking, you'll want to embark on making candleholders, too. On the pages that follow, you'll find instructions for making both.

Make this ensemble of candleholders easily in your home workshop. You will need expanded aluminum mesh, cardboard mailing tubes, wooden blocks, aluminum tubing from a plumbing shop. plastic foam, dowels, nails, and paint.

Handcrafted candle collection

Candlemaking basics

Today, candles come in a variety of sizes, colors, and shapes, but there are only two basic types: molded candles and hand-rolled beeswax candles. If you're unsure about which type to tackle first, discuss your project with someone who has mastered the techniques for making both types.

How to mold candles

Working with the right materials is essential when molding candles—as with anything else. Follow the recommendations here, and you're bound to be successful in your venture.

Several kinds of wax are suitable for molding candles. Each has its own qualities and characteristics. The best kind is a petroleum wax, 143/145 A.M.P. This wax is hard and can be used for most candle projects. Another wax, 128/130 A.M.P., is good for short candles only. *Caution:* do not use paraffin, a canning

wax that you can purchase in supermarkets. If you do, you'll end up with a candle that is likely to lose its shape.

Also, save your old, partly burned candles. Melt and remold them into new forms. Or melt and use them to decorate other candles.

There are two types of wicks to choose from: woven cotton wicking and wire-core wicking. Woven cotton wicking usually is used for pillar candles because it can be held erect inside the mold and anchored with a pencil or rod laid perpendicular to the mold. However, you'll get more consistent results with wire-core wicking because the wick burns more uniformly. If you use this type, make the candle first and unmold it. Then, push a heated ice pick down through the center of the candle, thread the wicking through the candle, and secure it with melted wax.

The size of wick you use will determine how well the candle will burn. If it is too

122

Candlemaking equipment

large, the flame will smoke. If it's too small, the flame will go out. Other variables include the size of the candle and the wax used.

The most common wire-core wick used is a medium-sized one such as #44-24-18. If you opt for woven wicking, try a #10 bleached woven wick in candles with a diameter of two inches or less, a 30-ply wick in 2- to 4-inch-thick candles, and a 40-ply wick in candles that measure more than 4 inches thick.

Additives are not new to candlemaking. During colonial times, homemakers added bayberries to tallow candles (made from grease) to cut down on the odor. And at the beginning of the twentieth century, coloring was used as a marketing tool by manufacturers of candles. Today, additives are used to alter appearance, texture, and fragrance.

Wax scent: a potpourri of fragrances are available in either liquid or solid form. Use only commercial wax scents. Perfume will not work, as it has a water or alcohol base.

Coloring: crayons, fabric dye, and candle wax color chips will all yield satisfactory color results. A ¼-inch piece of crayon melted in hot wax will color 3½ ounces of melted wax. When you use fabric dye, sprinkle the powder evenly over the completely melted wax in the melting pot. Then, stir to mix. If you use chips, shave off small pieces and melt them in wax that has been heated to 210°.

Crystalsheen: this is a plastic additive that gives the candle a glossy surface.

Stearine (stearic acid): adding this chemical will achieve three things—it makes the candle wax harder, gives it an opaque quality, and intensifies the candle's color.

Mottling oil: adding mottling oil will result in tiny internal cracks in the wax. It is used primarily with colored candles.

You can purchase candle molds in a variety of shapes and sizes at hobby and craft shops. Or, if you're an avid recycler, use household throwaways. Milk cartons, tin cans, cardboard boxes, and egg shells are likely candidates. Regardless of the type of mold you use, be sure that the inside is clean and dry and that the bottom has a hole for the wick.

In addition to a mold, you will need a double boiler or an old coffeepot with a lid, a candy thermometer that registers 375°, a large container to hold water, a clean, soft cloth, and a knife or cheese cutter. Also, keep an ample supply of newspapers on hand, as wax spillage is common. Next, find an area in which to work. (The basement is an ideal location if you have a heat source nearby.) With this done, you're ready to start your project.

Follow candlemaking steps given below:
1. Place small chunks of wax into the top section of a double boiler and fill the bottom section of the boiler with water, making sure no water gets mixed with the melting wax. If you don't have a double boiler, use a coffeepot set in a large pot of water.

Caution: take care that wax never comes in contact with an open flame, as it is flammable.

2. Prepare your mold while the wax melts by spraying the inside of the mold with mold release. This product facilitates easy removal. Wipe the mold with a soft, clean cloth, making sure the surface is evenly covered.

3. Thread the wick through the hole in the bottom of the mold and bring it up through the mold. (You may have to enlarge the hole in a new mold so that it will accept the wick.) Tie the wick to a pencil or a metal rod and pull down on the wick so the pencil or rod is held firmly across the top of the mold. Holding the wick, press plastic clay over the hole and around the wick to prevent melted wax from seeping through. Let one inch of wick

extend underneath the mold and tape it to one side. (Candles made in metal molds are formed upside-down, so this one inch of wick is necessary to light the candles.)

4. Next, heat the wax to 210°, and add any additives such as coloring or scent. (If you are using fluorescent colors, do not heat to more than 175°.) To make sure you have the color you're trying for, put a few drops of the hot wax into a container of cold water. When the wax hardens, it will be the true color.

5. Transfer the hot wax into an old coffee-pot or other container with a spout if your double boiler does not have one. (Make sure that you have some protection for your arms and hands.) Then, using a hot pad, hold the mold at a slant and slowly pour the wax down the side of the mold. (This prevents air bubbles from being trapped in the liquid wax.) It's also a good practice to tap the mold repeatedly to free air bubbles that do get trapped. Place the mold in a container filled with cool water—and weight down the mold. Make certain that the water level is lower than the height of the mold, but that it is higher than the wax level. (The water bath will eliminate candle's surface imperfections.)

6. As wax cools, it also shrinks. So, after 45 minutes, break through the crust close to wick and refill the well with 210° wax.

7. After letting the wax cool for eight hours, the candle should be hardened. Squeeze the mold gently and tap the end of it on a padded surface to release the candle. If the candle does not release, place it in the refrigerator for about 45 minutes and try again.

8. After you dislodge the candle, scrape off the ridge left by the mold, using a cheese cutter or knife. Polish the candle with a soft, dry cloth and then with a paper towel.

Surface decorations convert an ordinary candle into a one-of-a-kind art object. Starting with polished candles, you can add surface decorations with decoupage or dribble wax, or by wax painting, antiquing, or candle sculpturing.

Decoupage is relatively easy to do. The only materials needed are candle wax and motifs cut from paper. First, place the motif on several layers of paper toweling in an electric skillet set at 230°. When the design is heated, brush it with uncolored 210° wax. Then transfer the design onto a smooth candle. To secure the design to the candle, hold the wick and dip the candle into the 210° clear wax. Finally, immerse in a cold water bath.

Dribble wax will add dimension to any plain-colored candle. Use as few or as many colors as you wish. To prepare it, heat each color separately at 175° in a small pot with a spout. Then, pour the wax, one color at a time, around the top edge of a smooth-surface candle. The wax does the rest—it dribbles its way down the sides of the candle.

Wax painting, as its name implies, is painting designs on candles with melted wax to achieve an embossed effect. The beauty of wax painting is that if you're not happy with the design, you can remove it and try again.

The first step in wax painting is to heat the candle wax to 200° and separate it into small quantities in individual containers. Then, place the tins in a pan of boiling water and dye the wax in the colors of your choice. Use cotton swabs for painting the design unless you want fine detail. In this case, use a sable brush. If you use cotton swabs, use a different swab for each color. If you use a sable brush, clean it with carbon tetrachloride or alcohol when you change colors.

If you want an antiqued effect, apply a coat of oil wood stain over the designs with a cotton swab or sable brush. Let the stain dry briefly, then wipe off the excess.

Candle sculpturing involves shaping thin layers of wax into designs, then securing the designs to the sides of polished candles without damaging the designs. Following are directions for making flowers and leaves, but directions would apply to other motifs, too:

First, prepare the sculpturing wax by mixing equal parts of low-temperature and medium-temperature petroleum wax and beeswax. Heat to 170°. Divide the wax into two pots and dye one for the petals and one for the leaves. Wipe a cookie sheet sparingly with cooking oil to prevent wax from sticking to it. Then, pour a thin sheet of wax onto the sheet. When the wax has cooled, lift it out and place on layers of paper toweling in an electric skillet set at its lowest setting.

Next, while the wax is warm, cut petals and leaves with a knife. Then shape them. (If you wish, make cardboard patterns, and cut around them.) Cut a 2-inch circle of warm wax for each flower. (This will be the backing.)

Adhere the petals to each other and to the backing with melted wax. (Overlap each petal.) Warm the leaves again, thin the edges, shape, and add veins. Secure the leaves to the flowers. Pour a small amount of 170° wax on backing of flowers and press onto candle.

How to make beeswax candles

Beeswax candles always have been the aristocrats of tapers. In the era when candles were the main source of indoor lighting, hand-rolled beeswax candles were used only in homes of the rich and in the church. They burned cleanly and without unpleasant odor. For this reason, they are still popular today.

They are easy to make, too. Simply hand-roll either smooth or honeycombed, pre-dyed 8x16-inch sheets of beeswax around woven cotton wicking.

Beeswax usually rolls easily at room temperature, but if you have difficulty, hold the beeswax sheet under warm water for a few minutes to soften it. Then, place the sheet on a smooth, clean working surface. Cut the wick one inch longer than the size of the sheet you are using. Lay the wicking along the edge of the beeswax and press the wax firmly over the wicking so it will be held securely in place. The wax may crack a little, but this is not important. Roll the wax once more over the wicking and gently pull the wick at the top of the candle to make certain that it is held tightly in place. (The candle will burn longer if the wick is tightly covered.) Now, continue rolling the beeswax candle evenly and snugly until you reach the end of the sheet. Thicker candles are just as easy to make, only you use more sheets of beeswax.

Although beeswax candles are beautiful even when left plain, you may want to decorate them. If so, add glitter, sequins, or other small ornamental trims in an eye-catching arrangement. They will adhere without glue because the beeswax is naturally sticky.

Here are instructions for a variety of beeswax candles. Some of them are ordinary, others are not so ordinary.

Make 8-inch beeswax candles by bending the 8-inch side of the sheet over and around a 9-inch wick. Each time you wrap beeswax around candle, diameter increases by ½ inch.

Make 16-inch beeswax candles in the same manner as the 8-inch models, except that in this case bend the 16-inch side of the sheet over and around a 17-inch piece of wicking.

You can make beeswax candles of any height under 16 inches by carefully scoring a straight line across the wax sheet with scissors. Cut along this scored line, using scissors, a razor blade, or a craft knife.

Two 16-inch spiral candles can be made from one 8x16-inch sheet of beeswax. Score first, then cut the beeswax diagonally from one corner to the opposite one, making two triangles. Place a 17-inch wick along the 16-inch side and roll over the wicking as before.

Make two-toned spiral candles from two contrasting-colored sheets of beeswax. On each sheet of beeswax, score and cut a straight line diagonally from corner to corner. Place an 18-inch wick along the 16-inch side of the wax sheet. Then, place the contrasting colored triangle on top of the first triangle, with the bottom edges even. Roll the candle. Pinch the top of the candle tightly around the wick so that the wick won't pull out. For a decorative touch, gently flare out the edges of the candle with your fingers.

Alternating two-toned spiral candles are made by cutting the beeswax sheet and wicking the same as for the two-toned candle described above, except you will need to cut the second triangle shorter and narrower than the first one. Place the smaller triangle under the larger one, set the wick in place on the 16-inch side, and roll. (Or, make a triple-toned candle by adding a third triangle.)

Sculptured beeswax candles offer a real adventure in creativity. Experiment with various sizes and shapes of beeswax to see design motifs you can come up with.

With just a little practice at sculpturing candles, you can make them in the shape of Christmas trees, snowmen, flowers, mushrooms, birthday cakes, animals, or anything else your imagination conjures up. If you need inspiration, look around your home for ideas you can adapt to sculptured candles.

Safety precautions

Candlemaking is not hazardous if you follow these safety procedures:
1. Keep hot wax out of children's reach.
2. Turn pot handle to back of stove.
3. Always use a thermometer.
4. Never heat wax in excess of 300°.
5. Use hotpads when handling hot wax.
6. Never leave melting wax unattended.
7. Keep baking soda and a lid handy.

In the event that the wax catches fire in melting pot, smother fire with lid and remove pot from stove. If fire is caused by spilling wax on the burner, turn off burner and sprinkle with baking soda.

If hot wax spills on your skin, hold burned area in cool water. If the burn is serious, do not peel off the wax. Call your doctor.

The Three Kings

Angel, jester, and soldier

The Three Wise Men

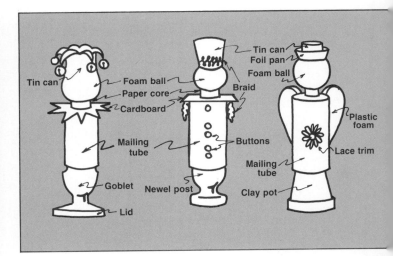

Tin can
Foil pan
Foam ball

Tin can
Foam ball
Paper core
Cardboard

Braid

Plastic foam

Mailing tube

Buttons

Lace trim

Goblet

Newel post

Mailing tube

Lid

Clay pot

Use drawing above as a guide for assembling and trimming the jester, angel, and soldier candle-holders at the left. This trio, attired in vibrant-colored costumes, will delight young and old.

Classy candleholders

As soon as you've mastered the simple techniques of candlemaking, you're bound to want to make your own candleholders to hold them. When you start, though, be sure to keep these things in mind:

• Candles should always stand upright in the candleholder.

• The purpose of the candleholder is to hold the candle so it does not drip wax on the furniture on which it is displayed.

• Unless it is to be placed on a mantel or buffet, where it will be viewed only from the front, the candleholder should be designed so it is appealing from all angles.

• The candleholder should have some kind of bobeche (a slightly cupped collar around the candle) to catch dripping wax.

• The base of the candleholder should be sufficiently weighted to balance tall or large candles without danger of tipping.

Now that you've heard the do's and don'ts of candleholders, let your imagination go and create designs that project that custom-made, handcrafted look that's always in fashion.

Materials for candleholders

If you're an inveterate saver of scraps of wood left over from carpentry projects, or cartons and containers of plastic, glass, and cardboard, you have all of the basics. Add to these your collection of string, yarn, tape, foil, beads, pasta, paint, white glue, and ink, and you have an assortment of materials with which to trim candleholders.

The candleholder designs that follow will complement your handmade candles and your holiday decorating scheme.

The Three Kings candleholders shown at the upper left of the opposite page exhibit their elegance no matter where you put them. Each of these stately characters is made of "play clay." (See recipe in next column.) To fashion these holders, bend a 4x5½-inch piece of chicken wire to form a cylinder measuring 5½ inches high. Weave the ends with wire to hold shape. Next, bend a 3½x1¾-inch piece of chicken wire into a cylinder 1¾ inches high; wire to larger piece.

Place each wire form onto a protected work surface. Starting at the bottom, add flattened balls of "play clay" to each wire form. Press each new section of clay firmly into the other. Mold the clay and add for arms, head, gifts, and facial features. Moisten edges slightly to adhere better, if needed. Mold and add crowns to fit around candle bases. Glue 'jewels' onto moist "play clay." If, when you're making these candleholders, you run out of time, simply cover holders with a plastic bag, and finish the project the next night.

The finished shapes should dry well before you try to move them—at least overnight. Complete drying takes three or more days, depending on the temperature and humidity.

To speed the drying process, place the figures on cardboard on oven rack in a preheated 350° oven and turn off heat.

When the figures are completely dry, paint them gold. Dry. Paint them with leather dye, using desired colors. As a finishing touch, brush holders with a coat of liquid floor wax.

"Play clay" recipe: in saucepan, stir together 1 cup cornstarch and 2 cups (1 pound package) baking soda. Mix in 1¼ cups cold water. Heat, stirring constantly, over medium heat until the mixture reaches a slightly moist, mashed potato consistency. Turn out on plate; cover with a damp cloth. When it is cool enough to handle, knead like dough into shapes. To store "play clay," keep it in a tightly closed container.

The Three Wise Men candleholders shown at the upper right of the opposite page are much simpler to construct than you would imagine. All you have to do is glue wooden turned posts (3½ inches in diameter) and finials (4 to 7 inches tall) together in the desired arrangements. Next, paint them with gesso, then with acrylic paints, using the photo as a guide. To make the extended arm candleholders, attach brass cafe curtain rod brackets. Coat arrangement with varnish.

The angel, jester, and soldier at the lower left of the opposite page are whimsical characters with an imposing appearance. (They are about 20 inches tall.) They are all made from sections cut from cardboard cylinders, tin or foil pans, glass goblets or tumblers, clay pots and saucers, combined with bits of fabric, cord, or lace. As a finishing touch, they are specially treated with papier mâché.

To make the angel, jester, and soldier heavy enough to support the weight of a large-size candle, pour plaster of paris or a tile-setting compound into one or two of the hollow sections of the candlestick base—either the tin cans or the goblets—and allow it to dry thoroughly. Glue together objects such as the cardboard mailing tubes or pieces of paper toweling cores, as indicated in the sketches shown here. If your 'junk' shelf contains different-shaped parts than those that are illustrated here, you can always improvise and find something of a similar size, shape, or texture to substitute.

After assembling the candleholders, cover them with a layer of papier mâché. (Use small strips and squares of torn newspaper dipped into a mixture of wheat paste and water solution.) After the papier mâché dries on the angel, glue on the delicate lace and cord trims. Follow the sketch for placement. (For a sturdy put-together solution, don't forget to put to use any large-size metal washers or disks you may be hoarding from discarded or second-hand pieces of fixtures.)

Give all three characters a coating of gesso. When this is dry, paint on the facial features and simulated clothing with enamel or acrylic paints. Embellish the candleholders with an antique finish. Cushion the bottoms of the candleholders with pieces of felt or velour-textured adhesive-backed paper to protect against scratching the surface that the holders will be resting on.

To make the curled tin candlestick at the far left of the opposite page, select five tin cans—two small ones the same size; the remaining three in graduated sizes. Using 7-inch wire snips, cut through the rim on one side of the can joint on the open end of the can. Cut the rim off to the other side of the can joint. Remove the joint by bending it back and forth until it breaks off.

Cut a strip of paper and measure around the can from the first cut to the last. Fold the paper in half three times, making eight sec-

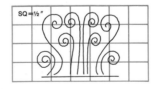

tions. Mark the divisions on the can with a ball-point pen. Draw lines on the can. Cut on the lines to the bottom rim of the can to divide the can into eight sections. On one section of the can, cut down at center of section. Cut each half of section into four strips.

With round-nose pliers, grasp the bottom of the first strip on the left, and turn the pliers so that the strip is at a right angle to the can rim. (See drawing in left column.) Repeat this technique for the first four strips and then reverse, turning strips so that they are at a left angle to can rim. Starting at the tip of the strips, curl them as shown in the pattern. Pinch center four strips together and hold them together with wire. Continue around the can on each section. (Be sure to keep the curled strips same length, and keep pattern even.) Follow this same technique for all five of the cans.

Drill a hole in the center of each can bottom to fit the stove bolt that runs up the center of the holder. Put the top two cans bottom to bottom. Put the stove bolt through the center hole. Thread on the next can, bottom end up. Even the strips, bending them to the slope of the rim of the larger can. (The strips should fit just behind the rims of the cans.) Continue stacking the cans in the same manner, then add a washer and nut to the bottom of the bolt to secure the cans. Spray-paint the candlestick, if desired.

The tall jug candleholder (second from the left) is a handsome decoration for the holidays or any time of the year. To make this stately holder, glue a 6-inch-tall cardboard rug tube to the top of a 1-gallon glass jug. Next, glue a terra-cotta flowerpot tray, 7 inches in diameter, to the top of the cardboard tube. (See the drawing below.)

Attach a band of aluminum foil around the center section of the glass jug, using adhesive. Glue small blocks of wood to the foil. Decorate the entire area with foil and colored tapes.

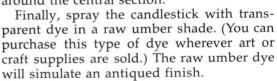

CARDBOARD TUBE

Trim the cardboard tube with foil and strips of leather. Push upholsterer's tacks into the tube around the central section.

Finally, spray the candlestick with transparent dye in a raw umber shade. (You can purchase this type of dye wherever art or craft supplies are sold.) The raw umber dye will simulate an antiqued finish.

There's no better way to display chunky Christmas candles than in these imaginative candleholders. And they are yours for the making. Try making some or all of them.

Candleholder collection

Can and candle concoction

Centerpiece candleholder

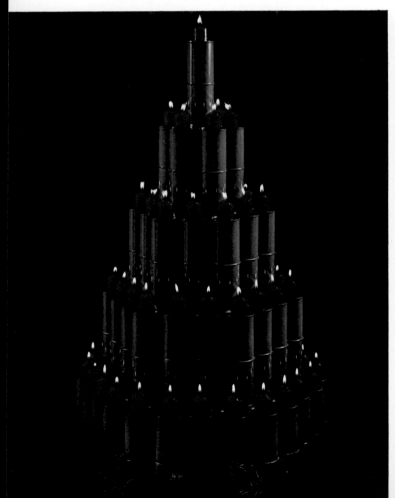

The **triple-ball candlestick** (third from the left on page 129) is easy to make. The only items you'll need to purchase are three large foam balls and three drapery rings.

To fabricate this candlestick, remove one end of a can the right size to hold the candle. Push the open end of the can into one of the foam balls and remove it, forming a mark for cutting the ball. With a knife or a serrated grapefruit spoon, dig out the center of the ball to fit the can. Then, push the can into the plastic foam ball again.

Next, cut a circle of wood for the base. Glue a wooden drapery ring to the center of the base. Then, glue the foam ball to the drapery ring. Continue in this manner until all parts are glued together.

Let the glue dry thoroughly. Mix instant papier mâché as directed on the package, and smooth a light coat onto the foam balls. Wipe excess off of the drapery rings and the base. Let this dry, then sand smooth. If desired, dip a heavy string into some glue and outline the top at the opening edge and the tops of the drapery rings and the base. Paint the finished candlestick with acrylic paint in a pleasing color combination.

The jumbo square candlestick (at the far right on page 129) adds a welcome contrast to the cylindrical shapes of the first three. To construct the square candlestick, make or find a 6x6x6-inch wooden or cardboard box. Glue four wooden blocks in a cross pattern on each side of the block. Then, push a brass tack into the center of each block. (See the diagram at right.)

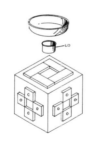

Next, glue a 6-inch-diameter salad bowl to a spray-can lid, and glue the lid to the top of the block. (See drawings below, left for details.) Spray the entire unit with transparent dye in raw umber. To add luster, finish with a coat of clear plastic spray.

The collection of candleholders shown at the top of the opposite page, each one an art object in its own right, is an inspiration to the budget-minded hobbyist. You may already have all the materials necessary to construct these, but you just never thought of combining them into candleholders for the holidays.

To duplicate these, look through your woodworking and craft supplies for materials to use. (Wooden drapery rings, wooden blocks, cardboard cylinders, assorted wooden beads, round molding, triangular wood cutouts, golf tees, knobs, cardboard cones, and cord are all used in one or more of the holders.)

Follow the photo for design ideas, then set up the components you have available and glue them together. The holders shown here vary in height from 4 to 15 inches tall, but you can make them as tall or short as you wish. Sand the wood, if necessary, and give them an antiqued or painted finish in colors to harmonize with your decor.

The can and candle concoction pictured at the lower left of the opposite page offers those who are ecology-conscious an opportunity to participate in an exciting recycling project. However, unless you use a can of frozen juice daily for at least eight months, you better enlist the help of your friends to collect the 250 cans needed to complete the tiered triumph. The one pictured here was designed as a table decoration, but you can adapt it to any use by varying the size of the cans used, and by adding or deleting tiers. If you have enough room, why not make a room-size version for the living or family room and put an end to needle fallout? Assembly of this model will take you a while. For the outside row, you will need 48 cans arranged in stacks of two; for the second row, use 72 cans, in stacks of 4; for the third row, 72 cans, in stacks of 6; for the fourth row, use 48 cans, in stacks of 8; and for the center, use 10 cans glued together. Glue each stack of cans together, with the closed, bottom side of the cans in an upright position.

Spray the assembled stacks with two or more coats of green paint—enough to cover the cans completely. When the paint dries thoroughly, arrange the five stacks into a tree shape. Buy enough red vigil candles to top each can on each tier of the tree.

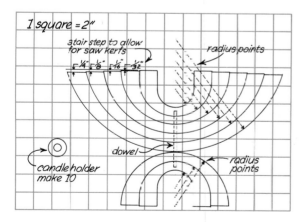

1 square = 2"

stair step to allow for saw kerfs

radius points

candle holder make 10

dowel

radius points

The **centerpiece candleholder** that is pictured at the lower right of page 130 folds flat for storing after your holiday entertaining is over. To duplicate this candleholder, you'll need a 1x12x30-inch white pine board, a 5 1/16 x 7 1/2-inch wood dowel, and acrylic paint.

First, cut five half-moon sections for the candle arms, and two more for the base with a saber saw. (Follow the sketch shown on page 131.) As you cut the candle arms, keep in mind that each saw kerf eliminates about 1/16 inch of the board. As a result, when the arms are stacked on the dowel, each arm is 1/16 inch longer than the one next to it. To make all the arms the same height, lay a straightedge across them after stacking them on the dowel. Sand the outer arms or cut each of them the same height as the shortest arm.

After drilling 1 3/16-inch diameter circles in the tops of the disks that hold the candles, glue a disk to each arm. Sand the entire candelabra and paint with acrylics.

Plastic sheets, tubing, and wire adapt well to contemporary designs. Here, they complement candles, but actually are not candleholders. If you wish to further a contemporary decorating scheme for the holiday season, these novel treatments are for you.

The plastic tubing shown at the upper left of the opposite page yields to a sleight-of-hand trick as it takes an easy sweep and turns into an exciting, contemporary holiday decoration. It can be displayed on a shelf, mantel, buffet, or chest. Simply purchase 1/2-inch plastic tubing from a plumber's supply shop and cut it into two pieces. Paint the pieces with automobile lacquer and shape them into the design of your choice. Add a pillar candle and green branches for a simple, yet elegant decoration.

This glistening forest of holiday trees, shown at the upper right of the opposite page, accompanied by the flickering dazzle of candlelight, is made from sheets of plastic. The simple pillar candles, which you can make yourself, or buy, accent each one of the table decorations' three sections.

To make the tree designs, use 1/4-inch-thick sheets of clear plastic that measure 8x10, 9x12, and 10x15 inches respectively. Apply masking tape to the plastic panels, leaving only the tree outline exposed. Next, spray-paint the exposed tree outline areas. Use aluminum window screen channels (these are available in hardware stores) to support the trees in an upright position.

To cut the acrylic plastic sheet material, follow these directions:
- *Do not* remove the protective masking paper before cutting the plastic.
- Using a straightedge as a guide, place the point of the acrylic sheet cutting tool at the edge of the material, and, applying firm pressure, draw the cutting point the full width of the material (5 to 6 times for thicknesses from 0.1000 inch to 0.187 inch and 7 to 10 times for 0.250 inch).
- Position the sheet with the scribed line face up over a 3/4-inch-diameter wood dowel running the length of the intended break.

To break the sheet plastic, hold the sheet with one hand and apply downward pressure on the short side of the break with the other hand. Keep your hands adjacent to one another and successively reposition them about 2 inches in back of the break as it progresses along the scribed line. The minimum cutoff width is about 1 1/2 inches.

To smooth the cut edges, scrape the edge smooth with a sharp knife, sand with medium-grit (60-80) sandpaper, or file with a fine-tooth metal file. To further improve the appearance of the edge, sand with 'wet or dry' 150-grit sandpaper.

Arrange the grouping of holiday trees, place a pillar candle behind each panel, and scatter a few green boughs around them.

The free-form flower burst shown at the bottom of the opposite page is an artistic tangle of wire combined with three pillar candles. Use plastic florist's wire for the tangles and spray it white. Place the tangled wire and candles on two rectangles of smoke-colored sheet plastic, one atop the other.

A word to the wise

Christmas wouldn't be Christmas without candles, but you must handle them with extreme care. Observe the following precautions for a safe holiday season:
- Never use any candles on or around a Christmas tree.
- Never insert candles in plastic foam holders. Plastic foam is exceedingly flammable.
- Give particular thought to where you place candles. If you have youngsters, do not arrange candles on a low coffee table, for instance, as they could ignite a small child's clothing in a few seconds.
- Keep candles high above furnishings—a safe distance from any ignitable substance.

Plastic tubing surrounds candle

Free-form flower burst

Glistening forest of trees

Chapter 8

Inviting Doorways

Your front door at Christmas, decorated with greens and red and white striped peppermint candy canes or any number of other items, is a personal Christmas card to the people who pass by your home every day.

The materials for converting ordinary doors into ones that project the holiday spirit are numerous. Greens are plentiful during the winter months. Scraps of material or yarn may turn into an angel or a wreath. Or, cut scraps of plywood into trees or snowmen. Enjoy the endless possibilities of plastic foam or add a note of sophistication with a rattan door decoration. And if you live in a warm, sunny climate, don't bemoan the lack of pine trees in your area—use palm fronds instead of the traditional greens for your door decorations.

Your decorating plans for the inside of your home should determine the design of your door decorations. A contemporary reindeer suggests the same type of stylized decorations within. The traditional green wreath says welcome to a house full of pine boughs and red and green Christmas ornaments. If you like a foreign flavor, try a Greek key or a Spanish gourd design, and make your whole house resemble a foreign land.

Your entranceway should infect everyone with your holiday spirit. And you should have fun decorating it, too.

Pine boughs are the key to creating this handsome door decoration. Boughs are wired together and tacked around the door; sprigs of pine ornamented with a gold cherub are tacked to a sturdy backing and held in place with a waterproof ribbon.

Outdoor holiday show-offs

During the holiday season, when exuberant greetings of "Merry Christmas" fill the air, why not extend the Yuletide message to all who pass by your home with a handsome door decoration? Not only will it welcome all the friends and relatives who stop over to see you during the holidays, but it will make the day brighter and the load lighter for mailmen, delivery men, and paper delivery boys when they make their daily rounds. The only limitation in designing door decorations is that you choose a theme that harmonizes with the architectural style of your entry.

From the great outdoors

Take a good look at the holiday door decorations on the opposite page. All four are natural beauties with heart-warming appeal.

The stunning bells pictured at the upper left of the opposite page, backed by a sheaf of evergreen boughs and topped off with a bow and streamers of red ribbon, will add grace and beauty to any doorway.

Begin by tracing three circles on a piece of newspaper in the size you want for the bottom of the bells. Following the outline of the circles, glue sweet balls (the fruit of eucalyptus trees) together. If sweet balls are not available in your area, use acorns or tiny pine cones. For the best results, use the type of glue you heat. Keep grouping and gluing the balls in circular layers of decreasing size to form the bell shapes.

Allow finished bells to dry overnight, then spray them with a glossy wood-tone paint. For the clappers, cut 18-inch lengths of wire and attach a large sweet ball to one end. Insert other end of wire up through top of bell.

Wire the bells to the pine branches and finish with a red bow and cascading ribbon.

A youthful singing angel is the focal point for the door decorations that grace this colonial doorway (pictured at the upper right of the opposite page). You can purchase the blue plastic cherub at a gift shop, variety store, or florist supply shop. Tape the figure securely to the door (with waterproof tape) atop a half-circle of snow-flocked evergreen sprigs. (You can use this same angel year after year to enchant passers-by.)

Next, wrap strips of wide red weatherproof florists' ribbon around the door columns in candy cane fashion, anchoring the ribbon with waterproof tape at the top and bottom. Wind natural holly branches and berries around the poles between the red ribbon, and finish the design with poinsettias (the permanent type) tucked into the ribbon at the bottom of one of the columns.

The traditional-looking berry wreath shown at the lower left of the opposite page originates with two loops of wire that form the outline. Cut sections of plastic foam three inches wide and fit them between wire loops. Wrap waterproof tape around the loops to hold the plastic foam in place, then wrap the entire wreath in dry cleaners' plastic bags. Next, condition magnolia leaves by soaking the stems in water for several days; and pin them over the wreath to completely cover the background material.

Obtain several sprays of evergreen that follow the natural wreath curve as closely as possible, and wire them to the wreath until they completely cover the base. Next, form an inner circle of red artificial berries. (Be sure to use full sprays of berries in order to ensure a luxurious-looking wreath.) Pin the berry sprays to the wreath with floral picks, and, as a finishing touch, add a large red velvet bow to the center top of your wreath. Hang the wreath from the door knocker with cord covered with red velvet ribbon.

The Spanish-inspired gourds-and-greens arrangement shown at the lower right of the opposite page will give a Mediterranean flavor to your holiday door decoration.

To make this one, first wire a four-inch-long dowel to a plastic foam block, leaving a wire loop for hanging. Then, wire several sprigs of cedar, a string of brightly painted gourds, and artificial peppers to the dowel. Add several bright red velvet bows.

For the rose-type bows, cut short oval lengths of red velvet ribbon. Hold several layers together, and wire the middle of the ovals with enough wire to go around the cluster. Use floral picks to insert the bows into the plastic foam base. Top off the arrangement with a wicker wine bottle cover spray-painted to match the red bows.

Bells and boughs

Singing angel

Traditional wreath

Gourds-and-greens

Gingerbread doorpiece

Santa Claus

Winsome drummer boy

Handsome harlequin door ornament

Fashioned from ready-mades

Here's an array of traffic-stopping door decorations that will cause all who pass by to pause in admiration. Unless you examine them closely, you'd never imagine that they originated with such unlikely materials as metal wastebaskets, oilcloth, cardboard, paper towel cores, and a simple lawn rake retrieved from your garden tools.

The gingerbread doorpiece that is pictured at the upper left of the opposite page will delight children and adults alike. To make the collection of gingerbread people, you will need lightweight cardboard; corrugated-on-one-side cardboard; soft, heavy white string; brown paper bags; white glue; acrylic paints; and clear, plastic spray.

For each cookie character, cut two patterns from lightweight cardboard and three from corrugated cardboard. To increase the textural effect, cut the corrugated pieces so that the corrugation does not run all in the same direction. Hold all of the pieces together (corrugated pieces on outside) with a rubber band at neck and another at ankles.

Cut a 5-inch piece of string for a hanging loop. Tie an overhand knot in the ends and glue the hanging loop at the top of the head, with the knot ends tucked in between the layers of corrugated cardboard.

Tear brown paper bags into strips, and then into pieces about 1x2 inches. Pour white glue into a flat container and dilute it with two parts water. Dip the paper pieces in the glue solution, and press the paper pieces on the cookie edges, beginning at the top of the head on both sides of the hanging loop. Paper from one side over the edge to the other side, continuing down the body, and removing the rubber bands when you are adding paper at the neck and the ankles.

Cover both the front and the back of the cookie with one layer of paper strips, overlapping the pieces slightly. Next, hang the cookie up until it is dry.

Draw on details with a pencil, and paint the clothing with acrylic paints. Dip a piece of string in the glue, squeeze out the excess glue, and outline the penciled details. Let the string dry. Cover both sides of cookie with clear, plastic spray.

Hang the gingerbread people on a background of green branches; add satin balls.

The winsome drummer boy in his colorful uniform (pictured at the upper right of the opposite page) is all ready to beat out a welcoming roll on his drum when guests approach the front door.

To make this lovable character, you will need inexpensive metal wastebaskets for the body, head, hat, and drum; cardboard rug tubes for the legs; strips of cardboard for the arms; dowels and tiny wooden balls for the drumsticks; and cord for hanging the drum.

Cover the various parts of the body and the hat with oilcloth, using the photo as a guide, and assemble the pieces. Paint the facial features with acrylic paints on one of the wastebaskets. Attach a small wooden ball to one end of each drumstick, and attach the drumsticks to the ends of the extended arms. Fasten a length of cord to the drum and hang it around the drummer's neck.

Santa Claus, who evokes such good cheer, is pictured at the lower left of the opposite page where he keeps a constant vigil over this front door. He's charmingly colorful and a perfect guarantee to bring a smile or chuckle from anyone who appears on the threshold. And just think, the grand old fellow you see here was once just a part of a plain, old-fashioned garden rake.

To duplicate this jolly old gent, remove the rake handle and daub some red and white paint in the proper places to simulate a hat and hair. Make pompons for the facial features — two black ones for the eyes, a red one for the nose, and six white ones for the beard. Make a larger white pompon for the tip of Santa's hat. Secure the pompons in place with short lengths of heavy thread.

After the holidays are over, you can remove Santa's yarn features so he can get back to raking the lawn!

The handsome harlequin door ornament pictured at the lower right of the opposite page features a dramatic black, white, and gold color scheme. It is simplistic in design and contemporary in spirit. Its overall dimensions are 30x20 inches.

To make this door decoration, you will need black and white yarn, paper towel tubes, glass ball ornaments (40 mm.), lightweight cardboard, heavy thread, and a needle.

First, cut four 9-inch-long sections from paper towel cores; flatten the centers and staple them. Wind black yarn around each tube from one end to the center. Then, wind white yarn around each tube from the opposite end to the center of the tube. Secure the yarn ends with glue.

Next, mark two 18-inch-long sections of tube at the centers and 4½ inches from either end. Flatten and staple the centers and ends alike. On the 4½-inch marks, flatten and staple at right angles to the center and end staples. Wrap half of each tube with black yarn, and half with white yarn. Mark a 21-inch paper tube at center and 4½ inches on either side of center. Flatten, staple, and wrap with yarn as you did for the two 18-inch sections. (If you don't have 18- or 21-inch paper towel cores, improvise by using two shorter tubes and inserting a piece of cardboard at a flattened area before stapling.)

Cut eight 1½-inch sections from a paper core that measures 2⅛ inches in diameter (available in fabric departments). Wind half of each ring with white yarn and half with black yarn, at right angles to circumference.

Arrange the units as shown in the photo, then saturate the surface with glue at all of the contact points. Hold units in place with clothespins until the glue is dry. If you're doubtful about the glue holding parts together, stitch adjacent arm-ends together.

For curved top and bottom sections, cut eight pieces of cardboard 9x1½-inch. Leave last four inches of one end tapering to a point; glue pieces together by twos, bending and holding them in a curve until glue is dry. Wind two units with black yarn, and two with white yarn. Glue these pieces in place with middles touching end 1½-inch sections and points touching ends of arms first.

Insert a shiny glass ball ornament in the center of each 1½-inch tube section. To secure gold balls, stitch heavy thread through back of section and through ornament hanger.

Sections from sisal place mats and dark green plastic webbing are the principal ingredients for the graceful decorations that adorn the door grouping at the top of the opposite page.

To construct the wreath, wrap an 18-inch foam ring with half-width green plastic webbing. Cut apart the red and yellow 'daisies' from three sisal place mats. Attach six large red 'daisies' on the front of the wreath; put a 1½-inch round mirror in the center of each flower. Border with yellow green straw braid, glued to the edge of the mirrors. Add six 5-inch yellow sisal coasters, topped with red 'daisies.' Wire the 12 'daisies' to the wreath. Around the inner edge, place 12 small 'daisies' each topped with a palm leaf bead and pinned in place. Around the outer edge, arrange 24 leaf clusters—each cluster is made from three 5-inch lengths of webbing. Fold each in half; cut one end like a leaf base—the other like a leaf point.

For leaf stem, make a ½-inch loop at one end of a 3½-inch length of wire. Staple three leaf bases, folded in half, over loop. Wind stem with green floral tape; spray leaves green to cover white line in webbing.

For side doors, assemble smaller clusters of leaves centered with a single flower.

The colorful wooden wreath shown at the lower left of the opposite page will appeal to everyone, but especially to the person who is handy with tools. It is made from white pine and trimmed with birds and flowers.

To fabricate this wreath, draw two concentric circles on wrapping paper—the inner circle has a radius of 6⅛ inches; the outer one, 12½ inches. Saw a ½x6-inch piece of pine into following lengths: four 9 inches long and two 21 inches long. Saw edges to form wreath shape, following your paper pattern for placement of strips. (Or cut a circle from plywood—25 inches in diameter on outside and 12¼ inches on inside.) Draw notches on wreath and cut with a saber saw.

Lay the wreath face down; tack or glue strips of lath in areas at top and bottom to join strips together. Stain wreath green. Trace bird and flower motifs onto orange crate slats. Cut with a saw, stain or paint with acrylics, and glue in place. Seal with a coat of varnish.

The young shepherd door ornament shown at lower right of the opposite page measures 21 inches from tip to toe and 20 inches from hand holding crook to cowl in back.

To make the ornament, draw an outline on corrugated cardboard; cut with scissors. Mix ½ cup wheat paste with one cup water. Cover cardboard with strips of newspaper dipped in paste solution; let dry overnight. With a felt-tip pen, trace features, clothes, and sheep onto cardboard. To prevent warping, coat with shellac. Let dry, then shellac again. Cover design with papier mâché.

Cover the surface with white tissue paper dipped in wheat paste solution. Let it dry. Mix two parts of white glue with one part of water. Soak the yarn in this mixture, then outline the shepherd's features, the sheep's wool, and the crook. Paint both sides with white acrylic. Paint the features. When paint is dry, coat with an antique glaze. Rub off excess glaze. Let dry thoroughly, then weatherproof with a coat of polymer gloss.

Sisal place mats and plastic webbing

Wooden wreath

Young shepherd and sheep

Double-exposure door decorations

You can make the front entrance of your home do double duty during the Yuletide season if you decorate both sides of the front door. When guests are greeted with this display, they'll have no doubt of the hospitality and goodwill abounding in your home.

If you have any doubts about how to tackle a door decorating project, let the architectural style of your home and the color scheme you employ guide you in the design and colors. Be sure to attach the decorations securely to the door so they will remain intact in spite of frequent openings and closings, and sudden gusts of wind.

Two one-sided seasonal evergreen trees are the starting point for the decorations on the exterior panels of the antique doors on the colonial home below.

The first step in making these elegant decorations is to attach the small one-sided artificial evergreen trees to the center panels of both doors. Next, completely cover the minia-ture Christmas trees with iridescent blueberry trimmings that highlight the painted finish of the antique doors.

To strengthen the holiday theme, use two-section topiary trees (only one of them is visible in the photograph) to flank either side of the doorway. Decorate the topiary trees with greens and blueberry trimmings to complement the door decorations.

To further the holiday spirit, place a wicker basket of ample proportions on the red brick steps at the base of the door. Fill the basket with mock Christmas gifts wrapped in red and green waterproof paper, and tuck in sprigs of holly to add a decorative accent.

The elegant decorations on the inside of the same antique double doors serve as the center of interest in the foyer (right).

Start with two commercial topiary-type trees, which you can purchase from your local florist. To each segment of the topiary trees, attach sprigs of artificial evergreen, clusters of gilded leaves, green velvet bows, and assorted sizes of shiny gold Christmas balls. Arrange the materials in a tight cluster at the center of the topiary balls, then let the evergreen branches, gilded leaves, and velvet ribbon fan out gracefully. At the bottom of each of the 'tree trunks,' fasten a small sheaf of the same gold and green materials and let it cascade downward.

Continue the gift basket theme that started on the front stoop by placing another one inside the front door on the floor of the foyer. Give this second basket of gifts a different twist, though, by wrapping the packages in shiny metallic foil gift paper and embellishing them with lustrous red and green satin bows. For a special effect, tuck in clusters of artificial fruit or berries.

When you plan a decoration of this type, be sure that you keep it in scale with the size of the door and the overall dimensions of the room in which it is placed.

Greens and blueberry trimmings

Here is the interior view of the pair of paneled ▶ antique doors shown at the left, complete with topiary tree decorations that fairly sing out a friendly greeting to all who enter.

142

Pine roping wreath

Three wreaths—topiary fashion

Nuts, pods, pine cones, and seeds

Greens and pine cones

Dapper doorway decorations

When you trim doors that are protected from the elements — the front door to an apartment or condominium, or an inside door in a house — you can select whatever materials you want. With inside doors, you don't have to be concerned with whether or not the ravages of weather — snow, wind, rain, or sudden fluctuations in temperature — will damage your door decorations. This allows you freedom to be as inventive as you desire.

From woods and fields

In addition to the natural materials that you might choose for outdoor decorations — greens, berries, pods, pine cones, and leaves — you can add fragile feathers and less hardy varieties of greens and flowers to your indoor holiday decorations.

The simple wreath of pine roping that is shown at the upper left of the opposite page has a ruggedly masculine look.

To duplicate this wreath, attach a loop of pine roping to a heavier wire shaped in the form of a wreath. Fasten a spray of dried wheat and a cluster of assorted-size pine cones to the top of the wreath. Add a loop of wire at the top of the wreath for attaching the wreath to the door.

Three wreaths arranged in topiary fashion provide the focal point for the inside door shown at the upper right of the opposite page.

The decoration looks hard to make, but actually it's easy. First, cover the door with shiny red oilcloth. Make the three double-needle balsam wreaths in graduating sizes. Wire bunches of ready-made gold grapes to the wreaths. Attach gold leaves to the wreaths and grapes. Add small gold poinsettias and back wreaths with gold paper. (As an alternative to the gold grapes, you can thread small gold Christmas balls to tie wire and twist into a figure eight.) Frame the door and surrounding panels with pine roping.

Nuts, pods, pine cones, and seeds are the major components for the stately wreath at the lower left of the opposite page.

First, cut a 24-inch diameter wreath shape from heavy cardboard. Next, wrap wreath with strips of sheeting. Cover the wreath with spaghnum moss dipped in glue. Then,

glue on nature's handiwork — nuts, cones, pods, and seeds — and plastic fruit.

Use the same materials and techniques to build the topiary tree at left of wreath.

Greens and pine cones star in the wreath at the lower right of the opposite page.

To make wreath base, use 11 metal rings from instant popcorn and wire together, with handles toward center. Using fine wire, secure rings in overlapping position at intersection points. Wind surfaces with floral tape; wire sprigs of greens to cover all surfaces.

Cut two sizes of weatherproof red velvet petals and place them in center of wreath, with small petals over larger ones. Glue red ornaments in the center. Spray pine cones gold, and wire at intersection points.

Along the outer points, wire small cones and red ornaments. Finish with a red bow.

From cord, board, and things

Dramatize your doors by concocting decorations featuring cardboard, paper doilies, yarn, wood, felt, and plastic. As you pursue your door decorating project, you will probably think of many other unlikely materials.

The high-spirited angel pictured at the upper left of page 147 is perfect to doll up the door of a child's room.

Make the figure from a 28x42-inch sheet of cardboard. The colored triangle pocket should be 22 inches wide at the top. On the bottom side, space at intervals six tabs one inch long and ¼ inch wide. These fit into six corresponding slits on the angel and extend to the backside, which will be anchored with glue.

Outline halo, pocket for gifts, and skirt with heavy yellow yarn. Add paper doily and seal trims. Wrap tiny gift packets of inexpensive surprises — one to be opened each day for the twelve days preceding Christmas.

The folk art original pictured at the upper right of page 147 will brighten up a door during the Yuletide season. Later, transfer it to a wall where it will reign as a permanent, handcrafted work of art.

According to the Indians of Mexico, Central America, and Peru, *"Ojo de Dios"* or *"God's eye"* will protect the home and all those who enter and keep away evil spirits.

For the framework of this door decoration, use two pieces of ¾-inch-square wood that measure 48 and 28 inches long, respectively. Taper the ends to points with a hacksaw, beginning two inches from each end. Sand the points smooth. With a wood rasp, score the outer edges of each stick. Cut notches ¹⁄₁₆ to ⅛ inch apart. This provides a gripping surface to hold the yarn in place.

Cross the 28-inch-long piece of wood behind the 48-inch-long piece in the center. Nail the two sticks together with two or more finishing nails. Stain or paint the sticks black. Let them dry thoroughly before proceeding with the weaving of the yarn. (Wool yarn works best because it does not sag or wilt if it is exposed to moisture.)

To start weaving the yarn, wrap the white yarn diagonally from left to right, making a knot on the backside. Wind the yarn from the center outward. (The loops on the frontside are smooth, while on the reverse side the sticks are plainly visible.) Tie the yarn at the intersection; go over and around each stick, keeping the yarn fairly taut.

Check the straightness of the crossed sticks often, as the yarn places great stress on them. If you place each strand of yarn side-by-side, the "Ojo" will be uniform and you'll be able to see each strand distinctly. When changing from one color to another, knot one color to another on the backside and tie the knot so you can slip it underneath and out of sight. Clip the end of the color of yarn not being used before proceeding. Hold the end of the yarn in place with glue, if necessary. Use the photo as a guide for placement of rows of yarn.

You can adapt this same design to smaller versions and use them as tree ornaments.

The elegant needlepoint tree at the lower left of the opposite page will make you the envy of all your holiday guests. It is stitched on diamond-shaped plastic grids that you can buy in knitting or craft shops.

To make the tree, you will need 21 diamond, 1 square, and 1 hexagon plastic motifs; knitting worsted in 1-ounce skeins—hot pink, vermillion, red, orange, rust, magenta, and green; a tapestry needle; 51 small green beads (³⁄₁₆-inch size); and a 12x18-sheet of

poster board, which you can buy at an art supply store. Use the plastic motifs just as you would use needlepoint canvas. Using the diamond motif, follow figure 1. Make long stitches, using two colors—one for the upper half and one for lower half of diamond.

Make seven motifs of each of the following color combinations: hot pink and vermillion; red and orange; and rust and magenta. Start at the middle of each diamond and work to the tips. Be sure to cover the edge of the grid.

Follow figure 2 for the hexagon, using all of the colors except green to form the star. Use green to fill in the background.

For the square, make center long stitches with green and fill in two side sections with hot pink and vermillion yarn, using the cross-stitch.

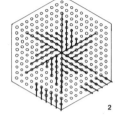

Cut cardboard into shapes to fit all of the worked pieces. Glue the pieces of cardboard to the backs of each and weight them down until they are dry and flat. Then, lay the pieces out in the tree shape. Attach the sections together at the corners with beads and heavy thread. Attach a hanging thread at top.

The pagoda tree design at the bottom right of the opposite page originated in the Orient. This decoration is a good example of how designs from other countries help contribute ideas that you can adapt for holiday decorating. This tree will add a dramatic note to an apartment or inside door.

To duplicate this gem, first cut seven cardboard pagoda shapes ranging in size from 5 to 19 inches, tip to tip. Next, cut the same number of pieces from velvet, but add an inch of margin to allow for pulling the fabric around to the backside of the shapes later.

Pad the frontside of each section with cotton batting, cut to size. Lay the velvet fabric, right side up, over the padding. Carefully stretch the fabric tightly, then glue the edges down to the backside of the cardboard. Glue matching paper cut a little smaller than the size of each section to the back of each piece, covering the raw edges of the velvet. Glue gold seals, red tassels, and other trim in place.

Cover a narrow slat the length of the tree with fabric. Glue the sections of the pagoda to this slat, starting at the bottom. Overlap each section slightly to give a slightly raised and dimensional effect.

High-spirited angel

Folk art original

Needlepoint tree

Pagoda tree

Chapter 9

Outdoor Decorations

Make your home stand out from the others in your neighborhood this Christmas by fashioning imaginative decorations for your yard, patio, fence, gate, or porch. You may prefer outdoor decorations that have a serious theme or you may enjoy those with a touch of humor. In either case, there are many designs from which to choose.

If you've always relied solely on a string or two of outdoor Christmas lights strung around the front of your house and perhaps a wreath on the front door or window, you will be inspired by the many ingenious Christmas creations presented on the following pages.

Let your holiday spirit soar by creating a Yuletide banner with an appropriate message. A cheerful phrase adorning a banner flying above your home leaves little doubt as to your family's Christmas spirit—and brings smiles to the faces of all who pass by. Add a holiday flourish to an ordinary fence with bold and colorful contemporary Christmas designs and messages. Or, enliven an everyday entryway with handcrafted decorations that are compatible with the architectural style of your home.

With the great outdoors as your canvas and a few inexpensive materials as your palette, you can create personalized outdoor decorations that convey your own special Christmas greeting to all who pass by your home.

The shepherd with flock grouping that is pictured on the opposite page is an updated version of an age-old Christmas theme. You'll find complete, easy-to-follow instructions for making this life-size outdoor scene on page 155.

Christmas flags unfurled

Message of joy

Noel flag

Banners with holiday spirit

Whether it's unfurled and flying gently in the breeze or hanging flat against a wall or door, a Yuletide banner is bound to attract the attention it deserves.

Fly Christmas flags unfurled (see those at the upper left of the opposite page) to announce to visitors that the eggnog's on!

To duplicate this handsome grouping, first cut wood closet poles into three different lengths and paint each in a different color. Paint three 1-gallon plastic paint buckets to match the flagpoles. Mix plaster of paris according to the package directions and pour it into the gallon paint containers. Place a pole in the center of each bucket and prop the poles in an erect position until the plaster sets (about 20 minutes).

Cut the banners, a back and a front section for each one, from sailcloth or other firm cotton fabric. Decorate the front section of each flag with fabric circles, snowflakes, reverse applique 'holes' and Mylar. Applique each of the pattern pieces to the banner with a zigzag machine stitch.

After the banner front is completed, stitch the front and back sections together, with the right sides facing, leaving the end open. Press, turn the flag to the right side, and press again. Cut a piece of cardboard to fit the flag shape and size, and insert it between the two layers of fabric. Zigzag the raw edges of the opening closed.

Finally, wrap the zigzag-stitched edge of fabric around the pole and tack it through the cardboard liner of the banner, through the fabric, and into the flagpole. (Use decorative upholstery tacks.)

The Noel flag pictured at the upper right of the opposite page is hoisted on a flagpole that is fastened to the roof of the house. You can let it fly during the entire holiday season, or you can establish your own tradition of hoisting it only when you're home. If the latter is your choice, let it be known that the flag at full mast signifies you would welcome drop-in guests.

Make this Christmas greeting flag from sailcloth, denim, or other firm, washable cotton fabric. Cut it whatever size you wish, and stitch a ½-inch hem along one end. Attach shower curtain eyelets that will fit over a standard flagpole along this hem. Narrowly hem the other three sides of the flag.

Using the pattern at the left as a guide, trace the letters and the flower motifs onto contrasting material, then cut them out. Spread newspapers on the floor to protect the work surface from glue, and coat the backs of each of the applique sections with glue. Glue one piece of applique at a time, and immediately smooth it in place on the flag, taking care not to stretch the fabric.

When the appliqueing procedure has been completed, stitch around each one of the applique motifs. Then, glue rug yarn borders around each applique design over the stitching line. Add a border of cotton fringe around the edge of the flag.

The brightly colored ensign shown at the lower left of the opposite page is made from plastic-coated material in a printed pattern, and it is trimmed with huge tassels. This 'message of joy' will make each person who enters your home a little bit happier.

To make this joyous banner, first select plastic-coated fabric in the print of your choice and cut it in an elongated triangular shape. Turn the top edge under 1 inch and machine-stitch it to form a casing for a ½-inch dowel rod. Reverse the pattern for the letters and flower designs (see illustration), and trace them onto the paper side of solid-color self-adhering plastic; cut out the designs. Peel away the paper backing of the plastic material and press the letters smoothly in place on the pennant. (If the pennant is to be hung where it's directly exposed to the weather, machine-stitch the letters and flowers close to the edges.)

Cover the back of the pennant with glue (spread newspapers to protect your work area) and press it onto a length of matching fabric, wrong sides together. Trim the edges of the pennant, and machine-stitch around the two long sides. Slip a dowel through the casing and glue large wooden beads or cabinet knobs to each end of the dowel. Mark the corners of the pennant with huge, color-keyed tassels. If you prefer to hang this banner from a flagstaff, attach shower curtain rings along the hem, as you did for the NOEL flag, and let it waft in the breeze.

Fences with flair are in vogue

Gone are the days of the backyard fence that simply marked the dividing line between the yard and the alley. In its stead, there is an ever-increasing demand for fences of good architectural design to surround patios, gardens, and swimming pools. In keeping with this trend, it's only natural that attention is focused on fences when it comes to outdoor decorating for the holiday season.

Even a privacy fence such as the one pictured at the top of the opposite page can present a dazzling appearance when it takes on a new and important look for the holiday season. These brilliantly painted, large-scale designs make an outstanding showing.

To construct the four stylized Christmas ball ornaments that spell out NOEL and the forest of colorful, modernistic Christmas trees, cut the designs from ⅛-inch-thick weatherproof hardboard. Decorate the motifs with paint in phosphorescent colors. Mount the hardboard sections to the fence in this manner: screw through the designs, then through the openings between the fence slats, and then through blocks of wood positioned on the other side of the fence. Tighten the screws with wing nuts to hold the sections.

To light the outdoor scene dramatically at night, install two black-light fixtures.

When the Christmas season is over, be sure to store the fence decorations in a dark place, as sunlight can deteriorate the glow quality of the phosphorescent paints.

The Yuletide banners with crossed standards shown at the lower right of the opposite page display your own favorite Christmas colors. These square, decorated banners make an effective decoration for a fence.

To make these banners, you will need sailcloth, denim, or other firm cotton fabric; fabric adhesive; thread; rug yarn; finials; dowels; paint; and tassels.

For each one of the flags, cut an 18-inch square of background fabric, and stitch a narrow hem around three sides. Turn under the fourth side 1 inch and machine-stitch to form a casing for a ½-inch-diameter dowel.

Trace the entire pattern onto the flag, using the illustration on the opposite page as a guide. Then, trace the individual sections of the design onto material of a contrasting color. Next, coat the backsides of the applique designs with fabric adhesive (protect your work area with several layers of newspaper) and attach them to the flag. Work with one pattern piece at a time and immediately smooth it in place on the flag, taking care not to stretch the fabric. Machine-stitch around the edge of each of the appliqued designs, then glue on a row of rug yarn.

Make the finial for the top of each staff by gluing a golf tee to a small cabinet knob. When the glue is dry, glue the finial to the end of a ½-inch dowel that measures four feet in length. Paint the completed staffs to harmonize with the colors of the flag; slip the flagstaff through the casing, and add a large-size tassel at the bottom of each flag.

Outdoor lighting tips

- Use only electrical equipment expressly designed for outdoor use. Check package label to be sure.
- Wherever you can, run cords above ground level. If this isn't possible, drape cords over wooden stakes high enough to avoid contact with snow and slush. As an added safeguard, wrap electrical tape around connections.
- Keep cords away from doorways or other areas where people might possibly step on or trip over them.
- Never fasten cords to side of house with nails; instead, secure them with insulated staples or drive rings.
- To keep moisture from getting into light sockets, use rubber gaskets when inserting bulbs. Then, hang sockets so they point toward the ground.
- Before installing or repairing outdoor lighting (even replacing a burned-out bulb), turn off electricity. Any little bit of dampness in the presence of electricity can be disastrous.
- If lights inside your house flicker or fade when you turn on your outdoor display, you've probably overloaded the wiring system. If this happens, turn off all other lights on that circuit when outdoor lights are turned on.

Glowing privacy fence

Yuletide banners

NOEL greeting

Greetings from many lands

South-of-the-border wall panel

Angel decoration

Enticing designs for entryways

Handsome doors and entryways have a basic appeal that's unequaled. Keep this in mind when you plan your outdoor decorating.

The shepherd and his flock assemblage pictured on page 148 will make your yard the focal point of the entire neighborhood during the holiday season. This gentle group should reflect the serene atmosphere that prevails in the home at Christmastime.

Although this scene is displayed in a mild climate where there is a readymade pastoral background, you can set it up in any locale. The shepherd and his flock would be just as spectacular with a backdrop of pure white snow as they are in a sunny climate.

To construct the figures, cut life-size sheep and shepherd shapes out of ¼-inch-thick plywood. Next, paint the figures the desired colors. (Use weather-resistant enamel for durability.) Here, a wood carving that was acquired on a trip is used for the head. If you don't have access to something similar, make the head of plywood and paint the facial features. Use wooden serving spoons for the hands, and use reeds to form the diagonal lines on the shepherd's cloak. Make the sheep's eyes and ears of black felt or black oilcloth, and glue them to the bodies.

Fasten two poles on the back of each figure, and anchor them in the ground. Arrange three wooden poles of varying heights in a triangular grouping and top them with Mexican tin and glass stars. Embellish the poles with red felt streamers.

The NOEL greeting pictured at the upper left of the opposite page follows the principle that to be effective from a distance, an outdoor decoration should be bold and simple. The overscale letters stand out smartly and clearly against the red background.

To construct these hangings, first cut ¼-inch-thick hardboard into four pieces, each one measuring 14x24 inches. Then, cut four pieces of red oilcloth that measure 16x26 inches each. Cover each panel of hardboard with red oilcloth, bringing the material around the edges and gluing it securely to the back of each panel.

Cut out the letters from white oilcloth, and the floral motifs from flowered oilcloth. Position letters, and glue in place. Glue floral sprays on top of letters in random fashion. Fasten a hanging cord at the top of each section, and hang them on small hooks.

When the holiday season is over, remove the hangings from the wall, wipe them with a moist cloth to remove soil, and pack them away until next year.

The intriguing decoration pictured at the upper right of the opposite page is bound to bring enthusiastic comments from everyone who sees it. The Mexican artist who designed the panel interjected a south-of-the-border influence with the lettering, which, translated into English, means Hallelujah.

To construct an outdoor decoration like this one, cut a piece of ⅛-inch-thick hardboard to measure 41x24 inches. Cut a piece of orange felt that measures 42x25 inches and glue it to the board top, wrapping felt around the board edges. Cut out the angel, rooster, and letters from wood. Paint and trim them, using the photo as a guide. Cut another piece of hardboard 49x22 inches; cut scallops across top and bottom. Stain or paint it a deep shade, and glue on a glass marble at the top of each scallop. Center the felt-covered board over the longer wood panel, and glue or nail it in place securely.

Then, fasten a 14-inch-wide floor-to-ceiling felt panel to the house, and mount the banner over it. For a finishing touch, hang a brass Shinto temple bell close to it.

The entryway pictured at the lower left of the opposite page expresses universal goodwill. It features placards with Christmas greetings in many different languages.

To begin this project, cut laths or narrow boards into equal lengths, one for each greeting (here, 11 are used on each side of the door). Paint wood strips red, and paint the greeting on each one in white. (Consult foreign language dictionaries for greetings.) Attach strips to each side of door; space them about two inches apart.

In the center of the door, hang a wreath with a lavish red bow at the bottom. Frame the entranceway with garlands of pine roping, laced with red cord. Place poinsettias on either side of the door (the permanent type if you live in a cold climate) and a jolly elf at one side to welcome visitors.

The contemporary angel pictured at the lower right of page 154 is a stunning outdoor decoration. Through the ages, angels depicted in paintings, poetry, and pious chants have been the bearers of momentous tidings, and this updated version is no exception.

Start this project by making the body of the angel. Cover a long, slim box with vinyl-coated paper or oilcloth in different colors, following the photo as a guide and giving the package the effect of an angel's robe. Cut the head, wings, arms, and feet out of sturdy cardboard and cover with the same type and colors of paper or oilcloth used to cover the package. Glue sections to back of box—arms, head, and feet first; the wings last.

Cut the hands, face, and neck out of heavy-duty aluminum foil, and cut openings for the eyes, nose, and mouth. Fasten these pieces in position and bend each piece slightly to give a three-dimensional effect. Mount the angel on a wall or door.

Rather than duplicating this design, you may decide to let this angel give you inspiration for your own designs.

The giant-size kissing ball (pictured at the bottom of the page) hanging above this front entranceway makes a simple but beautiful greeting for guests.

To make this overscale outdoor decoration, start with a 10-inch diameter plastic foam ball (or a larger size if your entranceway can accommodate it). Next, cover the entire ball with sprigs of boxwood cut in varying lengths. Then, stick fresh tangerines or oranges onto floral picks and intersperse them throughout the greenery around the plastic foam ball. Fill in any bare spots with clusters of orange berries.

Finally, use orange velour or velvet (weatherproof) ribbon to make a cascading multi-looped bow for the top of the kissing ball and streamers to hang gracefully below.

Hang the ornament high enough above the door so it won't interfere with traffic.

The graceful grouping of outdoor decorations pictured on the opposite page literally is the sweetest adornment you've ever seen.

To reproduce this trio of colorful holiday wreaths, start with plastic foam rings that measure 16, 14, and 12 inches in diameter. Purchase an ample supply of cellophane-wrapped candies in colors that harmonize with your Christmas decorating scheme.

To fasten the candies to the wreath bases, stick a straight pin through the candy wrapper at one end and insert the pin into the plastic foam wreath. Then, cut off the exposed twisted end of cellophane. Place the pieces of candy tightly together to completely cover the wreath base.

Back each wreath with small sprays of evergreens, and trim the wreaths with tailored bows and streamers of velvet (weatherproof) ribbon. Hang the wreaths on the front door, each one suspended from a different length of velvet ribbon.

This jewel-like outdoor decoration will gather added interest if you accompany it with bare branches liberally studded with tiny twinkling tree lights. To keep the branches secure, position them upright in a planter filled with pebbles and sand. Start stringing the tree lights at the base of the 'tree.' Secure the strings of lights firmly to the branches with green floral tape.

Giant kissing ball

A trio of cellophane-wrapped candy wreaths ▶ backed by gracefully arranged greens highlights the door at the right. The bare branches are studded with tiny Christmas lights.

156

Chapter 10

Dazzling Window Dressings

The windows of your home at Christmas, dappled with frost and overlooking blankets of pure white snow, are a natural stage for handcrafted holiday decorations. The sparkle of sun-on-snow provides a magnificent backlighting effect for your one-of-a-kind creations. And, if some of your windows are located near a street or a sidewalk, passersby will catch an intriguing glimpse of your home dressed up in its Christmas finery.

Think of your windows as large frames to outline beautiful Christmas scenes. Use wreaths, floral arrangements, hanging plants, and decorated window shades to achieve spectacular window treatments.

Your window decorations should join together the themes presented in your outdoor and indoor decorations. If, for example, your outdoor fashions lean toward the contemporary, but your indoor treatments are more traditional, your window ornamentations should combine elements of both contemporary and traditional design.

The design ideas presented in this chapter are guaranteed to make both Santa and your guests look twice. Duplicate those shown, or try some of your own.

Let your windows help to make your home look its holiday best this Christmas by fashioning scenes that will sparkle with the spirit of the season.

In the window at the left, an antique scale and a variety of candles rest on the sill. Green ornaments and an elaborate red bow adorn the scale. A brandy snifter filled with more green ornaments adds to the red and green color scheme.

Using what comes naturally

Make your windows look extra-special this holiday season by decking them with living decorations. Whether you wish to focus attention on the outside view or the interior room setting, flowers, fruits, and greens will add classic beauty to the windows.

The stately tiered floral arrangement pictured at the upper left of the opposite page presents a good solution for making the most of a tall, narrow window. This rather formal adornment is completely at home with the sweeping swag and jabot window treatment.

To concoct this tiered arrangement, start with a footed, flat cake stand for a base. Center a wide compote on the cake stand, and a footed water goblet on top of the compote. Use floral clay to secure the containers in pyramidal form, and attach the figurine finial to a block of wood.

Fill the unusual container with red—nandina berries, apples, and carnations. Cluster the material more profusely toward the bottom to give the proper balance.

A traditional wreath of evergreen is featured in the small-paned window pictured at the upper right of the opposite page. This ever-popular Christmas decoration extends the theme that starts with the spruce ropes around the double doors, the lengths of pine roping twined around the porch columns, and the large kissing ball that is suspended over the doorway.

Use a plastic foam wreath base or a wire frame to make the wreath. Cover the form with lustrous, dark green boxwood leaves. (If boxwood is not available in your area, use pine boughs.) Decorate the wreath with artificial fruit, and add a luxurious red satin bow as a finishing touch.

The holiday hang-ups pictured at the lower right of the opposite page will add character to any window in your home. They're also ideal gifts for those 'hard-to-buy-for' people on your Christmas list. These creations are easy to make, and the materials are inexpensive. And when you're finished, no one will believe that these hanging planters (food or juice cans) barely escaped the degrading experience of being thrown away.

All you need to make a collection of planters for hanging plants is a variety of tin cans, vinyl, buckskin strips (or scraps of leather and suede), and glue—the kind that is recommended for use on fabric. You can find all these materials in craft supply stores and fabric departments—perhaps even in your own collection of odds and ends.

Begin by removing the labels and glue from the tin cans—an overnight soaking makes this easy to do and speeds up the process. Wash and dry the cans thoroughly.

Cut a paper pattern to fit between the top and bottom rims of the can; use this pattern to cut the vinyl covering. Spread a strip of white glue around the top and bottom of the can and along its vertical seam. Press the vinyl material smoothly onto the glue. If necessary, trim the vinyl at the seam to make a neat fit. Secure the vinyl covering to the tin can with masking tape until the glue is thoroughly dry, then remove the tape.

Make the decorative borders for the planters from contrasting shades of vinyl, as shown in the sketch on the opposite page. Use small paper punches to make the disks. Adhere the borders on the top of the vinyl-covered can with white glue. Use a damp sponge to wipe away any excess glue. Cut buckskin strips to fit around the top and bottom of the can; attach the strips with narrow lines of glue. Set aside and allow the glue to dry thoroughly.

Under the top buckskin band, use a large nail to drill or punch three holes about 1¼ inches apart on each side of the can. Thread lengths of buckskin thongs through each hole, and knot the thongs on the outside of the can, as shown. Pull the knots taut; place a dot of glue behind each knot, then clip the knotted ends of the thongs short.

At the top of the window, install hooks that are strong enough to hold the weight of the planter, plant, and soil. Hang the planters on the hooks. The containers shown here are planted with begonias, but many other plants are suitable for hanging planters. Choose from tropical and feathery ferns, English ivy and kangaroo vine, old-fashioned philodendrons, and ivy geraniums. All of these plants will thrive in bright light and will not suffer from the cooler temperatures found near large windows in wintertime, unless the temperature near the glass drops below 65°.

160

Stately tiered arrangement

Traditional green wreath

Holiday hang-ups

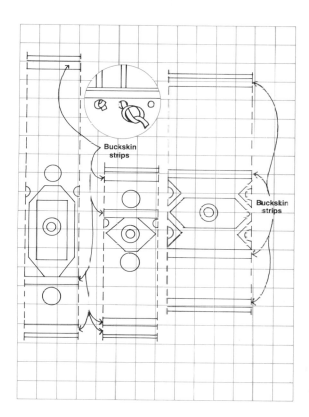

Buckskin
strips

Buckskin
strips

Stained glass wreath

Yarn wreath

Glittering window treatment

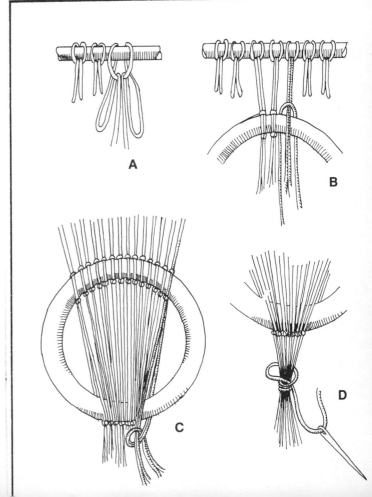

Windows with a magic touch

Display your craftsmanship by making unusual window decorations from unconventional materials. Assemble yarn, fringe, construction paper, wood dowels, tree ornaments, paper tubes, plastic foam shapes, window shades, and glue, and you're all ready to start decorating your windows.

The stained glass wreath at the upper left of the opposite page is a perfect window decoration. Rays of sunshine or beams of artificial light make this updated version of an age-old design gleam with jewel-like splendor when they filter through it.

To start, flatten a paper tube and cut crosswise into ¼-inch-wide sections with a scissors. (Because the tube has been flattened, these sections will be pointed at the ends, making a leaf form.) Set each section on edge into a shallow pool of glue, then onto colored paper—either origami, note paper, tissue, or construction. Trim paper when glue dries.

To make pears, shape sections of larger tubes between fingers to resemble outline of a pear, glue to paper. Shape another section of larger tube to form body of bird; glue to paper. Set more tube sections to body of bird to suggest wing and tail feathers. Arrange units to form wreath. Dot with glue at contact points; hold pieces in position with clamps until glue dries. Fasten a hook for hanging on the back at the top.

The glittering window treatment pictured at the upper right of the opposite page is a new approach to holiday decorating. The vertical blind effect is fashioned of lustrous gift wrapping ribbon, and the symmetrical Christmas tree design results from the grouping of the shiny Christmas ball ornaments. You can duplicate this window decoration in a very short time.

First, attach lengths of shimmering gold ribbon over the top and the bottom of the window frame with masking tape. Next, fasten two lengths of ribbon at the center of the top and extend them outward toward the bottom of the window to simulate the tree shape. Within the tree shape, fasten tree ornaments to the vertical ribbon lengths with straight pins. On a table beneath the window, stack a collection of gift packages wrapped in the same color combination.

The yarn wreath pictured at the lower left of the opposite page can be adapted to fit any size window. To make this captivating window decoration, you will need two 12-inch plastic foam rings, green crepe paper, red and green ball fringe, red yarn, and a spring-tension curtain rod.

First, glue the two 12-inch plastic foam rings together, with the flat sides facing. Next, wrap the wreath with narrow strips of green crepe paper. Mount a spring-tension rod in the window where the wreath will hang. Cut red yarn in strips about 2½ times the finished length to allow for loops. Wind a double length of yarn over the rod; slip-knot into position, pulling the knot taut. (See drawing A at the left.) Continue with the other lengths of yarn, butting the loops together until the rod is completely concealed. Count off to the center length of yarn, and place wreath form behind hanging lengths.

Loop another length of yarn that's doubled from behind the wreath around the forward lengths. Tie two lengths of yarn inside the rim of the wreath into a knot. (See drawing B.) Work outward from the center, slipping another yarn length around the ones tied to rod. Then, tie the two on inside rim of wreath.

When all of the lengths of yarn are tied, hang alternate strands of yarn in front of and behind the wreath. Tie the strands of yarn together along the lower outside rim. (See drawing C.) Gather the yarn together into a tight clump. Tie it into a tassel (drawing D) and trim at the bottom to the desired length. Pin on red and green pompons of various sizes, cut from ball fringe. Attach them to the wreath, graduating from small ones in the center to larger ones around the outside.

A golden angel of contemporary design glorifies the stair landing in the photo on page 164. This lightweight figure is easily fashioned of construction paper and wire.

First, consider the height of your window, and proportion your angel accordingly. Make firm underpinnings to support the figure—nail a long dowel to a cross base similar to those used under Christmas trees. Construct the basic shape of the angel from chicken wire and attach it to the dowel at the critical points. Cover the wire frame with sheets of

Golden angel

heavy construction paper, using more wire to support the folds and other details. Accordion-pleat the paper for the top and bottom of the gown. Attach a plastic foam oval for the head, a circle of raffia for the halo, and stiff wire wrapped with adhesive tape for the wings.

Spray-paint the entire figure gold. Or, use a deep brown or a dramatic black, depending on your decor. Arrange greens below the angel, a candleholder to one side, and an urn on the other side.

The decorated window shades pictured on the opposite page offer many intriguing design possibilities. The two shades at the top of the photo will appeal to youngsters, while the two at the bottom are elegant enough to hang in any room of your home.

There are many advantages to this type of window decoration. For example, you can trim them on both sides so they are equally attractive whether viewed from the inside or outside. And they are simple to make. When the holiday season is over, you can roll them up and store them until the next year. Use reverse roll shades, and be sure to use glue that

adheres to fabrics and vinyls and that does not stiffen the material when it dries.

To make the candy cane shade and valance, interlock and press red and white giant rickrack long enough for a border for both the shade and the valance. Glue interlocked red and white standard rickrack in candy cane shapes to the front of the shade. Glue the band of giant rickrack to the edge of the valance and just above the casing on the window shade. On the back of the shade, which is white, use green baby rickrack to form the greeting "Happy Holidays." Add a white plastic shade pull.

The red burlap-textured window shade, second from the top, provides a casual background for felt ornaments.

Cut the ornament shapes from felt, and trim them with scraps of braid glued on. Glue the motifs in place, and glue a row of gold middy braid just above the hem. Make the shade pull from two trimmed felt ornament shapes glued back-to-back, with stiff plastic or cardboard in between. Insert gold soutache braid cord through a reinforced hole in the shade pull.

Glittering stripes create a sari border on the third shade. Glue nine strips of braid across the bottom of the window shade. Select different styles of metallic braid in gold, red, and green to simulate the sari effect.

The pull is a tassel of metallic gold balls and red rickrack hung on a gold soutache cord. To make the balls, begin winding rickrack around two lengths of cord that are knotted together at the ends. Glue at each turn until a small ball is formed. Make a similar ball at the other end of the braid lengths. After completing 12 balls, gather the centers of braid together. Wrap with more braid; leave space at the top to insert cord.

The three-crown window shade requires a shade with a sawtooth edge. You can either order a shade with this type of edge or cut the edge yourself. Glue gold braid to the shade to form the crowns. Then, trim the edge of the shade with enough gold fringe for a double thickness, and add three gold tassels fashioned from middy braid.

Whether they're pulled down or partially raised, ▶ decorated window shades, such as those pictured at the right, amplify the festive holiday mood that prevails in your home.

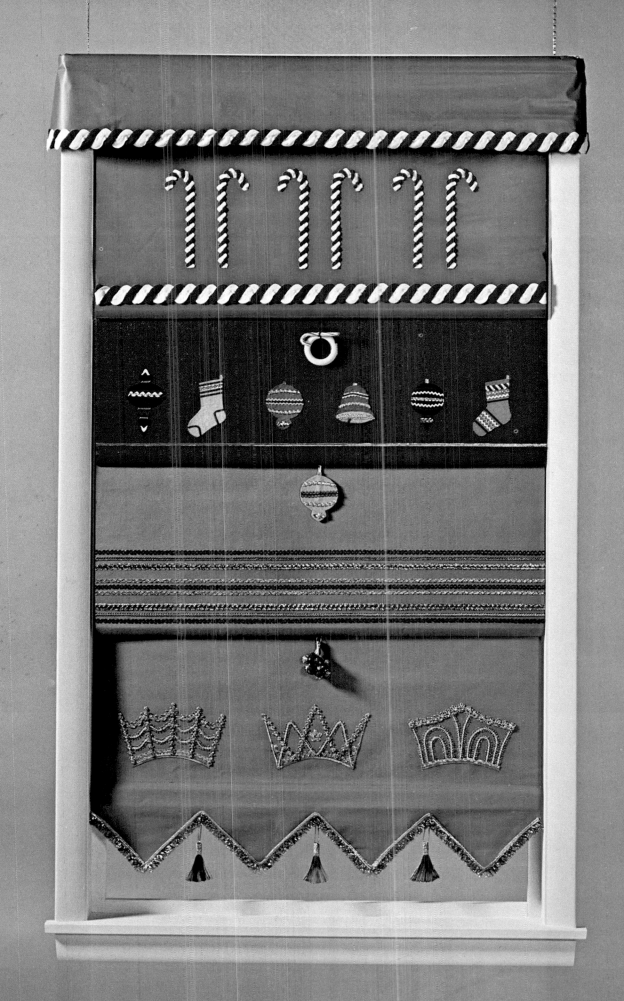

Chapter 11

Decorations Children Can Make

Children will enjoy Christmas more if they take an active part in all the exciting preparations for this fun-filled season. And, what better way is there for them to share in the family activities than by making holiday decorations of their own creation?

Encourage them to start with projects that are easy to do as soon as they can maneuver a pair of kindergarten scissors and a paintbrush. As the years go by and their creative talents and skills advance, you will still treasure their first childish efforts.

Paint, glue, paper, cardboard, fabric, yarn, and ordinary household string have always held a fascination for youngsters, so why not channel your children's boundless energies into producing a variety of colorful decorations with these simple items? You may have to do a little supervising when you launch their first few projects, but don't force your ideas on them. You will be surprised at their ingenuity when you give youngsters free rein.

Just be sure to have ample work area. Whether the children are working at a table or desk, the breakfast counter, or are sprawled out on the floor, protect the area with several layers of newspaper. Assemble all the materials and tools within easy reach, and let tomorrow's artists and sculptors follow their inventive impulses.

The brightly colored burlap and checked gingham ornaments that deck the tree at the left are a fun project for budding seamstresses. The only materials you need are scraps of fabric, cotton or foam rubber for stuffing, and leftovers of yarn.

Tree trappings to treasure

Your children's favorite Christmas tree ornaments likely will be those they make themselves. Encourage them in this activity, but be sure the materials they use—paint, glue, and clear spray coatings—are not harmful.

The colorful cardboard hang-ups pictured on the opposite page not only are fun for children to make, they'll enhance the appearance of your Christmas tree, too. And, they are easy to cut, paint, glue, and hang.

To construct these novel ornaments, you will need corrugated cardboard, clear plastic spray, gesso, fluorescent or ordinary opaque water colors, wire hooks and string for hanging, white glue, and chenille pipe cleaners for butterfly antennae.

Begin by drawing enlarged paper patterns, including all of the inner lines, following the sketches shown at the bottom of the opposite page. Cut the outline pieces from medium-weight cardboard, and the small individual pattern sections from corrugated cardboard. Cut the small pieces with the lines running in different directions on the corrugated cardboard, as this will produce a more interesting surface texture.

Paint each of the sections before gluing them to the backing. First, use a clear plastic spray for a primer. Next, add a coat of gesso. Then, paint each piece with fluorescent opaque water colors. (If you use ordinary opaque water colors rather than the fluorescent type, you can omit the gesso.) Finally, add a coat of matte finish fixative.

Attach a wire loop and string to the cardboard backing for hanging, and glue two chenille pipe cleaners to the cardboard backing of the butterfly ornament for antennae.

Assemble the tree ornament pieces and glue them to the cardboard backing with white glue. Glue small circles of corrugated cardboard to the tips of the butterfly antennae. Combine pieces of contrasting colors for greater effectiveness.

The perky paper ornaments pictured at the top of page 170 present a striking appearance that disguises the ease with which you can make this collection.

The materials for these tree decorations are easy to find and inexpensive—colorful tissue and gift wrapping paper, shiny metallic seals and ribbons to add an extra decorative accent, glue, and scissors. Children love creating handcrafted items with paper and glue, and even little ones take pride in being designers. If their first efforts don't produce the results they expected, encourage them to start over again. (In order to prevent needless accidents, have them use a pair of blunt kindergarten scissors.)

To make the cascading bells shown at the far left in the photo, trace small circles (each one a different size) on scraps of paper in a variety of compatible colors. Cut a slit to the center of each circle, overlap the edges, and glue together to form cone shapes.

Then, run a 10-inch string through several cones, knotting the thread between each to keep them evenly spaced. Arrange the paper cones in graduated sizes—the largest at the bottom, the smallest at the top. Glue on decorative metallic seals for trim around the bottom and attach an ornament hanger.

Cut the contemporary angel figure from medium-weight cardboard in two identical pieces. Glue gift wrapping paper to both sides of each figure. Fold the figures down the center and glue them at the centerfold to achieve a four-sided figure. Attach a hanger.

The gold spiral, which looks as though it is floating in the air, is easy to make. Start by cutting a circle of gold metallic foil. Then, cut round and round in a continuous strip to the center of the circle. Attach a hanging cord at the top, and let the gold rings droop gracefully from the branches.

For the attractive, fringed paper circle, cut a cardboard circle 3 inches in diameter for the backing. Cut strips of colored tissue paper, fringe them, and attach them to the cardboard backing with glue to resemble spokes. For the center decoration, pull strips of tissue paper across the open blade of scissors to make curls. Glue the curls in place, and add a cord for hanging. (Use this same curling technique for the cone-shaped decoration at the far right.)

Make the small scalloped decoration from two complementary colors of paper. Add strips of polka-dotted ribbon in a spoke design.

Construct all of the ornaments so they can be viewed from either side.

Colorful cardboard hang-ups

Perky paper ornaments

Santa Claus

Paint, glue, and string

Santa Claus is always a welcome sight at Christmas. The spirited version of the jolly old gentleman shown at the lower left of the opposite page will enliven any tree. The only materials you'll need to duplicate this genial character are cardboard, paper, glass beads, excelsior, and glue. This is a fun project for children of all ages.

To make this delightful decoration, cut three cardboard triangles that measure 8 inches high and 3 inches wide at the base. Glue or tape the triangles together to form a pyramid, and cover the pyramid with red paper (or you can spray-paint it red).

Glue small circles of black paper to the cardboard pyramid for the eyes. Pin a shiny red glass bead to the face with a corsage pin to simulate Santa's nose. Pin another bead ornament to the tip of his conical-shaped hat. Use white excelsior to fashion the flowing whiskers, the shock of hair, and the fluffy balls on the tip of the hat. Glue the excelsior in place. Attach a tinsel-covered tree hanger at the very tip of Santa's hat.

Paint, glue, and string are the ordinary household items used to make the fragile-appearing tree decorations shown at the lower right of the opposite page. Although these ornaments have a gossamer-like appearance, they are completely shatterproof. They require no special techniques or skills, and children will enjoy decorating the tree with them after a fun-filled day making them.

First, organize all of your materials on a large work surface—the kitchen table, a desk, or even the floor. Protect the work surface with several layers of wrapping paper or newspaper. Pour ¼ cup of a creamy white glue into an aluminum foil pie pan or bowl.

Next, cut a piece of cotton cord into one-yard lengths, and soak the lengths of cord in the glue bath until the cord is thoroughly moistened. (See photo 1.) This will take from 15 to 20 minutes. Before proceeding to the next step, remove the excess glue by pulling the string through your fingers while the cord is still moist. (See photo 2.) Remove the excess glue from only a few lengths of string at one time so the cord will not dry out while you are wrapping and shaping the designs.

Wrap the moistened cord tightly around cardboard tubes pressed into a variety of shapes, or around pencils, wood dowels, or plastic bottles. Let the wrapped cord dry until it is stiff, then carefully remove it from the forms around which it is wrapped by cutting the loops with a knife, single-edge razor blade, or a pair of scissors. Next, glue the ends of each piece together, making a closed loop. Combine an assortment of both small and large round and oval loops in the various designs, as shown in photo 3. Paint the designs in the colors of your choice.

To make designs other than those composed of circular or oval shapes—the bird, cat, or Christmas tree motifs—prepare each from pieces of string dipped in glue (removing excess glue), as you did before. Lay the string out free-form on a piece of waxed or freezer paper to form the outline of the design of your choice. Then, glue the extra smaller string parts to the larger outline shape. Glue a small round loop of string at the top of each ornament for hanging on the tree. Let them dry until the string is firm and stiff. (To make an assortment of designs, copy other holiday motifs that embellish Christmas cards and gift wrapping paper.

1

2

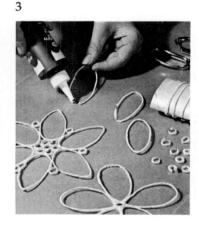

3

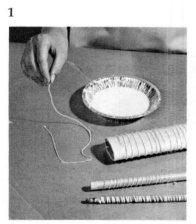

After the glue is thoroughly dry and you have the desired shapes, paint each ornament with water-based paint in several harmonious colors. To preserve the ornaments, coat each one with colorless nail polish, or spray with a clear plastic spray. For a more glamorous effect, brush the ornaments with white glue after the preservative dries, and sprinkle them with glitter. Let the glue dry, then gently shake off the excess glitter.

You can put these designs to other uses, too. Children can fasten special personalized ornaments onto gift boxes for the family. Try using solid-color paper for the background to show off the fragile snowflakes or bright stars. Or hang several designs in a doorway or over a table.

The menagerie of captivating animals pictured on the opposite page nestling in the branches of a flocked Christmas tree is an entertaining cut-and-tape project for children. In addition to having lots of eye appeal, the animals are quick and easy to construct—even for small children. The fanciful designs will appeal to their imagination, too.

All that you need to make this fanciful collection of paper animals is construction paper in a variety of colors, a pair of scissors, tape, a marking pen, bits of yarn, paper, and sequins to make the features.

Assemble all of the materials on a table or a desk, and let the children get started. If the youngsters who undertake this project are very young, you may want an older brother

The 'Zoo Story' could well be the name for the ▶ collection of engaging characters on the opposite page. The drawings below will make duplicating these cut-and-tape animals easy.

Paper chain variations

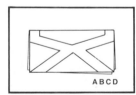

ABCD

Cut 3x6-inch rectangles. Fold and cut. Fold arms up when chain is complete.

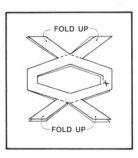

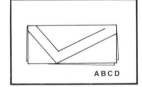

ABCD

Use 3x9-inch pieces of paper. Fold center strip in half and outward.

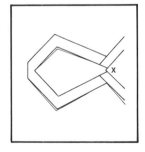

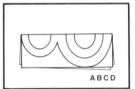

ABCD

Use 3x9-inch paper. Add extra circle after each link is added to previous one.

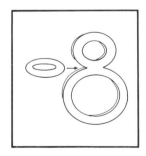

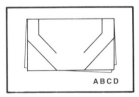

ABCD

Cut from 3x4½-inch paper. Open links, cut center in half, fold on dotted lines.

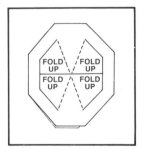

or sister to supervise the cutting and folding operations. But, leave the fancy embellishments to the 'budding Picasso's' imagination.

To construct these one-pleat animals, cut a sheet of 9x12-inch construction paper into two 9x6-inch pieces. You can make one animal from each half sheet. Fold the paper vertically so that you have a double rectangle measuring 9x3 inches. Using the reindeer, dog, and bird patterns shown at the bottom of page 172, trace onto the folded paper, with the animal's feet on the cut edge.

With a sharp knife or other sharp instrument, score along the broken lines on the pattern drawings, being careful not to cut all the way through the paper. This will enable you to fold along the curved lines. Mark both sides of animal for folding.

After cutting out the animal shapes, fold the diagonal crease by the tail of the bird or the head of the animals. Fold back and forth several times to make a good, sharp crease. (The angle of the fold will determine how straight up the tail or the head will stand, so experiment with these until you're satisfied with the results.)

To form the shapes, open the animal and pull up on points A and C while you are pressing down on B. Pinch and smooth the creases. Then, tape the figure underneath so it will hold its shape. Once you become proficient at the technique of folding, don't

hesitate to design other animal figures, following the basic shapes given on page 172.

Now, it's time to add the finishing touches to these clever creatures, and this is when youngsters can give vent to their fanciful impulses. They can use beads, yarn, bits and scraps of paper, and sequins to make the eyes, wings, and spots. Just because you've never seen a green dog with purple polka dots leering at you with a blue sequin eye doesn't mean they won't enjoy concocting this unique breed to hang on the Christmas tree. Glue the trim in place, and display the animal collection on the branches of your tree.

Paper chains have been around for a long time, but the Swedish chain variations pictured on the opposite page offer a greater challenge than the traditional paper chains ever have. And, the results are a great deal more gratifying. Your Christmas tree will take on a new and exciting look when it is adorned with long chains of multicolored paper circles and geometrical-shaped links made by the children.

The only materials needed to make these decorations are construction paper in assorted colors and a pair of scissors. The chains shown here have been constructed so that the dimensions fit standard construction paper size. The dimensions given with the small diagrams at the left are for the paper before it is folded. The diagrams illustrate the standard fold used in making chains. It is a common fold, also called the box fold. (See the large drawing below.) The letters A, B, C, and D in each diagram indicate the spot where the four corners of the paper meet.

The chains will not develop correctly if the cutting diagram is put on upside down, so be sure to have the corners matched exactly the right way according to directions.

The extra center pieces of some of the chain designs are curled around a pencil, folded in the middle, or folded into a 'V' shape. The pieces of the chain that are cut separately can be added over the chains by folding the chain link in the middle and slipping the extra ring over the link.

Join the links together by slipping the succeeding open link through the closed previous link. Bend one half of the open link carefully in the middle so that it will slip through easily. Close it and add another. The spots that are marked with an X on the diagrams indicate where to add new links during the assembly operation.

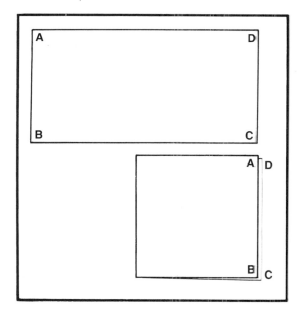

Party-perfect decorations

Holiday time is entertaining time, and children's affairs can be smashing successes with careful planning and a colorful theme. Let the youngsters participate by making the party decorations and invitations while you concentrate on what to serve the hungry hoard.

The Santa-in-the-box shown on the opposite page is a holiday version of the ever-popular Jack-in-the-box. This clever pop-up centerpiece will delight both youngsters and not-so-youngsters and will set the mood for a jolly Christmas party. Add to this paper hats and favors in the same color scheme, and the party's bound to be a success.

To make the Santa-in-the-box, line an 8-inch-cube white gift box with gold foil gift wrapping paper. Bind all of the sides with strips of gold foil tape. Stick red velour paper cutouts on the outside of the box, or design your own Christmas shapes on red construction paper and glue them to the box.

Next, coil a 2-foot length of armature wire (available at art supply stores) around a salt box or similar cylindrically shaped carton, and stick the box into a 2-inch-thick 8-inch-square plastic foam block. Wedge the foam block firmly into the bottom of the box. Stuff tissue paper around the wire and plastic foam for stability. Insert small nails into the bottom of the box and into the foam.

Insert the top end of the wire coil into an 8-inch plastic foam ball for Santa's head. Shape nose out of white crepe paper and use small Christmas balls for eyes; glue them in place. Cut a moustache and 10-inch beard shape from white crepe paper. Slash the crepe paper and curl the narrow strips around a pencil. Pin on beard and moustache.

Make Santa's hat from a 10x24-inch piece of red crepe paper. Pin the piece lengthwise around the head and stretch the middle. Gather the ends together at the top with a running stitch. Seam the center back. For the white brim, gather 2 yards of a crepe paper streamer down the center with a machine stitch. Fold the edges toward each other and pin the brim onto the hat. Top the cap with a white fringed and curled crepe paper tassel.

Fill empty spaces in the box with cellophane-wrapped popcorn balls and attach other balls to the box with strips of ribbon.

Make place-mark favors by inserting 7-inch bamboo skewers into popcorn balls. Wedge the other end of the skewers into 2½-inch sections from the bottom of 6-inch plastic foam cones. Decorate the foam bases with gold lace paper as shown in the picture. Put the names of guests on with gold foil alphabet paper and attach with short sequin pins.

To construct the hats, cut sheets of white oaktag into 9x22-inch pieces. Roll each piece into a modified cone shape and staple it together. Curl the ends of red pipe cleaners and staple them to the seams of the hats. Ruffle a red crepe paper streamer and glue to the edges of hats. Decorate the hats with motifs cut from adhesive velour paper.

Place the Santa-in-a-box on a green or red tablecloth and suspend extra popcorn balls from the ceiling with narrow red ribbon.

To make the box-shaped invitations (one is shown at the left in the photo), follow the patterns below. Cut the box shape (A) from red oaktag. Score and fold along the dotted

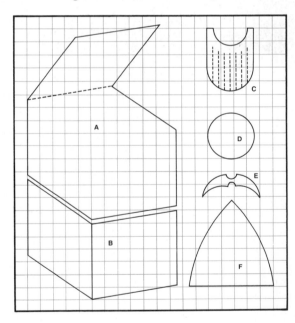

Here's an exciting array of children's party decorations—a centerpiece, party favors, place cards, and invitations—that will cast a magic spell over the holiday festivities.

line. Bind the edges with gold foil tape. Cut the smaller overlap piece (B) from white oaktag and bind the two box shapes together on the four outside edges with gold foil tape. Decorate the white sides with sequins in the form of snowflakes.

For Santa's beard, follow pattern (C) Cut the beard out of white crepe paper, slash on the dotted lines, and curl the ends of paper around a pencil. Make the round head (D) of white oaktag. Cut the moustache (E) of white crepe paper and the peaked hat (F) of red crepe paper slightly stretched in the middle and folded into a 'V' shape. Assemble the head and staple it to a red chenille pipe cleaner that has been curled around a pencil to resemble a coil spring. Tape the pipe cleaner coiled spring to the inside of the box. Let an invitation card peek out of the partially open box. Make the invitation out of white oaktag and bind it around the edges with the same gold foil tape.

Make your invitations to send to the guests well in advance of the get-together. Be sure to fill in the date, time, and place, and if you wish them to notify you whether or not they plan to attend, ask them to respond. It's always easier for the one who is preparing the food to know just how many people to prepare refreshments for.

When you entertain for children and use these holiday decorations, you might like to serve a hearty soup, assorted small sandwiches, a variety of crisp, raw vegetables on a relish tray, beverage, and Christmas cookies for dessert. Instead of the usual milk or hot chocolate, serve red or green punch.

Holiday goodies in festive wrappings grace the buffet table on the opposite page. This tantalizing display of homemade delicacies is ideal for an open house where guests come and go for several hours. They would be equally tempting as a treat for a band of carolers who stop by to sing "We Wish You A Merry Christmas." Or, you might want to send some of these homemade delights to friends as gifts. You'll probably want to prepare the sweets, but the children will be able to help you with the wrappings.

◄ **A potpourri of Christmas sweets** in their holiday finery are displayed on the buffet table at the left. Children will love helping you with these good-tasting decorating projects.

Below, there is a brief description of all the items in the photo, starting at the lower left and moving in a clockwise fashion.

Use an ordinary crystal-clear plastic bag to hold nut and cherry brittle. Add a brass drapery ring and a holiday nosegay to secure the candy inside. The nosegay is made of a gold, spray-painted pine cone, a shiny satin Christmas ball, and red berries.

Place chocolate divinity in tiny breadbaskets, spray-painted gold. Pad the bottoms of the baskets with evergreen sprigs before you put the candy in them.

Top small jars of homemade preserves with saucy ribbon bows in holiday colors. Arrange them in inexpensive straw baskets and weave red and green velvet ribbon through the sides of the baskets. Fill the baskets with shredded cellophane so the jars just barely peek out of the top. Or, you could use a small bushel basket and trim the rim and the bindings with strips of fabrics in bright colors. Glue the fabric in place.

Retrieve an about-to-be-thrown-away egg carton and convert it into an ornate pull-toy to hold marzipan. Make the wheels from plastic foam balls cut in half. Fasten them securely to the egg carton wagon with wooden skewers, and cover the entire egg carton with wide, decorative ribbon in holiday colors. For the handle, attach a short length of gold cord to the wagon and add a small ornament to the other end of the cord.

Here's another recycling project. Cover a three-pound coffee can with green burlap to hold cookies. Next, make a cone out of lightweight cardboard and glue on green burlap to cover it, too. Trim the cone with rows of red ball fringe; glue fringe in place. Fasten the cone to the top of the coffee can with glue. Fill can with toffee drop cookies, the same as those shown on the inverted cover.

Store sesame seed toffee bars in a tall, see-through canister and top it with a roly-poly Santa figure. To concoct this quaint character, use a plastic foam ball for the body and a smaller one for the head. Glue the two sections together. Use red velvet ribbon for hat, nose, buttons, and belt; a small gold buckle for belt; and white fringe for hair. Perch Santa atop the glass canister, and let a sprig of evergreen peek out from behind.

Apple-shaped wood cutting boards act as handy servers for fragile Christmas cookies. Wire a cluster of pine cones to the handles to add holiday flavor.

Merry medley of holiday decorations

Christmas delights children, and their excitement is infectious. To bolster your youngsters' already high spirits, plan a decorating spree for them. With your encouragement, they're bound to have surprising results.

Making posters such as those at the top of the opposite page is a Christmas craft that children will enjoy greatly. Construct these bright designs to adorn the front door, the hallway, or walls. The only materials you need are poster board, adhesive-backed burlap, decorative tape and seals, and velvet-backed ribbon. Cut 22x28-inch posters from white poster board.

To make the partridge poster, cut out the pattern pieces from wrapping paper first. Arrange pattern on poster board and trace around paper lightly with pencil as an aid in the final positioning of the design. Then, trace on the back of adhesive-backed burlap, placing pattern pieces face down. Cut designs, peel off paper backing, and press burlap down in the previously outlined areas.

For the holly wreath poster, make a pattern on paper first. Draw a 12-inch diameter circle 6 inches from the edge of the cardboard. Cut 34 leaves from adhesive-backed burlap and arrange them around the penciled circle on each side of the line. Punch out red and green dots to denote berries. Trace a pattern of the bow on the back of an 8-inch-wide velvet adhesive-backed ribbon and apply. Use a 6-inch-wide strip of velvet ribbon at the top of the poster. Trace the letters on the back of the strip, cut them out, and then attach the band to the poster.

For the poinsettia poster, cut out a petal pattern on wrapping paper first. Arrange the pattern on the board and trace around the paper lightly with a pencil as an aid in the final positioning of the design. Then, trace the patterns on the back of adhesive-backed burlap, placing patterns face down. Cut out designs, peel off paper backing, and press burlap down in outlined areas. Use this same procedure for letters and border.

To form the centers of the poinsettias, cut out $7/16$-inch diameter circles of green adhesive-backed burlap. Punch out $1/4$-inch circles from gold burlap or tape, and apply gold circles on top of the green circles.

The Christmas tree design features adhesive tape and seals. Draw guiding lines on poster, allowing a $3/4$-inch space for tape and a 1-inch space between each line. Start with a 16-inch-wide guideline. Then, reduce each line by 2 inches, with top line 1 inch wide. Apply tape along lines, finishing with a diagonal cut at both ends of each strip of tape. Repeat this procedure for tree holder with strips of tape 6, 5, and 4 inches long placed $1/4$ inch apart. Allow 1 inch of space between tree and holder and apply tape for tree trunk. Finish with a $1/2$-inch-wide strip of tape 2 inches from the bottom.

The Nativity scene pictured at the bottom of the opposite page will be the center of attention on a table, desk, or mantel. And, it is easy for children to reproduce this stately Holy Family, which is made from paper products and plastic foam balls.

For the heads of the figures, paint the plastic foam balls with acrylic paints in flesh tones. Paint the facial features, and make beards and hair of cotton or yarn.

For bodies of male characters, use paper drinking cups. Turn them upside-down and glue on inverted paper baking cups for necks; glue heads onto necks. Make hats of paper nut cups and trim them with braid glued on.

Make Mary's robe of construction paper, cut and glued to form a cone shape. Add gold braid trim down the front of the robe. Use a paper nut cup for the manger. Make all three halos from sections of lace paper doilies.

For the shelter, cut a rectangular-shaped gift box from corner to corner. Cover the outside of the box with a strip of brown construction paper, cut with pinking shears. Arrange the grouping on a rectangular piece of hardboard placed under the shelter.

Pomander balls add spice to the stunning felt hanging ornament that is pictured at the upper left of page 182.

Make the pomander balls by studding two oranges with whole cloves. Cut a paper pattern for the hanging piece first, following the illustration below the photo on page 182, to determine if it is the right size for the ball. Then, cut it from felt in the right size.

Paint the tops of 1-inch wooden beads and a wooden drapery ring. Wire the ring to the

Christmas posters deck the walls

Tabletop Nativity scene

Pomander balls add spice

From wrenches to candelabra

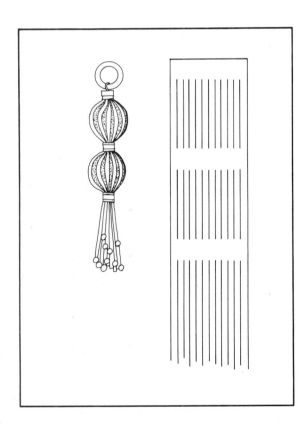

top of the painted bead. Glue the bead at the solid section of the felt casing. Place a pomander ball in the slit section, wiring the felt together below the ball and adjusting the slits to fit evenly around the ball.

Glue top and bottom beads in place; wire above bottom bead. Add beads to fringe.

From wrenches to candelabra without even waving a magic wand could well be the description of the table decoration shown at the upper right of this page. To assemble this unique candleholder, purchase twelve $1/4x5/16$ box-end wrenches, one $1/4$-inch threaded iron rod, thirteen $1/4$-inch nuts, and a precut wood base with a $1/4$-inch metal threaded insert.

Screw the threaded post into the base. Screw on the first nut. Slip on one wrench with the $5/16$ side on the bottom. Repeat the nut and wrench arrangement until all of them are on the post. Position the wrenches, starting at the bottom. Tighten the nuts as wrenches are positioned. Cut off any excess post and stain the base as desired. Place tall, slim red tapers in the wrench holders.

The snowball and shovel door decoration shown at the upper left of the opposite page

Shovels of snow

Frosty house plant container

Garlands of popcorn

can be assembled in a hurry. To make this last-minute door decoration, start with children's snow shovels and treat them to a fresh coat of red paint. Then, pile the shovel scoop with various sizes of plastic foam balls glued together and glued to the shovel. Cut some of the balls in half and glue flat side to shovel.

For an eye-catching effect, trim the handles with bright red Christmas ribbon bows and streamers. To add glamour, brush glue on top of the balls and sprinkle glitter on them.

A dramatic container for a Norfolk Island pine house plant is shown at the upper right. To fashion this frosty container, cover a flowerpot with aluminum foil and decorate it with plastic ball halves. Glue the balls on in alternating rows. Arrange a grouping of angels at the base of the planter.

Garlands of popcorn add a seasonal touch to the lamp shown at the right. Place ornament hooks on the top of the rim of the shade to secure the garlands. Then, cover the hooks with shiny foil reflectors. If you'd rather, substitute tinsel swags or ribbons for the popcorn. Place small packages bedecked with ribbons and flowers beneath the lamp.

Chapter 12

Decorations for Other Holidays

Celebrating the joy of holidays throughout the year can range from an impromptu get-together to an elaborately detailed gala event. Entertaining is definitely in order, and to make your parties come off with a flair, make fresh, imaginative holiday decorations.

Ring in the New Year with style—centerpieces for the table, favors, and wall decorations in vibrant colors are the order of the day.

Invite friends and loved ones to share St. Valentine's Day with you. Set a pink hearts-and-lace table and create dainty decorations for this special lovers' holiday.

St. Patrick's Day also is an excellent time for party-giving and for holiday decorating. Shamrocks, clay pipes, harps, and leprechauns add a lighthearted touch to the festivities.

Decorations for Jewish holidays, with designs that are dictated by history, are truly an inspiration to all. When they are handcrafted by family members, they take on even greater significance.

Red, white, and blue patriotic decorations that make you want to cheer for 'the grand old flag' add zest to holidays that are special to Americans everywhere.

Add Easter, Halloween, and Thanksgiving to this list, and make each holiday a memorable one by decorating your home with appropriate handcrafted creations.

On the opposite page is a sampling of the holiday decorations you will find on the pages of this chapter. Directions for these and many others that are appropriate to the occasion are detailed and easy to follow.

New Year's Eve centerpiece

Crepe paper flower

New wall is a cardboard facade

Welcome the New Year

New Year's Eve is apt to be the climax of the year's entertaining, a festive finale to the busy holiday season. It's a special occasion to radiate end-of-season cheer.

It is a gala evening, a time for sharing memories of good times during the past year and the promises of the year to come. Plan your food, beverage, and decorations so that the evening will be a memorable one.

The decorations on these pages will establish a holiday mood as you ring out the old year and welcome the new one. And, best of all, you can store these artful arrangements and bring them out another year.

The New Year's Eve table decorations pictured at the top of the opposite page combine all of the elements associated with this auspicious time of the year.

To duplicate this one, first pick any large, flat (this is important) container or tray to be the base of the arrangement. Next, cut two blocks of 2-inch-thick plastic foam. One should be 1½ inches shorter and narrower than the shallow container; the other should be the same size as the clock base. (This places the clock two inches higher than the rest of the base.)

The leaves here are magnolia leaves sprayed gold. If you wish, you may substitute salal, lemon leaf, camellia, or other foliage for the magnolia and spray it gold. Also, spray a tall branch of pine gold.

If you don't have a black and white square clock like the one pictured, either use another color or shape, or make a clock face from black and white poster board.

Purchase balloons in a variety of colors, noisemakers, and party hats in colors and designs that harmonize with the balloons.

Arrange the decorations at the end of the table against the wall, following the photo as a guide. Add a cluster of eucalyptus pods, small pine cones, or other pods. To complete the New Year's theme, add two candles—one almost totally burned down to represent the old year and the other a freshly lit one to denote the new year.

The massive paper flower pictured at the lower left of the opposite page is guaranteed to create a carnival-like atmosphere at your New Year's Eve party. Suspended from a light fixture above the punch bowl setting, this masterpiece is the pivot around which the table setting theme revolves. Its vivid, dazzling colors add gaiety to the holiday season, and a busy hostess will find it easy to construct, even at the last minute.

To duplicate this lofty centerpiece, first make a large ball from chicken wire. (The one in the photo is approximately 22 inches in diameter.) Cut 7x7-inch squares of tissue paper (the colors shown here are hot pink and red) and fold them twice so that the squares measure 3½ inches. Stick the tissue squares in the wire openings and leave the ends protruding through the holes in the chicken wire. (Cut enough paper squares to completely cover the ball.) Suspend the huge decoration above the table and attach ribbon streamers of the same colors. Let the streamers sweep out to encircle the festive table.

Cover the table with a tablecloth in one of the same bright colors, and center the punch bowl. Arrange plates, napkins, mugs, and snacks so they are easily accessible for guests. Serve a punch that harmonizes with the colors of the artful decorations.

The new wall pictured at the lower right of the opposite page converts your family or game room into a sophisticated New Year's Eve spot, and offers a creative project that is great fun for the whole family.

The materials for the new wall consist of various colors of poster-weight cardboard, colored tissue paper, and cellophane straws.

To fashion, first measure your wall to determine the size and number of cardboard squares and rectangles you'll need. Be sure to use colors of cardboard that complement the color scheme of the room. Then, staple the large cardboard squares and rectangles to the wall. (Place the rectangles over the large squares and let them bow outward for a three-dimensional effect.)

Next, take lengths of green cotton string and thread, and alternate crumpled squares of the tissue paper, straws, and ornament beads on the string. Hang the strings from the ceiling, slightly in front of the cardboard facade. These hanging streamers will turn at the slightest breeze and cast interesting shadows on the wall behind them.

Fuchsia wreaths adorned with silver bells and bows reflect the gaiety of the season.

To make this centerpiece, you'll need thick plastic foam rings, table legs, crepe paper, silver ribbon, silver paint, and bells. Start by wrapping the wreath base with crepe paper cut across the grain into 2-inch strips. Next, cut more crepe paper strips 1½ and 2 inches wide. Place the narrower strips atop the wider ones, and machine-baste down the center. Ruffle both layers of crepe paper.

Pull stitching to gather strips. Glue strips to center of ring, holding with pins until glue dries. Glue two more gathered strips to ring's outer and inner edges. Fasten bells to wreath with chenille stems.

For each stand, cut an appropriate-sized circle from wood; drill a hole at the center for the table leg screw. Screw the leg to the base; spray-paint silver. Attach a wreath to the table leg. Finish with a silver bow.

The stroke-of-twelve wall decoration shown at the upper left of the opposite page is timely for a New Year's Eve party.

Cut two circles, 22 and 28 inches in diameter, from colored cardboard, or cover plain cardboard with paper or vinyl. Make or buy party horns, and glue them to clock face at the quarter hour marks. Glue the numbers onto the clock face and cover the dowel 'hands' with shredded paper.

The jolly jesters at the upper right of the opposite page are waiting for the new year.

To duplicate them, you'll need two sizes of party cups (either paper or plastic); glue or plastic cement; adhesive paper in blue, white, black, and red; gift-wrap paper for hats; yarn or ribbon for ties; cardboard scraps; and red fat yarn for hair.

For each jester, roll a party cup on adhesive paper, marking the path at the top and bottom edges, forming a pattern. Cut pattern and fit adhesive paper to cup. Cut the hat pattern from gift paper (use two pieces, back to back, if you want color on inside of hat). Roll the points over a dowel or pencil to curl them. Glue hat to head.

Cut out facial features. Cover cardboard nose with adhesive paper; glue to face. Add eyes and mouth. Make hair from snips of red yarn about 2½ inches long, folded and glued to the head just under edges of hat. Stack and glue cups together to get the desired height. Add yarn ties when the glue is dry.

The suspended blue ball shown at the lower left of the opposite page is a quick-and-easy centerpiece to make for a gala New Year's Eve party. Buy a big honeycombed ball ready-made, and hang it from the light fixture with monofilament line. Attach circles cut from origami paper to the strings.

The spangly, tassel-trimmed triumphs shown at the lower right of the opposite page are so versatile and varied that they'll be a decorative asset all during the holidays.

To make them, cut cardboard in various shapes and conceal the forms with brightly colored thick yarns. You can shape some designs like flowers and others like tassels with tiny bells or balls that swing and sway at the slightest movement.

To make the wall tree, cut a 39x39x17-inch triangle from heavy corrugated cardboard. Cover the tree with bright green fabric. Cut the fabric 2 inches larger all around. Pull it taut to the backside and glue it securely. Hold the fabric in place with pins until glue dries.

Fill in flower designs with yarn, and blanket-stitch around circles and rings. On some, wrap small-size curtain rings with yarn and tack to centers of flowers. (Follow picture for placement.) Glue shapes to tree.

Fuchsia wreaths

Stroke-of-twelve wall decoration

Jolly jesters

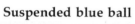

Suspended blue ball

Spangly, tasseled triumphs

St. Valentine's Day

St. Valentine's Day is the most sentimental of all holidays. It brings to mind traditional, dainty valentines decorated with hearts, flowers, birds, ribbons, paper lace — and an endearing message. Or, it could be a spoof on the old familiar sentimental theme — a comic valentine that lampoons the recipient.

Whatever meaning St. Valentine's Day has for you, it's still a good time for entertaining and decorating in a festive manner.

St. Valentine's Day party plan

This is a perfect plan for a junior miss valentine party because the teen-age hostess herself can carry out the decorating projects.

To set up this arrangement, first cover the round table with a circular pink tablecloth. Then, arrange the heart-shaped reversible place mats, alternating the sides. If you have both red and white dinnerware, alternate the two as shown in the photo. The centerpiece consists of a red flowerpot studded with colorful hair bows fastened to wire stems cascading out casually in a flowerlike arrangement. The napkin rings are made from 2-inch lengths of cardboard mailing tubes covered with red and white checked gingham.

To make the place mats, cut the heart-shaped sections from fabric pieces that measure 13½x17½ inches. Use red and white checked gingham for one side and red printed calico material for the opposite sides. Place the two right sides of the fabric together and machine-stitch around the edge, with a strip of 1-inch-wide white eyelet embroidered ruffling stitched into the seam between the two layers of fabric. Leave a small opening at the top of the heart (large enough for turning), and turn the place mat to the right side. Press the raw edges of the opening to the inside so they are not visible.

Leave this opening unsewn until after the meal is finished. Then, let each guest stuff

◀ **The party decorations** on the opposite page are bound to catch the fancy of teen-agers. If you wish to entertain adults instead, just remove the flowerpot of hair bows and substitute flowers.

her pillow-place mat with polyester filling and sew the opening shut. This provides part of the party entertainment, and each guest has a dainty pillow to take home as a remembrance of the happy event.

To make six place mats, you will need 1⅛ yards each of red and white checked gingham and red print calico, and 8 yards of 1-inch-wide white eyelet embroidered ruffling.

To re-create the floral imposter, use a flowerpot that measures about 5½ inches in diameter. Paint the flowerpot red, or cover it with red fabric. Using grosgrain ribbon that follows the same red and white color scheme, make bows and fasten them to green florist's wire stems. (Use 1 yard of 1½-inch-wide ribbon for each bow.) Place a chunk of floral foam in the flowerpot, and arrange the ribbon bows in a flowerlike composition. After the festivities are over, let each guest choose a bow to take home as a favor.

The best part of entertaining for holidays such as Valentine's Day is that you have a ready-made theme to guide you when planning your decorations. And, not only does the theme lend itself to decorating, it also influences the type of food you serve.

Here are some menu suggestions for a teen-ager's Valentine's party. For the soup course, choose a hearty soup such as clam, cheese, or corn chowder; vichyssoise; or creamed broccoli or asparagus soup. Accompany the soup course with an assortment of crackers, Melba toast, or breadsticks.

Let the sandwiches be the dainty variety. A frosted sandwich loaf with ham salad, egg salad, and tuna salad fillings can be just as pretty as the party decorations. Frost the loaf-style offering with cream cheese tinted pastel pink, and decorate it with strips of pimiento arranged in the shape of hearts. Place the sandwich loaf on an oval platter and surround it with garnishes of radish roses, tiny beets, and celery curls.

Serve cake for dessert. Bake it in heart-shaped cake tins and frost it with pale pink icing. Or serve gelatin heart cutouts or pink meringue hearts filled with ice cream.

Punch is peppy, well-suited to a party, and easy to mix. For this special occasion, serve a delicious and refreshing red fruit punch.

St. Patrick's Day

Even though it's not a national holiday (yet), and even if you're not from County Cork, St. Patrick's Day offers a happy excuse for entertaining friends and relatives.

To begin with, use lots of green in your decorating scheme. Add to this the traditional motifs that go along with this special day—shamrocks, clay pipes, potatoes (a reminder of the potato famine in Ireland that resulted in many of the sons of Erin leaving the old sod), bowlers, pigs, and leprechauns.

If you have dinnerware with a green design, this is the time to use it. If you haven't, you can always find paper plates and cups with a St. Patrick's motif. And, don't forget to let Irish coffee goblets be an important part of the total theme.

The traditional menu for this day includes corned beef and cabbage, and green beer if it's an informal get-together, or Irish coffee if you wish to add a more elegant touch. Instructions for creating the St. Pat's centerpieces on the opposite page are given below.

Green bowler centerpiece

Here's additional proof that non-floral centerpieces can be effective for a special event. This distinguished decoration, a salute to old Erin, is simply a green bowler resting on an isle of plastic foam.

For the base, use a sheet of plastic foam in a rectangular shape, or if you want it to be more realistic, cut the foam in the shape of the Emerald Isle. Wrap candy pipes and harps in see-through food wrap and arrange them around the brim of the bowler. Place beribboned party favors around the base of the centerpiece and let green foliage peek out from under the base all around the edges. Use a vivid green tablecloth to strengthen the holiday decorating theme.

St. Patrick's dinner

For many people, St. Patrick's Day isn't complete without a meal featuring corned beef, cabbage, potatoes, and green beer or Irish coffee. To set the stage for the meal, first cover the table with a bright green tablecloth. And if you have some, use white dinnerware sprigged with green. Then, center the table with a pedestal-base bowl and fill it with Irish potatoes, clay pipes beribboned with green bows, and trailing sprays of shamrocks. For still another touch of green, garnish the boiled potatoes on the platter with chopped parsley.

St. Patrick's buffet

Here's a setting that will delight all St. Pat's revelers. It's easy to achieve and it is inexpensive. In just a few hours, you can make the patchwork table runner, the clay pipe plant container to hold the shamrock, and the pipe cleaner napkin rings.

Make the table runner whatever size is best for your buffet serving table. The runner shown here measures 16x48 inches. To duplicate it, first cut 48 patches 4½ inches square. (Use prints that have a predominance of green for most of the squares.) Join 12 patches in each of four strips first, then join the four strips. Use ¼-inch seams to join the patches. Cut a lining piece in a harmonizing print the same size as the runner. Place the right sides together, and insert jumbo rickrack between the two sections along the seam line. Stitch the seam, leaving an opening long enough to allow turning the runner to the right side. Whip the opening shut by hand.

The large clay pipe is so realistic that you would have to look closely at it before you'd realize that it's simply a clay flowerpot covered with papier mâché.

To fabricate the pipe, use a 7½-inch-diameter clay flowerpot, and attach the pipe stem with tape. (Use a cardboard tube about 2 inches in diameter for the stem, with one end angled to fit the side of the pot.) Cover the pipe with papier mâché, and paint it brown. Or, you may wish to paint it a putty color instead so that it will resemble a clay pipe. Place a thriving shamrock plant (in its pot) into the plant container so it appears to be bursting out of the top of the pipe.

It takes only a few minutes to make the green pipe cleaner napkin rings. Use green pipe cleaners and bend them around a 2-inch cardboard mailing tube. Twist the ends of the pipe cleaners to form a shamrock design.

Green bowler centerpiece

St. Patrick's dinner

St. Patrick's buffet

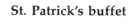

Easter breakfast

Easter brunch

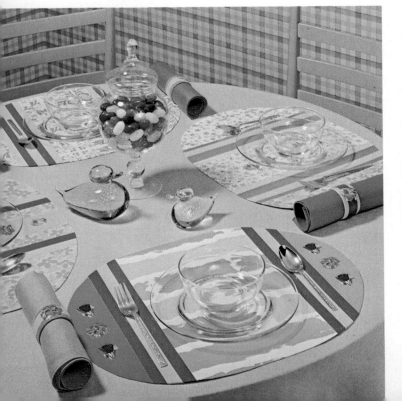

Easter buffet

Easter table finery

Easter Sunday is a day for rejoicing, and a time for families and friends to get together. To small children, it may suggest the annual hunt for Easter eggs and the thrill of expectancy that goes along with exploring the contents of their Easter baskets. For the family, there is the fun of testing creative talents during the pre-Easter egg decorating ritual.

In keeping with the festive spirit of the day, Easter is a perfect time for entertaining. And, with the theme already established, it's easy to decorate the table for this important event. Some people prefer to entertain at an Easter breakfast, while others favor the Easter brunch after church services. Still others enjoy entertaining friends at an Easter buffet later in the day. Here are suggestions for decorating for all three of the occasions.

Easter breakfast

The table decorations for this breakfast are so bright and cheery that everyone's bound to start out the day on a happy note.

The centerpiece is the focal point, and what could be more natural—a clear glass bowl of pure white eggs surrounded by green leaves. Both rest on a white cake plate and are guarded by a lavender hyacinth plant on each side. The green table linens, yellow and white dinnerware, white-handled flatware, and green tumblers follow the spring theme.

Even the food is part of the decorative plan for this Easter breakfast. There's a fruit course of orange sections and strawberries, poached eggs in toast cups, crisp bacon, pink cereal, hot cross buns, and beverage. To make the cereal pink, prepare farina or creamy rice according to the package directions and add a few drops of red food coloring (use coloring sparingly to achieve a delicate pink color). Top the hot cereal with strawberry jam, preserves, or currant jelly. Serve the cereal in the white ramekins with the bunny covers.

Easter brunch

The highlights of the table decorations shown at the bottom left of the opposite page are the handcrafted place mats and napkin rings.

To make the place mats, cut white cardboard into 12x17-inch, egg-shaped pieces. Cover each egg-shaped place mat with adhesive-backed or gift-wrap paper in bright, cheerful designs. For added decorative effect, add bands of vinyl tape in harmonizing colors. To duplicate napkin rings use ordinary plastic napkin rings and add bands of the same vinyl tape that trims the place mats. Adorn the bands with small floral stickers.

Cover the table with a yellow tablecloth first, then arrange the place mats. Use a napkin of a different color at each place setting. The clever centerpiece is the easiest ever—just fill a glass compote with jelly beans in assorted colors, and arrange clear crystal ducks around the base.

Easter buffet

A tall, graceful centerpiece is appropriate for this Easter buffet (opposite page, lower right) because it is positioned against the wall and to the rear of the food. To duplicate this Easter-egg tree, a symbol of new life, anchor a manzanita branch to a shallow tray with florist's clay. Fasten ribbons to eggs, and suspend eggs from branches to form balanced design.

To empty eggshells, first wash eggs. Then, make a small hole in each end of eggshell with a pin or tiny skewer; enlarge holes slightly. Run a long pin through center of the egg to break yolk. Hold the egg over a bowl; blow gently in one hole. Rinse the empty shell in cold water; let it dry thoroughly. To be sure you get an even color, just before dyeing, rinse eggshell in hot water and dry. Follow package instructions for dyeing.

Complete the centerpiece by filling the shallow tray with greens and spring blooms.

Let your menu follow the season's traditions. The pièce de résistance is ham, beautifully glazed and trimmed with a candied orange daisy. Add springy accompaniments such as frilly leaf-lettuce salad, asparagus tips topped with almonds, parslied potatoes, rolls, and beverage. For a novel dessert, make meringue shells shaped like Easter baskets. Fill the shells with egg-shaped ice cream balls and top with fresh strawberries.

Happy haunting

Halloween's a time for fun; and witches, ghosts, pumpkins, and black cats provide the theme for this occasion.

To make the flying witch on the opposite page, you will need black rug yarn, black satin fabric, cotton batting, 2 old nylon stockings, crinoline, red and black felt, 2 wire coat hangers, adhesive or masking tape, and 4 small buttons.

To make the padded coat hanger body, cut crossbar of hanger in half, and straighten wires. Close loop of hook to form head. Cut bar off second hanger and tape to twisted area of first hanger to form arms. Tape two straightened wires of first hanger together 4 inches below arm wire (hip line). Bend end of each wire up 9 inches below tape; bend remaining 4½ inches into oval foot shape. Loop ends of arm wires for hands. Pad hands and feet with cotton batting; wrap with a 2-inch-wide spiral-cut strip of nylon stocking.

For the head, cut a 6-inch-wide section from stocking. Wrap wire loop with cotton and slide hose section over it; gather and fasten. Slip a ball of cotton under hose and thread it around to form nose. Stuff extra cotton in head where needed; gather and tie off top edge of stocking. Cut eyes and mouth from felt and glue in place.

For the hair, wrap rug yarn around a 4½x8½-inch piece of paper to form the loops. Machine-stitch through paper and yarn 4¼ inches from the outer edges. Pull the paper off and adjust wig on head; sew in place.

Cut shoes following pattern; make adjustments to fit feet. Hand-stitch in place on sole section; side seam, turning under ¼ inch on raw edge. Add buttons next to seam.

For pants, fold 8½x8-inch black fabric in half to 8½x4-inch-size. On fold line, cut slit 4 inches from bottom for legs. Seam 8½-inch-long raw edges together to 4 inches from lower edge. Match the leg edges and seam. Run gathering stitches around the waist and legs. Put pants on witch and draw up to fit.

For the slip, hem a 1½x72-inch piece of print fabric. Gather for ruffle, drawing up to 35½-inch length. Join the ruffle to a 7½x36-inch piece of printed fabric; hem edges. Run gathering thread on top edge. Slip on doll, gather to fit waist, and secure.

From the same print, cut a 24x1½-inch piece for apron ruffle and a 4½x12-inch piece for skirt. Straps are two 1½x2-inch pieces, and the waistband is 3½x1½ inches. Hem ruffle and gather to fit skirt edge; stitch in place. Hem sides of apron; gather the top edge to 3 inches. Hem the ends and sides of ties. Join the waistband to the skirt. Add ties.

For the hat brim, cut two 4½-inch diameter circles of black fabric and one of crinoline. Place crinoline on wrong side of black circle. Stitch right sides of black fabric together along edge, leaving opening to turn. Turn; handstitch opening closed. For crown, cut a semicircle (4-inch radius) of crinoline and a 4¼-inch radius semicircle from black fabric. Turn under raw edge and blindstitch fabric. Overlap edges of crinoline to form cone; baste to hold. Cover the cone with black fabric, turn under raw edge, and blindstitch. Turn ½ inch under at base of cone, center on brim, pin, and handstitch. Add ribbon ties.

For the cape, cut one printed and one black piece of fabric (see drawing). With the right sides together, stitch ½-inch seam, leaving a section open for turning. Turn and handstitch the opening closed. Add ties.

For the dress skirt, cut a 7½x36-inch piece of black fabric; cut two 5x7½-inch pieces for sleeves, and cut bodice according to pattern shown. Hem sleeves along 5-inch measurement; stitch underarm seam. Slide sleeve on arm, gather top, and sew to doll shoulder. Cut two bodice pieces and slit back of one piece on fold line. Hem both sides for back closing. Sew shoulder and underarm seams, leaving armholes. Turn under hem at neck. Hem skirt and join back seam (7½-inch edge). Gather waist edge of skirt to fit waist measurement of bodice; join bodice to skirt. Slip doll into dress, turn under raw edges at armholes, and catch in place around armholes.

To make nut cups, cut a 2-inch-diameter mailing tube into 2-inch sections; cover with orange construction paper. Cut a second piece of orange paper 3x6⅜ inches; make slashes ½ inch apart and ⅜ inch from top and bottom edge. Glue onto covered tube so top and bottom edges are flush, causing strips to bulge. Glue on black paper features, attach pipe cleaner handle, and set nut cup inside.

A witch riding her broomstick over a gnarled, leafless branch is the focal point of the Halloween centerpiece shown above. To further the theme established by the centerpiece, serve typical Halloween snacks such as doughnuts, cider, apples, and an assortment of packaged snacks (pretzels, potato chips, and peanuts).

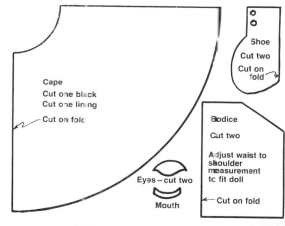

Cape
Cut one black
Cut one lining
Cut on fold

Shoe
Cut two
Cut on fold

Bodice
Cut two
Adjust waist to shoulder measurement to fit doll
Cut on fold

Eyes—cut two

Mouth

Thanksgiving and autumn

Thanksgiving is much more than roast turkey and dressing, cranberries, and pumpkin and mince pie. Though a bountiful repast is definitely in order, the holiday is important because it is a reminder of that first Thanksgiving Day, when Early American settlers gave prayers of thanks for the food that sustained them through their first rigorous year in the New World. In keeping with this rich heritage, it's symbolic to feature autumn and Thanksgiving decorations that revolve around fruits and vegetables, and natural dried materials.

All of these finds from nature combine to set a festive mood for the entire autumn season, as well as for Thanksgiving Day. You can get marvelous effects when you display these offerings tastefully.

The fruit tree pictured at the upper left of the opposite page becomes a harvesttime hallmark when you display it on the dining table at an autumn breakfast.

Start with a strong manzanita branch that has graceful configurations. If it isn't as shapely as you would like, prune the excess branches until you have the desired form. Anchor the branch firmly in a low bowl, using a needlepoint holder plus floral clay. Fill the bowl with pebbles and stones to conceal the clay. For this type of autumn decoration, a bronze, ceramic, or wood bowl is especially appropriate.

Tie the fruit onto the branches with velvet ribbons, and urge each guest to untie his choice for dessert. When you use a tall centerpiece, such as this one, be sure to place it where it will not interfere with across-the-table conversation.

The rest of the table appointments are also in keeping with the autumn theme. You can make a similar table cover from a length of fabric in autumn colors simply by hemming the ends. The earthenware dinnerware and the copper coffee server strengthen the theme.

The seed-covered squirrel pictured at the upper right of the opposite page is a happy choice for any fall occasion.

To duplicate this fanciful woodland character, start with spheres and rectangles of plastic foam. Cut the plastic foam into the general parts for the body. Assemble the body parts with glue-dipped toothpicks. Do the final shaping, using the photo as a guide. Then, cover the figure with a coat of rubber cement; cover the body with seeds. For a lifelike appearance, use lighter colored seeds for the front of the squirrel and a dark shade for the nose and eyes.

Center the squirrel centerpiece on a bed of colorful autumn leaves. Choose table linens, dinnerware, and glassware that are harmonious with the overall theme.

Apples and gingerbread men star in the holiday scene at the lower left of the opposite page. They project a simple charm for a country-style kitchen or family room.

Assemble apples that are fairly uniform in size and shape, polish them until they shine in the reflected glow of the candlelight, and arrange them in a large wood bowl. Circle the bowl with gleaming brass candlesticks holding white candles, a spray of trailing ivy, and another red apple.

The gingerbread men, mounted high on the wall, are made from authentic eighteenth-century molds. The antique wagon wheel serves as a base from which the trailing ivy reaches out in many directions.

Although all of the elements in this decorating plan appear casual and unrestrained, there is a unity of purpose that radiates warmth and hospitality.

Truly rural could well be the description of the rustic vignette pictured at the lower right of the opposite page. It is an unconventional arrangement for a back-of-the-table composition. Or, you could place it on the floor in an entrance hall or on the hearth next to a fireplace. This long-lasting arrangement can be used for both the Thanksgiving and Christmas holidays.

Start with a peach basket with tastefully grouped apples and sparkling Christmas balls spilling out of it. Alongside the basket, place an antique wood butter churn filled with an arrangement of long-needled evergreen branches, cattails, and sheaves of wheat, all left in their natural state. Add color interest with shorter stalks of heavily berried bittersweet. If you don't have a wooden peach basket or old-fashioned butter churn, look for other seldom-used objects.

198

Fruit tree

Apples and gingerbread men

Seed-covered squirrel

Truly rural

Jewish holidays

Jewish holidays are steeped in tradition, and the manner in which they are celebrated has been bequeathed from generation to generation for many centuries. Only four of the holidays—Rosh Hashanah, Hanukkah, Purim, and Passover—are singled out in this section on holiday decorations.

Rosh Hashanah (New Year)

The Jewish New Year begins on the seventh month of the Jewish calendar. This is a deeply religious holiday and is bound up with prayer, the synagogue, and self-assessment. During the synagogue service, the shofar, or ram's horn (pictured at the lower right of the opposite page), is blown to remind the Jewish people of their agreement to obey God's law.

To make the shofar, shape baker's clay (see page 55 for recipe) by rolling it with the palms of your hands as you would to make a rope. Make the strip 8 to 9 inches long, one end about 2 inches in diameter, and the other end about 1 inch in diameter. To give the horn a curved shape, lay the clay strip in an oven-proof bowl with a curved bottom. Bake in a 350° oven about 45 minutes, or until it holds its shape.

Roll out dough with rolling pin to about ¼ inch thick. Lay a 5x8¼-inch rectangle on cookie sheet and prop partly baked horn on sheet with moistened dough. Decorate with flowers cut with cookie cutter, or make bunches of grapes. Place in oven again and bake for at least an hour, or until hard.

Finish the decoration with a coat of gesso or white latex paint to smooth the surface. Then, spray with white enamel and gold. (Spraying with gold while the white is still wet gives an interesting effect.)

The candleholder centerpiece pictured at the center right of the opposite page is a replica of the famous Chagall windows at the University of Jerusalem. With symbols of peace and hope on it, this candleholder signifies the sacredness of Rosh Hashanah.

To make the cylindrical candleholder, cut a 10x20-inch sheet of thin, clear plastic. Draw a pattern on it with a marking pen, then paint with stained glass paint. Outline the designs with liquid lead. To shape candle-holder, warm it in an oven a short time, wrap around an oatmeal box, and glue together. Place cylinder over a votive candle.

Hanukkah (Feast of lights)

This holiday, which means dedication, celebrates the rededication of the Jewish temple in Jerusalem after Judas Maccabeus recaptured it from Syrian invaders. A legend is told that when the service was ready to begin, the worshipers could not find oil for the holy lamp that hung over the Ark. (It was supposed to burn day and night.) At last, one small jar of oil was found that held enough to burn only a single night, but miraculously it burned for eight days.

To remember this miracle, the menorah, a candleholder that holds eight candles, plus the shammash, or servant candle (upper left of opposite page), is used. One candle is lit each night during Hanukkah with the shammash until all eight candles are lit.

To make a baker's clay menorah, roll out dough about 18 inches long and 1½ inches in diameter. Use a sharp knife, and cut off outer edges to give four flat sides. Place on cookie sheet and shape as desired. Build up one end with another square of dough to make it higher (this will hold the helper candle). Cut out the candleholders with cookie cutters, using the candle that will be placed in it to make a hole in the center of each. Moisten the bottom of each candleholder and fasten in place on the menorah. Add other clay decorations, if you wish. Bake in 350° oven for an hour, or until hard. When it is cool, coat with gesso or latex paint and spray-paint with white enamel and gold—or any color you wish to feature.

The dreydle (three are pictured in the center of the opposite page) is a top that is used in playing games. It has four sides, each of which has a Hebrew letter standing

The collection of handcrafted items at the right ▶ are closely integrated with Jewish holidays. Instructions are given for making decorations for Rosh Hashanah, Hanukkah, Purim, and Passover.

for "Nes Gadol Hayah Sham," meaning "a great miracle happened there." A penalty or reward is given, depending on which letter comes up when top is spun. Gifts or treats can be given to children each night during Hanukkah.

To make the dreydle, remove top of a half-gallon milk carton. Measure 3¾ inches up from bottom on all sides and draw a connecting line all the way around. Using a sharp knife, score this line. Find center of each side and mark at top. Draw a line from center mark to the outside corners of  the carton on the scored line. Cut on these lines, removing the rest of top portion of carton. Find the center of the bottom of the carton and make a small hole. Place a screw through the hole from inside the carton and screw a cork to the end of it. Fold the points inward until they meet; tape points together.

Paint dreydle with latex paint or cover it with fabric. Decorate with gold braid and foil ornaments, leaving space in center of each side for letters (see bottom of page).

To draw a Star of David, begin with a circle. Draw a line through center, as indicated by dotted line in figure at right. Trace an equilateral triangle on the circle, with one point touching center line. Invert circle and trace another equilateral triangle in same way.

Purim (Feast of lots)

This holiday symbolizes the casting of lots to determine the fate of the Jewish people. It is a fun holiday that usually occurs in March and celebrates the story of the Book of Esther in which a beautiful Jewess named Esther saves the Jewish people of Persia. Today, to celebrate Purim, children masquerade in costumes reminiscent of the days of Queen Esther and munch hamantaschen, delicious three-cornered cakes with prune or poppy seed filling. During Purim, it is a custom for Jewish families to exchange treats and to give gifts to needy persons.

Follow these instructions for making the figures of Esther and Mordecai shown on page 201.

To make body, bend two wire coat hangers, as shown in drawing at right, using one for upper body and one for lower body. Hold in shape with masking tape, and tape the two wires together at the waist. Stuff body with tissue paper to give it shape, and cover body, arms, and legs with crepe paper. Use plastic foam balls for head. Make clothing from bits of cloth, and sew or glue in place. Use wool yarn for hair and beard.

Here, Esther is in a sitting position and is taped to the chair before her clothing is placed on her. (Chair is made from a milk carton.) Use only the upper portion of the body for Mordecai and tape it to the neck of a tall bottle so he will stand erect.

Passover

Passover, or Pesach, is a reminder of the momentous crisis in the life of Jewish people —the departure from Egypt. The *Holy Bible* dictates the date of Passover, how long it lasts, and prohibits eating anything that is leavened during this time. The Passover seder is the evening meal, which is followed in a special order to remind Jewish people of the first Passover. During the seder, the Haggadah (the story of the exodus from Egypt) is read. The centerpiece for the Passover seder (top of page 201) is a plastic mobile, a modern version of the seder plate. It displays the passover symbols.

To construct the mobile, start with a strip of clear plastic that is 24 inches long, ½ inch wide, and ¼ inch thick. Warm the middle of the strip over a stove burner by holding it 2 to 3 inches from the burner so it can be bent to fit in a large paper bag. Place the bag with the strip in it in a 350° oven for 5 to 10 minutes. Remove with oven mitts and shape the mobile (keep base of strip flat). The strip will be very flexible when it is warm, but will hold its shape as soon as it cools. Using plastic cement, glue sculptured strip to a plastic base (hold on with masking tape while gluing). Make symbols of cardboard and hang from mobile with clear thread.

Hebrew letters used on dreydles

Centerpieces for patriotic holidays

Patriotic holiday decorations

Red, white, and blue set the scene for patriotic holiday decorations that you can use throughout the year—Washington's and Lincoln's birthdays, Memorial Day, Flag Day, Fourth of July, Labor Day, and Veteran's Day. Or, for that matter, use them whenever you want to let your patriotism show.

Eagle decoration

The eagle at the top of the page, with its majestic air, is a table or mantel ornament you will cherish. You can use it for many special occasions throughout the year. Wher-

ever it presides, it will add a regal touch. Following are step-by-step instructions.

Shield: using the paper pattern on page 205, cut a shield shape (C) from corrugated paper, and glue it onto a layer of plain white cardboard to stiffen it. Cut the smooth top of the shield (above dotted line in drawing) from lightweight cardboard and glue it in place on the front of the shield (corrugated paper side), as shown in the photo.

Stars: make three stars from typing paper to decorate the shield. Fold a 4x4½-inch piece of typing paper in half (4x2¼ inches). Mark 1¼ inches down from the outside top corner

203

and 1¼ inches up from the bottom outside corner. Make a mark halfway up the fold line. Connect the three points with lines (step 1 on page 205). Next, fold the top portion behind (step 2). Leaving this portion folded down behind, fold down again on the second line (step 3). Fold up the lower left corner to match the other folds. Measure ⅜ inch from the point on the top side and ⅜ inch from the point on the bottom side. Draw a line between these two marks and cut. Unfold the star and recrease the folds so the fold on each point is up (step 4).

Or as an alternative choice, use gold star seals mounted on cardboard (cut the cardboard in the same star shape) for depth, and glue the stars to the shield.

Arrowheads: cut three arrowheads (B) from plain cardboard (see illustration on page 205). Make the shafts from corrugated paper, tapering them slightly at one end; glue the arrowheads and shafts together to form the three arrows. Back each arrow with a wood stick, glued on to give support.

Olive leaves and stems: cut the olive leaves and the stem (A) from plain cardboard. Score down through the center of each leaf and bend it in slightly. Stiffen the back of the stem with paper-covered wire. Glue the leaves in place on the stem, using the photo on page 203 as a guide.

To assemble the shield, arrows, and leaves, cut a 1x6-inch piece of plain cardboard, and score and fold it 2½ inches from each end. To form a triangle, tape the folded piece of cardboard together. Fasten this triangular piece at the top of one of the six sections of the base. Glue the shield in place on the front of this piece, and glue the olive branch and arrows behind the shields.

Hexagonal base: draw three concentric circles with radii of 6, 9, and 17½ inches on lightweight cardboard (see drawing at the bottom of page 205). Along the 17½-inch arc, draw seven 4-inch chords; draw eight radii through the ends of the chords, all the way from the center of the 17½-inch arc. Draw the chords between the 6- and 9-inch radii on the other arcs. Cut out on the dotted lines of the largest chord (17½-inch arc) and the smallest chord (6-inch arc); cut also along the radii between each of the smallest chords to the 9-inch arc (seven slits). Dent and bend along the radii between the 9-inch and the 17½-inch arcs, and along the chords on the 9-inch arc. Overlap the end sections and glue

them together to make a hexagonal stand to hold the eagle; bend in the top flaps and glue them together to make a solid top.

Body of eagle: make a foundation for the body of the eagle out of two 8x12-inch pieces of stiff cardboard. Fold in the top corners at a point 2¼ inches from each side on each piece. Crease the top corners sharply to flatten them. Place one piece inside the other and staple them together (see L). Trim the bottom of the cone so that it stands about 11½ inches high.

Wrap this cone with a 12x13-inch piece of corrugated paper (corrugations vertical on the front), overlapping the paper on the back. Staple it together at the back. Cut 25 feather shapes of corrugated paper, each 1 inch wide and varying in length from 3 to 5 inches. Arrange the feathers in five overlapping rows, beginning three inches from the bottom (see M) and working up to the top. Use the longer feathers on the sides, the shorter ones in the center of the front. Glue a 3½x1½-inch cardboard rectangle across the top row of feathers to form a gluing surface for attaching the head. Cut out figure D from corrugated paper. Glue two 3x1½-inch ovals, folded in half lengthwise, to the backside of D. Glue the top portion of these ovals closed to form pockets (see N). Slip this section over the top of the body and glue it in position.

Head: cut out the shape of the head (F) and the eye (E) from plain white cardboard. Use a paper punch to make a hole in the center of the eye. Cut a small piece of a paper drinking straw, one end cut at an angle, the other end flat; glue this in place behind the eye to give it added dimension.

Cut the lower part of the beak, as shown by the dotted line on the drawing. Cut out another beak, using the upper part of the pattern only. Glue this upper part of the beak in place on the top of the beak that is a part of the head to give it added dimension. Glue the head to the body, using the rectangle in front of the feathers and the top part of D as the gluing surfaces.

Wings: cut the various pieces from the pattern—two each of G, H, I, J, and K. Lay the large piece unfolded and glue the smaller pieces in place as shown (see O). Close the wing and glue (see P) it in place over the smaller pieces. Repeat this same procedure with the second wing, but in reversed position. Fasten the two wings to the back of the body with push pins.

Paper balls

The red, white, and blue balls of varying sizes and heights, grouped in random fashion, also add a festive touch (see page 203). For a massive centerpiece, use them to complement the eagle. Or, let them stand on their own. Also, you can pile them in a large bowl, or hang them on monofilament threads from the ceiling or a chandelier.

To make a collection of the jaunty red, white, and blue paper balls, you will need gift wrapping paper with a glazed finish, a stapler, dowels (sharpened at one end with a pencil sharpener), small flowerpots or votive candleholders, white paint, cardboard, and spools (from thread).

For each ball, cut six circles of one color, and six of another color (5-, 6-, and 7½-inch circles are used in the paper balls pictured on page 203). If you use paper that comes in a roll, remove the curl by pulling a strip over a table edge before cutting circles.

1. Fold each circle in half. (If you are using paper with a white back, make sure the colored side is folded in.)

2. Fold again into a quarter circle.

3. Make a pinhole through all four layers of paper, ⅛ inch in from the circumference of the circle and halfway between the points of the quarter-circle.

4. Open each unit to a half-circle, and staple the half-circle just inside the circumference on the fold mark.

5. Join the six units of one color into a half-ball by stapling together the outer layers of paper of the adjacent units, and stapling them just below the top and as close to the fold as possible.

6. Join the two hemispheres (match the folds and spread the loops to admit the stapler) by stapling *crosswise* just inside the 'equator'.

7. Staple together the adjacent white sides at the pinholes. Set the paper balls on painted dowels in small flowerpots or in votive candleholders. Center a dowel in the flowerpot by pushing it through a cardboard disk placed over an empty thread spool, positioned in the bottom of the container.

8. For the fluffy trim at the top of each ball, cut a piece of typing paper to measure 3x8 inches, and cut fringe 2 inches deep on the 8-inch length; roll the fringed strip tightly and fasten it with tape. Insert the compact roll of fringed trim in hole on top of ball.

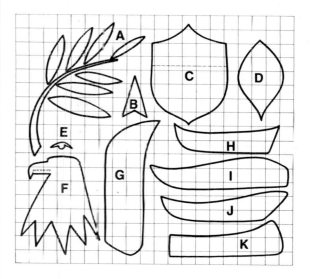

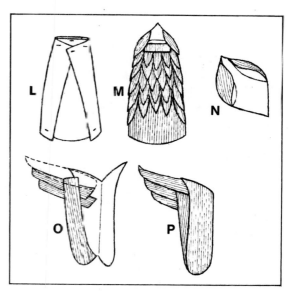

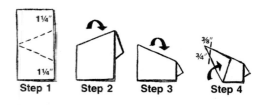

Step 1 Step 2 Step 3 Step 4

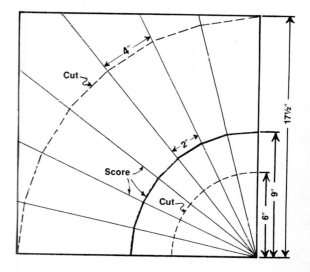

Index

A-C

D-F

We are happy to acknowledge our indebtedness and to express our thanks to the following who have been helpful in producing this book:
Arno Adhesive Tapes, Inc.
Jan DeBard
Gladys Herndon
Kay Myers
Sue Ruttenberg
Bill and Doris Wells